Finding Our Place in the Sun

... A True Story

By
Corry & Pierre de Haas
with Peter de Haas

© 2021 de Haas Publishing

ISBN: 978-0-646-83303-3

All rights reserved. No part of this publication may be reproduced, distributed or transmitted in any form or by any means, including photocopying, recording or imaging or by any other electronic or mechanical methods, without the prior written permission of the author and publisher, except in the case of brief quotations embodied in critical reviews and certain other non-commercial uses permitted by copyright law.

Copy editing and interior design by All-read-E
(http://philipnewey.com/All-read-E.htm)

Cover design by Glen Holman (glenholman.com), with artistic concept by Veronique Hambling, artist and daughter of Corry & Pierre de Haas

A catalogue record for this work is available from the National Library of Australia

Table of Contents

Foreword		*v*
Part One: Pierre's Story		**1**
1.	His Early Years	*1*
2.	It Begins … Forced Labour and Evasion!	*6*
3.	Courier, Spy and Fugitive	*11*
4.	'Jan' on the Atlantic Wall	*15*
5.	Commando	*19*
6.	Liberation and Elly	*28*
7.	On the Move Again … and Injured	*32*
8.	A Promise Made and Quickly Broken	*37*
9.	Island Hopping and Aussies	*43*
10.	'Anyone who came that close, deserves to know how close!'	*49*
Part Two: Corry's Story		**67**
11.	Her Early Years	*67*
12.	Some Memorable Firsts	*75*
13.	War Comes to Our Loungeroom	*81*
14.	Life Under Occupation	*89*
15.	Liberation of Oudenbosch … to VE Day	*92*
Part Three: *Their* story begins …		**113**
16.	First Letters	*114*
17.	Sparring Partners?	*121*
18.	Worried	*125*

19.	The Offensive ... and a Turn in Their Relationship	132
20.	Towards a Deeper Friendship	137
21.	Another Christmas ... Gifts of Disappointment, and Hope	152
22.	The Fight Goes On	161
23.	Confusion	167
24.	Preparing to Leave	173
25.	Departure	179
26.	Homeward Bound	183
27.	Homecoming	188
28.	First Meeting	194

Part Four: Building our life together ... and our family. — **207**

29.	'The Best Years of Our Lives'	207
30.	Engagement and Marriage	211
31.	Business and Babies	216

Part Five: Emigration — **225**

32.	No Way!	226
33.	A Possibility?	231
34.	Move Forward!	239
35.	The Decision	246
36.	Impressions of a Seven-Year-Old	254
37.	Living Rough?	260
38.	Stepping out ... in Faith	265
39.	Letting Go	271
40.	Farewell!	275
41.	Life at Sea	281
42.	Christmas at Panama	285
43.	On to Australia	288

44.	Overnight Train to Brisbane	294

Part 6: Wacol Migrant Hostel   **307**

45.	First Days	307
46.	First Separation	317
47.	Second Separation and Crisis	327
48.	Together Again	337
49.	House and Land Deals?	343
50.	Highs and Lows	353

Part 7: Moving On   **365**

51.	An Emotional Roller Coaster	365
52.	New Births …	377
53.	Aussies in the Making	381
54.	Settled	388
	Afterword	401

Foreword

> 'It is in your moments of decision that your destiny is shaped.'
> Tony Robbins

He dropped the bombshell just when I took the first sip of coffee. Did I hear right? 'What was that?' I asked my husband, hoping I had misunderstood.

'What would you say if I told you I wanted to emigrate?'

Life stopped, as if all the clocks had been put on hold. I felt the blood drain from my face, icy fingers travel down my spine. 'What would I say?' Panic tightened my throat. 'I would say you'd taken leave of your senses, that's what I would say.'

He sighed. 'Please don't start. At least allow me to talk this through. Just think …'

Really frightened now, I took a gulp of coffee and air at the same time, which made me splutter. 'I don't have to think, I can … I can tell you here and now, no way. If you want a change, that's fine by me, but I'm not going to emigrate. Just as a matter of curiosity, where would you have us go?'

'Australia,' was his prompt reply.

'To Australia? Good grief, going to the other side of the world? You might as well say Siberia; you wouldn't get back from there either.'

This conversation between my parents, Corry and Pierre, took place in a little apartment above their shop in Nijmegen, the Netherlands, in early 1959. The actual words are quoted from my mother's autobiographical account, on which the latter part of this book is based.

To fully understand what was at stake for each of them on that cold, dank evening in 1959, and why coming to any agreement about migrating to Australia would prove to be so incredibly difficult, it is necessary to 'wind the clock back', right back into their childhoods and their vastly different experiences as young adults. When their worlds collided, Corry was a teenager still living at home with her parents, while Pierre was caught in a whirlwind of war and conflict on the other side of the world, in what was then the Dutch East Indies. After narrowly escaping death on at least two occasions, he returned home safely in late July 1948 after three and a half years of active service; a commando sergeant and war veteran yet to celebrate his twenty-fifth birthday. However, there was a part of Pierre that never came back …

By way of a brief preview, Thursday, 16 January 2020, quietly and without any fanfare, marked the sixtieth anniversary of our arrival in Australia as a young migrant family. The year 2020 also commemorated other significant milestones: 10 May was the eightieth anniversary of the invasion of the Netherlands by Germany; and the seventy-fifth anniversaries of VE day and VP day were held on 8 May and 15 August, respectively. These historical events are not only inextricably interwoven into the lives of Corry and Pierre, but also are the very catalysts which brought them together in an extraordinary way.

So, this is an auspicious year to be editing their story.

While pivoting on an extremely difficult and challenging conversation (which continued for months!) about the possibility of emigration, this remarkable but true story of Corry and Pierre contains two quite separate periods and circumstances which, although interconnected as you will see, were the most formative for each of them individually.

For Pierre, it was the unrelenting turmoil and turbulence of the war years, which included evasion, spying, forced labour, commando training, and prolonged counter-insurgency operations against militia, and remnant Japanese troops who had not been convinced their war was over. Based on his carefully kept war diaries, Pierre wrote a four-volume work: *Dreams and Tears for Souvenirs*, an autobiographical account, completed in 2003, but never published.

While in the jungles of Sumatra, Pierre contracted a double dose of malaria and typhoid fever, a combination which almost killed him. During his lengthy recovery in hospital, he arranged for an advertisement for penfriends to be placed in *Tuney Tunes,* a music lovers' magazine of that era. Corry was one of over fifty young women who responded, the beginning of their story which then quickly moves—from being 'sparring partners' as they playfully tease each other—into a deeper, more intimate connection. Through their letters to each other over many months, we can follow their relationship slowly unfolding.

For Corry, the most pivotal and challenging time in her life came much later and commenced with the conversation quoted above. Pierre was asking her, and their five young children, to leave behind all that they had ever known in the Netherlands for an unknown and risky future in faraway 'Down Under'. Neither of them could possibly have known how quickly Corry would fall in love with Australia, its vastness and beauty, and its people; or that Corry, a most reluctant emigrant, would ultimately become an awarded bush poet!

In 2003, and based on her own diaries, articles she wrote for a Dutch newspaper *Wereld Post* (World Post) and letters to her mother, Corry wrote a three-volume work, unpublished, to record her feelings, insights and experiences during what would prove to be a three-year migration journey, with its many uncertainties, challenges and adjustments. Then, in 2006, Corry produced a further unpublished work, *The Early Years*, an autobiographical account of her early childhood in Oudenbosch, a small rural village in the Netherlands. She also wrote many poems, some of which were published and awarded.

So, to the best of my ability, I have knitted these separate but closely related stories (and some relevant poems) together into this one account, the story of Corry and Pierre, and how they eventually found their place in the sun. As much as possible, I have kept my own words to an absolute minimum, mostly used to bridge or fill gaps in their own writings, and to summarise or reduce details not essential to the overall narrative.

In editing and producing this story, *their* story, I hope I have honoured them as parents to whom I and my siblings owe so much. For myself, working on this book has, at times, been a very emotional and even a humbling experience, in awe of what they lived through and achieved, both individually and together. I feel that I have come to know my father and mother in a much deeper and more intimate way, and, in doing so, have also come to better understand myself.

I especially hope that this book will be of interest for Corry and Pierre's grandchildren and great grandchildren, and for our extended families both here and in the Netherlands. Hopefully, it will be treasured by future generations as well.

Perhaps it might also be of some interest more generally and, if that is the case, then my siblings and I are immensely proud to be able to introduce a wider readership to two amazing people. However, that is not my main purpose in publishing this true and quite remarkable story of their lives: a testimony of adventure, love and resilience; a story of sacrifice, for their country and for their family; and a migration odyssey, bravely leaving behind the old and familiar to discover not only their 'place in the sun', but also a deep love for their newly adopted country, Australia.

Peter de Haas
September 2020

PART ONE: PIERRE'S STORY

1. HIS EARLY YEARS

Pierre de Haas, officially named as Petrus Johannes de Haas in keeping with Dutch custom at the time, was born to Willem and Everdina de Haas on 11 November (Armistice Day) 1923, into a merchant family in Helmond, the Netherlands. Ultimately, Pierre became the middle child of five boys, in order: Jan, Koos, Pierre, Teddy and Willy. Sadly, the only girl in the family, Joke (pronounced Yokee), died at three years of age.

The de Haas family all lived in a small apartment, including all the available roof space, above a home-lighting and bicycle shop located in the centre of the Helmond business district. This business was owned and operated by Pierre's father and, as they became old enough, all the boys worked in the shop. Consequently, from an early age, Pierre necessarily learnt how to 'read' and interact with all sorts of different people. While undoubtedly adhering to the motto that the customer is always right, given what was so plainly part of Pierre's make-up later in life, he gained an early ability to judge not only the character of others but also developed considerable skills in detecting any insincerity or deception.

Running a family business at any time is very demanding and, if it is to be successful, always requires a priority of commitment and effort, no more so than during the Depression years. Pierre, like his young brothers, learnt that, to do well, one must work hard and be thorough. These became

Part One: Pierre's Story

his guiding mantra for the rest of his life, lessons he also passed on to his own family. (Even now I can hear Dad's voice: *Peter, if you are going to do something, do it properly!* This has certainly guided my life's journey, like a little tape playing in my subconscious, part of the fabric of my very being, and playing again now as I am tackling this book.)

As a very welcome break, and to provide an additional source of fresh food, the family maintained a sizeable and productive vegetable garden somewhere outside of town. At times, when the weather was kind, the whole family jumped on their bikes and rode out of town for a day in the garden. Surely, Pierre's lifelong love of gardening was nurtured right here, in the open fields and fresh air of the family 'vegie patch'.

From the surviving photos of his early years (sadly there are no writings), there were also trips to the beach to break the monotony of running a business; although in later years Pierre would often remark that in the Netherlands summer was only ever for one or two days!

Pierre's—at times wicked—sense of humour and fun started to emerge quite early. As a teenager, he learnt how to ride a unicycle and became very adept at this most unusual skill. Not content to show this off during normal daylight hours, after dark he sometimes donned a white sheet and went whizzing up and down the streets of Helmond pretending to be a ghost, terrorizing young and old alike!

But all was not always well within this busy merchant family. Pierre himself wrote:

> As far as fathers were concerned, our family suffered from a different problem. With a dozen pubs within walking distance from our shop, Dad had ample opportunities for indulging in a glass of gin with his many friends from the local business community. The strong liquid, consumed nearly every night, caused many heartaches and so much friction in our household. No matter how hard we tried to keep things in order, family life, and the running of our shop, suffered.
>
> Mam, as our mother was affectionately called, had been a tower of strength in the early part of our lives and it was she who guided us through the dark times of the Depression years. Trade then was at an all-time low and yet, somehow, we managed to survive.

His Early Years

It could have been a happy family, but it seldom was. Time and time again we were confronted with endless arguments about cash at hand when Dad in his befuddled state wanted explanations where all the money had gone. At least food-wise, once the war entered our lives, we were far better placed. We could barter with bicycle parts, especially tyres, when they were available. We became experts on the black market, trading and swapping, assuring the family (and often close friends as well) of food supplies.

Sadly, Pierre's relationship with his father was strained from an early age, and never recovered in later years; nothing that Pierre or his young brothers did in the shop ever seemed to be good enough, even after spending many hours setting up inviting window displays or spending long days at the counter or fixing bicycles. The day's takings were often secreted away so that they couldn't be used for yet another drinking binge.

Pierre always remained very fond of his mother, Dina; indeed, they shared a remarkably close and special relationship. Despite his father's drinking, Dina made sure that the family was well cared for as far as she was able. She recognised, and even encouraged, in Pierre a spirit of independence and adventure, qualities which increasingly set him apart from his brothers as, from May 1940, another war overwhelmed the Netherlands which would eventually pull him into a swirling vortex of upheaval and chaos.

(Interestingly, Pierre never wrote about the invasion by Germany, how he experienced this as a sixteen-year-old, or the impact it had on him. We can, however, clearly infer his underlying attitude and feelings from the way he responds to the harsh dictates of the occupiers, and when the opportunity to fight for liberation presents itself.)

It all starts, somewhat innocuously, about two years later:

I first met Elly on a Sunday afternoon in the Spring of 1942. Tony, the only friend who had kept contact after we finished school, used to drop in on a weekend, and together we would take our pushbikes into the country or watch a local soccer match. We were at that awkward age where school was already a faraway part of our history,

Part One: Pierre's Story

yet we often missed the friendship of our former classmates. We never knew if we had arrived at the adult stage of our life or were hovering somewhere in no-man's land, where nobody seemed too keen on accepting us.

As we passed through the outskirts of town that sunny April day, we noticed a hockey match in progress. Having nothing better to do, we decided on a visit. There weren't many spectators, so our roving eyes caught the look-alike girls behind the goal mouth at the same time and, after a quick, knowing smile at each other, moved in their direction.

They had seemed like twins from a distance. Now, as we ambled closer (we didn't want to be seen to be in a hurry), we could make them out as sisters. The older one had dark hair and flirtatious eyes that passed ever so casually over our approach. They were dressed identically in white silk blouses and brightly coloured skirts in the national colours of red, white and blue. As least somebody was silently demonstrating that, although we were occupied by the enemy, we were by no means conquered. That thought, however, stayed inside me.

My approach became slower and slower, postponing the inevitable. The reason was simple. I had very little experience with girls as I had grown up in a family of males, the middle of five brothers. Female contacts were in the form of young girls wanting their bikes repaired in our bicycle shop, and often their physical proximity gave me the shivers, although I liked what I saw … from a distance …

The younger girl had dark-brown shoulder-length hair with a rosette behind her left ear, giving the impression of a Spanish dancer. Her full lips stood out in a plain face devoid of make-up. A Grecian nose seemed to smell the blue sky where little white clouds were playing hide-and-seek with a lazy sun. Not until I asked my first question, 'What's the score, ladies?' did I lock eyes with her, and that short, penetrating look made an everlasting impression.

We didn't get far that Sunday, with only vague answers to our mostly feeble probing, but they did allow us to escort them home, or near enough anyway. Not wanting their parents to see us, we said our polite goodbyes around the corner from where they said they lived. The result of that first meeting: no names, no address, nothing whatsoever. Yet I had detected a slight curiosity in the younger girl.

The older one, left talking mostly with Tony, seemed too much of a flirt to be bothered with our company.

After that first contact, something had grown in me, a feeling not experienced with anybody at all. It took me a couple of days to find out where they lived and even longer to see her again. By passing the house as often as possible I finally managed to halt my bike next to her.

'You are a hard one to locate,' was my opening sentence.

'I didn't know you were looking for me,' the shy reply.

From then on, at a slow and careful pace, we got to know each other better, making trips on our bikes or going for walks in the countryside. With spring showing what can be done to nature, our awakening feelings blossomed as well. At a party for my parents' silver wedding anniversary, I stole the first hesitant kiss.

'I thought we were only friends,' she said with a smile.

'It was only a friendly kiss, Elly,' I replied, hardly knowing the difference myself. As she had only recently turned sixteen, I did not want to smother her with affection. Friendship felt more solid than the trauma of love, I thought, as I tried to keep in step with my dancing partner.

Shortly afterwards, Elly started work at the large Philips complex, some fifteen kilometres away in Eindhoven. Soon, at the insistence of my father, I found myself a job as an apprentice motor mechanic in a small repair shop in that same industrial town. From then on, we could travel together by train. In the crowded wagons or sometimes even sitting on the floor of the goods compartment, we felt at ease with the world around us, especially in the darkness of total blackout. Our arms seemed to link so tightly as if afraid of losing contact with each other.

So, life for Pierre, a young man in his last year as a teenager, was good, predictable even. Yes, the Netherlands was occupied and under harsh rule by Germany, but he was learning a trade and had a steady girlfriend; most young men, even today, would be quite happy to have both!

2. IT BEGINS ... FORCED LABOUR AND EVASION!

Then everything changed in an instant, and from this time onwards, Pierre's life would be filled with constant uncertainty and instability, grave risk, and separation from loved ones for the next five and a half years. Nothing would, or could, be the same again. Yet amid all the upheaval, we discover a man of great courage, an adventurer willing to *put it all on the line* to serve his country and, in doing so, push his own boundaries to the very limits, even to death's door.

> It was the second week in March 1943.
>
> I found out shortly after returning home. My mother stopped me before I even had time to close the door. 'Have you read the announcement, Pierre?' and from the tone of her voice I knew something was wrong.
>
> 'No, I haven't. Anything I should know?' I replied, unpacking my lunchbox and dirty work clothes.
>
> 'Pierre,' she said in a slow, sad tone, 'all men born in 1923 are to be transported to Germany to forced labour camps!'
>
> *Arbeitslager*, the propaganda machine called them; places where one did not come back from, except on a stretcher.
>
> 'When?' It took me a while to bring that question out.
>
> 'Monday morning at nine. A special train will be at the station.'
>
> 'And my *Ausweisz*, Mam, doesn't that count for anything?' I had obtained that important paper, working in the repair shop in Eindhoven. We maintained BMW motor bikes for the German army and this business was classified essential. That too must have changed.
>
> 'Not anymore, son, not anymore,' and then as an afterthought, 'All papers have to be handed in when you leave.'
>
> We were both silent then. No need for more words. My brain was already working overtime, desperately trying to find a solution.

While all the other young men obediently boarded the train on the following Monday morning to be taken to a labour camp on the far side of Germany near the Polish border, Pierre had somehow worked out a very daring and dangerous alternative. In short, he jumped on his bicycle, with a cut-lunch prepared by his mother, who had no idea what he was planning to do, and cycled into Germany, crossing the border near the town of Venlo, at a checkpoint named Nierderdorf.

He wrote about that eventful day:

> In front of the station thousands of people were gathered. Family and friends, most of them girls, were struggling with tearful goodbyes. I watched for a few moments, saw the long queue of young men disappearing into the darkness of an uncertain future and felt a lonely sadness. Using side streets, I came back to the railway line a kilometre further on and followed the narrow bike path, parallel to it.
>
> Two hours later the train overtook me. I saw the young faces behind dirty windows, hated to think what was behind their masks. Many of those deported that day I knew through the family business; some even had done exams with me when we finished school. We all had one thing in common: we were the wrong age! I counted twelve carriages. The German uniforms clearly visible at the exits.
>
> I crossed the border into Germany at eleven o'clock. The guards hardly paying any attention to me or my belongings. One official noted my ID card number and wrote it down. They knew, as I did, it was one-way only. I had a strange feeling entering Germany and, although landscape-wise there was not much difference to the Netherlands, I was now in enemy territory. The first village I came to, and still having one sandwich left, I stopped at a small café.
>
> 'Ein bier bitte,' I said to the plumpish woman when she appeared from a dark, dank room behind the bar. She did not offer any conversation; I was not a local and that entitled me to the glass of beer I had asked for and nothing else. At least I spoke the language and, even then, at that early stage, I realised how important it might become later on.
>
> It was past three when I cleared a long, tiring hill (near Moers, close to Duisburg, about 90 km from Helmond) and there it was: the might

Part One: Pierre's Story

of an industrial nation at war. As far as my eyes could see were belching chimneys, cooling towers, factory complexes. Stretching to the horizon was the Ruhr estate, an unbroken line of deadly war machinery in full production. It was an awesome sight, on that cold March afternoon of 1943.

A bus company in a side street caught my attention and, without giving it any more thought, I walked up to the front office. 'Ja, bitte?' a voice from somewhere behind an open window startled me. 'Komm doch hinein, es ist zu kalt draussen.' The window closed again.

Yes, I knew it was cold outside and accepted the invitation to enter. 'Have you got a job for me?'

My simple question was met by a machinegun-like response. 'Got a driver's licence? Are you a motor mechanic? Any experience with diesels?' He paused to reload. 'You speak French?'

At last, a question I could answer, 'Jawohl.'

He explained then that having to employ half a dozen French labourers in his marshalling yard tended to be difficult with no one from his staff able to converse in that language. 'You start tomorrow at 6 am sharp,' and, handing me some forms to fill in, including one to obtain food coupons, he showed me very vaguely on a street map where to find a boarding house. He stepped back behind his desk, desperately trying to hide a limp. Must be over sixty, I thought. Probably an early victim of war.

And so commenced Pierre's forced labour in Germany for the next seven months. However, in the afternoon of that same day, his parents received a visitor.

A police sergeant, making sure he couldn't be overheard, asked my mother what had happened to her son Pierre. 'He left at seven this morning, catching that special train. I know because I packed his bag and gave him food for the long journey.'

'The Germans informed us that he was not crossed off their list and they don't make mistakes.' His voice was sad. He was an old friend of the family and if he could help, he would.

'Just a second,' my mother said and disappeared into the workshop. She came back soon afterwards. 'He took his bike with him!'

'His bike?' replied the sergeant in disbelief and then softly, as if talking to himself, 'His bike?'

He looked at my mother and finally said, 'Forty-eight hours is all the *Sicherheitsdienst* (SS) allows for information to come forward. After that'—he shrugged his shoulders—'it's out of our hands.'

Thirty-six hours later the Germans informed the police force in Helmond that I had crossed the border. I had left the country. The hunt was off. A very relieved mother heard the news from the same friendly sergeant.

The last place they would be searching for Pierre was in their own backyard!

During his forced labour, Pierre barely escaped the devastating bombing of nearby Ruhrort by the Royal Air Force on 13 and 14 May 1943, noting in his writings that the air-raid bunker where he should have been sheltering received a direct hit, killing everyone inside, including one of the bus drivers who Pierre had been working with only that afternoon. This was Pierre's first close call with death …

Pierre kept up a continuous correspondence with his girlfriend, Elly, who remained extremely concerned for him, especially with his willingness to take such a grave risk by not complying with the dictates of the German occupation. However, not content with the limitations of letter writing, Pierre managed to cross the border back into the Netherlands with the help of a friendly bus driver who simply told the guards that Pierre (who was carrying no documentation at all) was a new driver learning the routes. Later, he managed to comprehensively manipulate the German border control arrangements to secure a border pass by simply changing his recorded Dutch address to a randomly selected place in the town of Venlo. As Venlo was within 10 km of the German border, he then qualified for a border pass that would enable him to freely cross the border without any other documentation.

Consequently, in between his rostered work shifts with the bus company, visits back to Helmond to see Elly and his family became quite regular. Nevertheless, Pierre had to be extremely careful. His face was a familiar one in Helmond because of his long involvement in the family business. Darkness and disguise were his closest friends. One could never know who the German informers might be, or who might be openly questioning why Pierre was back when their own sons were still far away with the *Arbeitslager*.

3. COURIER, SPY AND FUGITIVE

Pierre also became a courier and a spy while working in Germany, both initiated and encouraged by his mother!

Letters home from the young men, his peers, who had been dragooned into the *Arbeitslager* were heavily redacted and censored by the Germans before they were delivered in the Netherlands, but apparently not so if they were addressed internally within Germany.

'Pierre,' Mam said, 'what if you send these young men on the list your address in the Ruhr and ask them to reply to you only. When you next come on leave you can bring the uncensored letters with you …'

'Just like that, Mam?'

'Well, what's the trouble, son?' Her voice sounded bewildered. 'Sure enough it's a small favour to ask, seeing that they are in that *Arbeitslager* and have no choice in the matter of writing. But you … you'—and she shook a finger at me—'can give them the freedom of correspondence.'

'How many are there?'

'Six all told. Two cousins and four friends of the family. You know them well. That train, the one you didn't take, transported the lot to near the Polish border, and with these crossed-out lines in all of the letters, their families don't know anything about their well-being: health, food, work, bombing raids … It's all bloody deleted!'

For my mother to swear, even gently, meant she was upset, and from her tone I concluded a promise was already made. Something like, 'Pierre will look after the problem.'

'What if I get caught?' A simple question.

'They won't catch you, son.' An even simpler answer.

When I sat down preparing the list I said, 'You knew all along I would do it, didn't you?'

'Of course, Pierre.' And with a sly smile at me, 'And I also know

Part One: Pierre's Story

how you operate, how your mind works. That, however, should stay between you and me, eh?' With that typical Dutch way of ending a conversation, we went over the list again, and later had the last cherry pancakes.

Within four weeks some twenty letters had arrived from various parts of Germany, and that presented Pierre with the new problem of how to smuggle them across the border.

Folding my meagre wardrobe one night before going to bed I stood for a moment holding a pair of well-worn trousers. And started to laugh ... No border guard would ever suspect them there, even if a physical check were carried out! Years ago, my mother had sewn a large piece of leather to the seat of my pants. Because of my daily cycling I always ended up with shiny pants. Very carefully, I undid some of the thread and the mail disappeared inside, hardly visible behind the solid material. Not being a qualified tailor, it took me far longer to put my pants back to normal again.

Although I felt as if I was sitting on a time bomb when we crossed the border and the guards were going through my belongings, everything went to plan. My mother laughed even more than I did when she asked if any letters had been sent and I, turning around, showed my leather behind.

'I knew you could do it,' was all she said amidst our laughter, but there was also pride in her voice when she phoned people telling them I was home. 'Yes, there are four letters for you and five for you ... Yes, come over to collect.'

'For God's sake, Mam, don't advertise it. The phone might be tapped.' But the calls went on. She hadn't even heard my outburst.

This was followed a short time later by another conversation with Mam, during which she conscripted her own son as a spy.

'I have a favour to ask, son.'
'Mam, you've done nothing else so far.'
'This is important, Pierre.'
So, the letters were only a prelude for other things to come.

Looking across the room, to see if Dad or my older brother Jan were listening, she continued, 'Someone has been in contact and would like photos from the bombed cities in the Ruhr and Rhine areas.'

There was complete silence then. No need to look at her face for any sign of a practical joke. She was deadly serious.

'He saw the pictures you took after the bombing of the Philips complex in Eindhoven. He was impressed.'

'But that was only fifteen kilometres away. The rolls were quickly developed and that was the end of my effort. Taking a camera into Germany and then casually putting the damage of their devastated cities on film is a completely different story.'

'Your Voigtländer is still in perfect order and I managed to get one film. The rest you have to buy over the border.'

And so it happened. However, by November 1943 Pierre had had enough of the bombing raids on the Ruhr industrial complex so close to where he was boarding and working. He had seen more than his fill of death and destruction and had some close escapes himself. So, the decision was made to use his border pass one last time to cross back into the Netherlands for good and then go underground, into hiding. He also brought back with him five rolls of film, referred to in the phone call to his mother as 'samples to be collected', which she promptly arranged.

The safe house where I was staying was in an unobtrusive corner block, and the fact there was a back door to a dark alley made it even more useful as a hiding place. There was also another twist, that hardly anyone was aware of. The family had a son, Hubert, a couple of years younger than I, and roughly the same build and showing a marked resemblance to my features, which wasn't surprising as he was my cousin.

Hubert was intellectually disabled and preferred to spend his time indoors, quietly reading in a corner of the small living room. So, naturally, Pierre borrowed Hubert's ID, coat and cap, purchased similar items on the black market, and thus became 'Hubert' whenever he went out to spend time with Elly, or just to escape from his hiding place for a while.

Part One: Pierre's Story

He was nevertheless careful to avoid any German security patrols which were spotted, and avoided, long before they became aware of his presence.

After being such a tumultuous and unforgettable year for Pierre, 1943 then came to a comparatively quiet end:

> Saint Nicolas Day on 6 December came and went without presents. Shops were empty and food, even if one had coupons, became more difficult to buy as winter put its chill on our town.
>
> Elly and I went to Midnight Mass at Christmas and once again found peace within and with each other. We linked hands as we joined in the many carols, and when we sang 'Silent Night, Holy Night' there was more in our eyes than just the twinkle of candlelight.
>
> Afterwards we had breakfast at her place and, surprisingly, her parents made me feel at home. That same day later in the evening, we visited my home and had a festive dinner near the tree and crib. My mother always enjoyed giving the house a real feeling of comfort and this time, war or no war, was no exception. Dad had bought some wine on the black market and we toasted to a better and happier future.

For the next few months, through a bitterly cold February and into March, with the first glimpses of spring and its flowers, Pierre continued to live in hiding, carefully venturing out in disguise, mostly under the cover of darkness. Nevertheless, he was still able to manipulate the German 'system' with its manic record keeping.

> Walking briskly in the cool spring evening, I went to my friend's place. Paul van de Reek looked after my border pass, and on Wednesdays I picked it up, after it had been stamped by a foreign exchange bureau in Germany.
>
> Paul was a black-market dealer and used the daily smuggler's train to the Ruhr for boosting his finances. My pass allowed him to change German Marks into Dutch Guilders at the same time as the stamp provided me with proof that I was still working across the border. Every imprint was dated. A simple and effective way to bypass the German system—the deadly efficient application of paperwork.

4.   'JAN' ON THE ATLANTIC WALL

In late April 1944, Pierre's life was confronted with yet another challenge, again at the behest of his mother.

One evening when he was with Elly, taking her home on his bike, she casually remarked, 'All the shopkeepers are being deported to work on the Atlantic Wall.' After nearly crashing into a road sign in shock, Pierre asked her to repeat what she said and Elly then confirmed that the very next morning, all shopkeepers in Helmond would be put on a special train to the North Sea coast. The impact on his family was obvious, so Pierre then hurried home, arriving at about ten, an hour before curfew.

On arriving home, he found the family distraught. His oldest brother Jan would have to go, as no exemptions would be allowed for any reason, and both his mother and Jan's fiancée, Mieps, were in tears.

> Then Mam's voice very softly: 'Can I talk to you for a moment, Pierre?'
>
> We went into the lounge, closing the door behind us. 'It would kill him,' she exploded, but at the same time pleading with her eyes for me to understand. 'You are different, Pierre. You are a survivor. You proved that over the last year and it meant I never had to worry about you.' She rectified after a few hesitating seconds, 'Being a mother of course I still did ... '
>
> Again, she waited for my reply, which wasn't forthcoming.
>
> 'Jan is afraid of going. He could never cope. It would destroy him!'
>
> Only then did it dawn on me what she was trying to get across. 'Surely, Mam, you are not thinking what I think that ... ' The unspoken words hung silently in the room. She nodded, unable to say another word, the tears gone, but still a star somewhere in the corner of her eyes.
>
> I admitted to her how well she was reading my own feelings—if not for Jan or weakness, but for Mam's distress.

Part One: Pierre's Story

'Oh, you crafty mother, to cook up a scheme like that,' which brought the first hint of a smile on that lovely face of hers. 'But it won't work, Mam. We don't even look alike,' which was certainly true. My brother having freckles all over his whitish skin, blue eyes, a kind of upturned little nose ... My God, it was a far cry from my pronounced hawk-like overhang, receding brown hairline and grey eyes. The only thing we had in common were our voices ... If only I could talk my way through.

'You'll make it work, son, I know you will,' and, giving me a warm hug, she made it seem so utterly simple.

'Will you do it, Pierre?' Their voices were as one as we re-entered the kitchen.

'Let's have a brandy instead of tea while we discuss what has to be done, and yes I will do it!' My last words were smothered by Mieps, who embraced me as if I had just saved her life.

We took our ID cards outside, rubbed them through sand, leaving them basically intact but obscuring enough of the fingerprints and photos to make them passable as someone else's. The important thing for Jan to do, once I had taken his place, was to move upstairs and, on no account, to show himself to the outside world.

And so it happened: the real Jan hid himself in the attic, while Pierre became Jan and worked as a labourer on the Atlantic Wall for several months in the middle of 1944. (In later years, this story was retold over and over again, becoming family folklore. What Pierre did then and later remained a source of admiration among his younger brothers, Teddy and Willy.)

From his diary and writings, it appears that the work on the wall was mostly a half- hearted effort, as they dug in large poles which were intended to stop gliders from landing.

It took a while getting used to being called Jan. On several occasions I didn't react when someone yelled, 'Hey Jan, give us a hand with this pole,' or later in the evening, 'Jan, did you have your meal yet?' Pierre gradually faded from my memory, except deep inside, where I was desperately trying to hold on to myself.

Changing names had one advantage. The Germans paid me three

guilders a week extra for being two years older. For once their efficiency in keeping details worked in my favour.

Apart from a daily visit by a German SS officer on a motorbike, there was no supervision, as our old guard was quite content to wait at the end of the field we were working on. So, hearing the distant sound of the motorcycle in the otherwise deserted landscape, we would run to our holes and, looking terribly busy, let sand fly in all directions. There were always poles standing lopsided, ready to be firmly erected. Always men at work ... Always ...

Then, on the very last day, a hilarious episode to raise spirits:

One of our best-liked companions was a pub owner—living in the same street as I—who had an enormous beer-belly, stopping him from seeing his own feet while digging. So, from the very first day he was sent to farmhouses to try and obtain more milk or bread to supplement our meagre rations.

However, on the very last day he managed to dig a hole about forty centimetres deep. We found an extra-large pole and, with a combined effort, held it up, pushing sticky clay in the tiny hole. It stayed there (admittedly only just) but it looked normal enough from a distance. Later, as we gathered our spades and belongings, the old German guard appeared and shouted in an excited voice, 'Jetzt ist der krieg vorbei,' and to emphasise that the war was over, he started to use his hands, meanwhile leaning his bike against the suspect pole. Before our startled eyes, as if in slow motion, this giant started to move, first ever so gently and then with increasing speed, hitting the ground with an almighty thud. The old soldier just stood there in shock.

Probably to overcome his own feelings, the beer-belly man in that half-stuttering voice of his blurted out, 'These p-p-poles are for stopping p-p-planes and not for use as b-b-b-bicycle racks.'

It was too much for us, the crashed pole, the expression on the soldier's face and the stuttering of the bar owner. We needed the support of our spades to stop us falling over in helpless laughter. Later, we went back using a slow-march tempo and singing 'Moeder, onzen haan is dood ...' the slowest song every written in the Netherlands. Yes, 'Mother, our rooster has died ...' was a fitting goodbye to the spades, blisters and card games associated with our

Part One: Pierre's Story

stint on the Atlantic Wall.

So, on the day after the allied landings in France (D+1), 'Jan' returned home to Helmond, back to his hiding place, and became Pierre again. That evening, the real Jan threw a party to celebrate his own liberation from the attic, and Pierre's safe return. Their mother told Pierre amidst peals of laughter that Jan had only gone out of the house once, dressed up as a girl. He and Mieps, his fiancée, went for a bike ride, in the open country around Helmond, with him wearing a long skirt, newspapers under his blouse for padding, a wig and frilly hat!

5. COMMANDO

Some sort of normality now resumed for the de Haas family. However, by the end of August 1944, Helmond was no more than 30 km from the front line, with the US First Army pressing into Belgium, heading for Brussels. Pierre writes:

> The Germans panic and retreat and the population watches in amazement when on 'Dolle Dinsdag' (Mad Tuesday) the once mighty *Wehrmacht* walks in the direction of the fatherland. Yes, I use the word walk on purpose as no one was marching ... not when one pushes prams and wheelbarrows, has cows, with a rope around their necks, following, and the only type of transport are pushbikes ... for officers only. I took some pictures as the circus moved slowly en route to Germany through our Molenstraat where we lived.
>
> I met the first GI on Sunday afternoon, 17 September 1944. His emblem said he was a member of the 101st Airborne Division which had just landed 10 km north of Eindhoven. He was guarding a small concrete bridge on a country road only a few hundred metres from the main thoroughfare to Nijmegen. Standing on the side of the narrow track he was hardly visible as his camouflage uniform blended in with the shrubs bordering the vast expanse of lush green meadows.

A short time later, with the Netherlands only partially liberated, and against the advice of his mother as well as ignoring the distress of his now long-suffering girlfriend, Elly, Pierre and two friends joined the *Binnenlandse Strijdkrachten* (BS)—the Dutch Interior Forces—as volunteers. Pierre records how Elly pleaded with him:

> 'Why, Pierre, what's the urgency?' How do you explain to a girl you love that there is such a thing as a physical urge inside to do more with your life than waiting at an address called a safe house?

'Why can't you wait until the whole country is liberated? It won't be that long now. We can be together then without fear for your freedom and we can look at a future and ... and ...' but the flow of words halted. She was aware now I wasn't listening. Not with my heart anyway ...

So, Pierre joined what can only be described as a militia, although formally established by a royal decree on 5 September 1944, which founded the Interior Forces to be actively involved in the liberation of the Netherlands and the removal of the enemy. It was a motley force. Any and all training was strictly 'on the job' in a confused, rapidly changing combat situation, with constantly shifting positions and redeployments of his unit.

Without experience, just a few brief explanations how Stens and Lee-Enfields worked, and lacking discipline we were indeed raw ... but no one complained, we were so eager to be part of the Allied forces.

When we arrived, we were amazed that everyone, apart from a few NCOs and officers, were still in civilian clothes. The only indication that they were actually in an army, a band across one arm with the letters BS. Then, late on the first day, an army truck pulled up and unloaded English khaki uniforms. When we changed and looked at each other, we realised how these brand-new outfits made us even more aware of how inadequate we really were.

'The only way to learn this trade is to go into the streets and meet them head-on!' It was the longest speech our sergeant ever made. Our first contact with the enemy came after dark on Armistice Day.

After several weeks of fully living the old, well-proven army adage of *hurry up and wait*, intermingled with some actual combat in street and building-to-building clearance operations, Pierre's unit received a visitor, a young officer, who was seeking volunteers to train as commandos in the UK. Although there wasn't much time to consider the possibility—they were only given thirty minutes—Pierre records that he still managed to write down a list of pros and cons on a sheet of paper. The only thing against him volunteering was one word: 'Elly'; while he ran out of paper with the 'pros' column. So, a short time later, Pierre found himself in a jeep on his way to Eindhoven where all volunteers were being assembled; but not before fielding some insulting allegations of being a deserter from some of the members of his first 'army' unit.

For the next extremely hard and uncomfortable weeks, Pierre discovered what the real army was like. After crossing the Channel to England, the 120 young and enthusiastic volunteers were taken to a training camp near Petford, in the south of England, for intensive basic training in the fundamentals of being a soldier.

> As the days flowed into each other they became like one. The only time we knew there was a difference was on Sunday morning when we were allowed a visit to the chapel and a talk with the padre. Then, back to training. Nights were taken up with cross-country marches and complicated schemes to test our ability to approach unseen, to tread without noise, to infiltrate enemy positions.
>
> Our nerves got frayed at the edges in the process, friendships were hard put to survive for more than a couple of days. Arguments broke out over little things like snoring in an upper bunk ...
>
> Yet, I felt at home in this camp because so much was asked of us and so much of ourselves given in return. Our isolation was complete. No visits to local pubs or villages were allowed. No mail could be sent to the Continent, as postal services were not yet operating in our partly liberated homeland.

Then, on 6 December 1944, the recruits were taken to that very windswept, cold and bleak commando training ground in Achnacarry, Scotland, just as winter was starting to take hold. Following some further weeks of gruelling training—while accommodated in freezing tents—and after successfully completing a final test of extreme endurance and initiative during a blizzard, Pierre received his green beret with seventy-eight other 'survivors'. The rest were returned to their units.

On Christmas Day, a special surprise was in store. It was 0630.

> When our Dutch instructor, a corporal in his mid-twenties but

Part One: Pierre's Story

already a veteran of several assaults on the Continent, told us our destination, we looked at each other in surprise. Ben Nevis? On Christmas day? The highest mountain in the British Isles? A joke of course! All one thousand, three hundred and forty-two metres of it? They must be kidding ... there was half a metre of snow covering the mountain with snowdrifts several metres high ...

But it was no joke! About the climb, Pierre writes:

Our army boots had long ago given up hope of keeping our feet dry; the continuous onslaught of snow and frosty streams had taken its toll. They became soggy at first and, finally, completely waterlogged. It was past noon before we started on the last two hundred metres of a steep overhang below the summit. Ropes and grappling irons, part of our kit, were unslung and in a short while the face of the mountain looked like a swarming ant's nest.

It should have been routine really, with numerous mountaineer lessons behind us to boost confidence. But with more than six hours of forced, uphill marching, and detours because of snowdrifts, we were extremely tired. The frozen snow with its raw and sharp edges turned this section into a dangerous obstacle.

Cold, hungry, wet and sore feet, heavy clothing damp with sweat and fear, hampering equipment, near frozen fingers holding on for dear life: no, definitely not a favourite way to spend Christmas. Hanging on the ropes, balancing on the narrow ledges, I stretched out to reach the one above me. Then, unintentionally, I looked down to the figure following me. Something I should never have done because panic tried to dislodge my trembling body. I saw a thousand metres of emptiness below me. What saved me was a sudden surge of adrenaline flooding my insides like an injection of a powerful drug, penetrating my mind.

Finally, a thirty-minute rest period at the summit where they could admire the marvellous view of lakes, valleys and mountains which lay beneath them to the horizons.

Then, after making their descent in less than two hours, another surprise awaited them!

A festive Christmas dinner was waiting after our successful assault on Ben Nevis. The large mess hall, normally bare and uninviting, had been transformed into a truly welcoming atmosphere: brightly coloured tables; a real tree with decorations in the centre of the hall; greenery on the walls, and delicious food—that most of all—the turkey, served with roast potatoes and vegetables, hardly fitted in mess-tins, as we slowly made our way alongside the service counter.

The corps commander, Colonel A Lyons, made his speech short and to the point, comparing our commando training with the hardship of millions of people, still occupied throughout Europe. He asked us to join him in a silent prayer for relatives and friends of the Norwegian and Dutch servicemen. We prayed for a few minutes and lined up again for dessert.

After that typical English treat of rich pudding with rum-sauce was served, we started on Christmas carols. Each nationality sang their own special melody. The very last one—'Silent Night'—was sung together.

I was glad to be sitting at a table near the exit, where lights were dim, and shadows hung around corners. Because there are those ballads that haunt me. Not so much with the words but with memories attached to them. 'Silent Night' is one of them …

It doesn't help, thinking you are a trained soldier, a tough piece of fighting machine. In moments like these, weakness and strength go hand in hand … It only lasts a couple of seconds, with tears appearing and retreating, leaving the eyes with the gloss of emotional mist.

Pierre remained in Achnacarry till mid-January 1945, and then his unit, No. 2 Troop (Dutch) of 10 Commando, was relocated to Eastbourne in the south of England, joining other commando and special forces units. On leaving Scotland, Pierre records:

All in all, those six weeks of assault on our bodies and minds alike had been bloody murder. That much I care to recall. Perhaps in thirty or forty years my grandchildren might ask, 'Opa, whatever happened in Scotland?'

Part One: Pierre's Story

While Eastbourne was a much more comfortable base in that Pierre and his comrades were billeted with families and found themselves in decent beds for the first time in months, training continued unabated and became much more specialised. Pierre trained as a combat signaller and then as a paratrooper, completing his first jump in late March 1945.

> Wednesday, March 28, the first night jump took place. We boarded the Dakota at eight o'clock and were soon cruising at an altitude of 300 metres. Equipment was checked, static lines hooked onto the anchor-line. The door opened and an icy wind took our breath away. No one paid attention to comfort. All eyes on the red light, turning to green suddenly, and the first paratrooper went into space, followed in quick succession by two dozen others.
>
> I felt the fierce jerk as the silk unfolded, and hit the ground hard, because of the deceiving shadows of the full moon. I rolled, was half back on my feet again, started to wrap the parachute, hit the release button, all in a confused and wrong sequence. The instructor, a light on his stopwatch, was understandably not impressed. 'Too slow, too goddamn slow,' he kept repeating. His English swear words more familiar than his French.

Just over a week later, Pierre, with two fellow commandos, was given a mission to eliminate a double agent in the Netherlands who was considered a grave risk because he had a great deal of information on the British and Dutch secret services. Pierre records the following aspects of the briefing he was given:

> '... the target has lived in that area since 1936 and is a respected member of the local society. Since December 1942 he has been a trusted radio operator for the Dutch resistance. He is a Gestapo agent and top man in *Abwehr*. He is what we call a "PWM", a Pre-War-Mole. They are highly trained infiltrators operating in occupied countries.'

On the night of 6 April, the three commandos were inserted by parachute and their mission was successfully completed.

Shortly after, Pierre found himself back in the Netherlands for a further mission planned for early May, but the end of the war in the Netherlands occurred first, with all hostilities on land, on sea, or in the air by German forces ceasing at 0800 hours British Double Summertime on Saturday, 5 May 1945. VE day came three days later

Then, Pierre received the first news from home for months.

Helmond, 6 May 1945
Dear son and brother,

Well, well, at last after more than six months without any news—although Elly told me she had received a letter from you—three of those special 'on active service' envelopes arrived together.

One was from last year December—what a time to cover the distance— where you talked about snow and tents and mountains. Then, one from England, which was dated April, and a recent one posted somewhere on the continent, perhaps in the Netherlands then? You DO move around, Pierre, glad to read though that you are coping well, it must have been hard all that training under those cold conditions.

And ... a GREEN BERET! Congratulations, son, you deserve it. I've phoned a few friends telling them the good news and they send their regards and were glad to hear you came through the war INTACT.

I wonder when we'll see you again, hopefully you'll get some leave soon. Everyone in the family survived the war, so no complaints in that respect, but as far as business is concerned, and our income from that source, the situation looks grim.

The shop is nearly empty, there is no supply yet of any bicycle parts, and the surrender of Germany this week won't make much difference. All the factories and warehouses are in the western provinces of the Netherlands and God knows when they open for trading again.

Last Christmas we had a harrowing experience. To get at least some atmosphere for the festive season, we had decorated the shop windows with white paper and imitation snowflakes. We used your Raleigh bike as a centrepiece for the display, put a couple of tiny spotlights on (blackout was still in force then) and the result was an eye-catching fairy-tale look.

At midnight on the twenty-third, a stray V2 bomb exploded around the corner near the butcher shop, a mere hundred metres from here, killing some twenty people and wounding dozens.

You can imagine how the centre of Helmond looked like with thousands of windows shattered and glass and debris everywhere. Of course, with the cold winter we had, everyone was frantically trying to board up the gaping holes. Timber, cardboard, newspapers, pieces of iron, anything to keep the frost out.

It took us two days to pick up all the slivers of sharp glass, flown throughout our shop. Your bike survived but is slightly damaged.

You see, Pierre, we all thought war wouldn't touch us anymore, after the easy liberation by the Tommies, but Christmas changed all that. But we are thankful that we have been spared death or injury.

You asked for Elly's latest location, but I honestly don't know. She joined VHK that's all I have heard. Perhaps Army HQ could inform you.

Take care now and best wishes from friends and family.

Love from Mam and Dad and your brothers
See you soon, I hope …

The *Vrouwen Hulpkorps* (VHK), translated as Women's Help Corps, was a paramilitary organisation of volunteers.

What wasn't mentioned in the letter, probably because it had become the terrible experience of much of the Dutch population, was hunger. Since late 1944, food had become very scarce due to the impact of the war, and many thousands starved to death in the following months in what became known as the *Hunger Winter*.

Pierre records:

25 April. All central food kitchens in Amsterdam, The Hague, Rotterdam and Utrecht are now closed down through lack of coal or any form of heating. Emergency supplies of reserve food have also dried up. Thousands of people use their last reserves and walk hundreds of kilometres in an often-vain attempt to buy some potatoes or any type of food still left with the farmers.

The tulip fields had already been the target, right through that period, the *Hunger Winter*. The tulip bulbs and all the other varieties could be eaten as a staple diet, tasting like onions and at least filling the stomachs of those fortunate enough to live in the coastal area. But there was no substitute for coal or firewood. All tram and railway sleepers in the main cities had disappeared and had found their way to improvised little stoves made from biscuit tins.

From late April, and into the last days of the war, massive food drops were made across the Netherlands under *Operation MANNA*. Both Pierre and Elly separately found themselves (and their respective units) assisting with food distribution to their starving countrymen and women.

6. LIBERATION AND ELLY

Notwithstanding the backdrop of loss, destruction and starvation, nothing could stop the celebrations that sprang up spontaneously across the country when the news spread that the war in Europe was over … and in the town of Breda, two young lovers were unexpectedly reunited after many lonely months apart, with only an occasional letter exchanged while both their lives were in constant upheaval.

Breda, a city of around 50,000, had gone mad …

That's the only description one could give, watching this singing, pulsating mob trying to reach the city centre, where a large open-air dance was in progress. Germany had surrendered and the population was going to celebrate, not just the end of five years of occupation but also to rejoice in a new beginning.

It was a glorious May evening, the sun still out, with the warmth of her rays hanging in the air. Standing in one of the main streets, watching the crowd from the edge of the pavement, my two buddies Joep and Gerry somewhere behind me, I felt a kind of jubilation to see all those happy people singing and chanting. Although we didn't know anybody in this town, there was a friendliness in the air that was catching.

The amplified music from the nearby church square, where the dance was being held, drifted over the throbbing, undulating stream of people. As the sun settled below the horizon and the long twilight softened the contours of the old buildings, some streetlights came on for the very first time in five years.

Apart from the singing crowd, everything looked pre-war peaceful again. Suddenly out of the corner of my eye I saw a black beret moving and then it disappeared. Up it came once more and I could see a girl in army uniform about twenty metres away, trying to find an opening through the clinging mass of people.

Her features were still obscured. I stared at her in the fading light, waiting for her face to materialise. The beret moved closer, dark curls dancing underneath. Suddenly, I shouted, 'Elly, Elly over here, it's me!'

She turned … our eyes met. Two hands came up out of the weaving crowd. A cry followed: 'Pierre, Pierre!'

People smiled, yielding a passage for hungry arms, stretched out now to meet and embrace. We collided halfway. Words were impossible, a warm kiss shutting out the other world. My friends were forgotten and already discarded.

It seemed ages before we could disentangle and give our new appearances at last a chance to be noticed. Holding her by the shoulders I looked her up and down, taking it all in, the khaki shirt and blouse, the tie, the black beret with the Dutch lion, the emblem on her uniform, VHK. 'You look great, Elly, just great.' It sounded so banal. There must be a million different ways to describe a girl like her, yet I seemed unable to find them.

She had seen me once before in uniform late last year, but now my green beret held her attention. 'My own commando,' was all she said, but the way it came out was a promise of belonging, of sharing plans for a future together.

At last, away from the dancing people, we found a quiet café where we could order coffee and some biscuits.

It took us all evening and part of the night to open our hearts, and, as we walked through the still-crowded streets of Breda, I told her about the lonely winter months in Scotland, the training, the endless nights in the fields. Elly talked about VHK, how she had enlisted; the first weeks so emotive that she often thought of giving in.

We sat on a bench near the railway station. It was well past two in the morning; time had lost its meaning. We had to talk and get it all 'out of our systems'. All the worrying thoughts of months gone by …

We walked back to her barracks where the front gate had been locked in the night. Elly climbed the high steel fence with a helping hand from me; the bars were spaced just far enough apart to hold our lips a little while longer, with her standing on the inside now.

The only disturbing detail of that evening kept appearing in front of my eyes. Who was that soldier she was walking with when I first saw her? She didn't volunteer his name or their relationship. I hadn't asked either …!

Part One: Pierre's Story

Given Pierre's adventurous, risk-taking nature—after all, he had chosen to leave her behind to join the army as soon as it became possible to do so—who could blame her for finding friendship elsewhere? Indeed, when Pierre would again leave her stranded for his next adventure in a few short months, the hurt would be very deep and would mark the end of any future together they might have imagined possible.

Soon after their unexpected encounter in Breda, Pierre went back to the VHK barracks only to find them empty. Elly's unit had moved to The Hague.

> Dear Pierre,
>
> Sorry about our sudden departure, you must have wondered what had happened to our unit. Well, the above line 'on active service' says exactly what we are doing: working nearly 24 hours a day to feed, clothe and delouse thousands of people.
> I have never seen so many starving women and children (men are hardly present) who need our help. The food kitchens in our Queen's Messenger trucks operate day and night. The girls working in shifts to keep the meals flowing. I could never imagine while still a civilian how desperate was the condition of the population in the big cities.

This was part of a very warm-hearted letter to Pierre which he reciprocated in early May. However, in his diary Pierre notes:

> Yet, I was already in a different world, a restless one and confused. I loved the girl with the black beret, but perhaps my love was too special and becoming vulnerable as I moved from one village to the next. And met other girls, just friendly connections of course ... but dangerous nevertheless ...

Dangerous indeed! The war in Europe being over seemed to unleash in Pierre what we may now refer to as a 'party animal'. Elly's absence didn't deter him, and the month of June 1945 was filled with short leave periods, parties and dances.

But then, towards the end of the month, Pierre and Elly met up again, and they decided to become engaged. Perhaps this is reflective of the confused and uncertain situation in which they (and everyone else in the Netherlands) existed at the time, possibly giving rise to a certain impulsiveness aimed towards creating a sense of stability?

> One Friday, 22 June 1945, I was back in The Hague for another five days' leave. Elly had moved to Groenestein, an old mansion built after the first war. It held dozens of rooms, now all transformed into sleeping quarters for the VHK unit.
>
> I was allowed a visit to their domain and, from the safety of a spotless canteen, watched the comings and goings of many attractive girls in uniform. Some recognised me and made small talk with us while Elly and I were having a cup of tea. Others were going on with the daily routine or getting ready for an evening out.
>
> That same evening, we took part in street dancing, a new way of overcoming the shortage of halls and electricity. Army trucks would line up near a suitable square, put their headlights on, a jazz-band appeared from somewhere and hundreds of people could enjoy free entertainment. We danced till well past midnight when band and trucks had had enough and the quiet of the star-lit sky took over again.
>
> At noon on Sunday, 24 June, we went to a special Mass in the VHK canteen, talked for a long time afterwards with the chaplain and decided to get engaged.
>
> 'What about rings?' Elly asked. 'Do you think we can buy any?'
>
> 'We still have those thousand Senior Service cigarettes I sent to your BLA address, remember?'
>
> And so, unexpectedly for both of us, we promised each other everlasting loyalty. Photos were taken, again with cigarettes as payment, tulips were bought, and a happy couple smiled at the camera. The party later was a simple affair. Two bottles of Beaujolais gave the festive sparkle to celebrate the bond of two young people.

7. ON THE MOVE AGAIN ... AND INJURED

Then on 3 July, Pierre's life changed again. No. 2 Dutch Troop, 10 Commando, were redeployed to Recklinghausen in Germany to guard an SS POW camp.

Recklinghausen, 27 July '45

Dearest Elly,

As you can see by the above address, we have moved house again, this time into a real one, a row of solid German buildings where our unit is located.

I only stayed a few more days in Winterswijk before we had to move out quite suddenly. That's the way commandos operate, let you guess where you will go next. Not very good for young people in love—like you and me—because, actually, we still don't know where to find each other.

You at least will be stationed in The Hague for a while, but our movements are so erratic. It has all become part of everyday life. I am used to it now, in fact like it in a certain way!

I'm still thinking about that last leave with you, the dancing in the street, the sudden engagement, flowers, photos, rings ... like a distant dream! Don't even know if it actually happened, only my diaries say so. I'd better believe the words written down!

We are guarding a POW camp and the inmates are all ex-SS, so the word is out: 'be careful'. Many of them are expected to be charged as war criminals later. Two thousand men is a lot to keep an eye on!

A strange thing happened to me last night while on duty outside the perimeter. I noticed an SS member standing outside a hut and he was drawing something on paper. I stood underneath a spotlight and marched to the left and right as our instructions stipulate. Imagine my surprise, finding a rolled-up drawing stuck in the wire mesh, when I had completed my guard duty.

A picture of me in coloured pencil. So real in fact that it has become more than just a face, as if he portrayed my inner secret self. There is something there, drawn to perfection, like an internal affair, not often disclosed to anyone. I will show it to you when my next leave is due and let you make your own conclusions.

I shall always wonder though what kind of prisoner did this portrait of me, the only indication is a Capital S and a small k to the side of the paper and the words: "Lager Recklinghausen, 26 July 45".

There are rumours already of moving again, back to England even, but so far, no details. Please write soon. I can't wait to see that black beret again and hold all the goodies moving underneath!

Seeing we are in Germany, AUF WIEDERSEHEN FRAULEIN ICH LIEBE DICH! Pierre

Less than two weeks later, Pierre found himself back in England, even noting himself that his diary was having trouble keeping up with all his movements. Now he was at the 'Royal Military College—NCO School' located at the Royal Marine Barracks at Deal in Kent. Here the relatively relaxed military atmosphere of the past few months in post-war Europe was replaced by tough and very strict discipline. Open fields had given way to fenced-in barracks and the ever-present parade ground for marching and drill, instead of weapons and combat training. It was quite an adjustment for Pierre and his army buddies: to now being drilled in instant obedience to orders after all they had already been through. Normally, parade ground drills and marching are part of basic training for soldiers, not those already wearing green berets!

Then, very suddenly, the war in the Far East was over. The *Movietone* news, shown in the local cinema, revealed for the first time the devastating new weapons that had obliterated much of Hiroshima and Nagasaki, with actual footage of the mushroom clouds billowing up above ground zero. A few days later, VJ day was declared.

Pierre and his Dutch colleagues on the NCO course then received a pleasant surprise in the form of a request to take over the guard duties of the barracks. For the first time in the long history of the Royal Marines

Part One: Pierre's Story

foreign troops would 'hold the fort'.

> It was one of the proudest moments in my life when, together with five others, we changed guard at 12 noon. That evening, to the amazement of a singing and dancing crowd, Dutch commandos stood to attention in front of the barracks, then marched left five steps, made a smart about-turn, and marched to the right. Many friendly and inviting smiles were cast in our direction. Some girls even imitated our steps, laughing and giggling. But we had been warned not to forget about 'decorum'.
>
> Of course, no one mentioned winking, and as I stood at ease, just outside the sentry box, my eyes fixed at a point straight ahead, certain girls tried to stare me out. They would have succeeded if I hadn't winked, just a faint one mind you, but it made them laugh and they then re-joined the jubilant crowd. Yes, if ever I felt like a real soldier, it was on VJ day 1945. No one likes guard duties. Deal became an exception.

Then from what was clearly an absolute high point for Pierre, only a few days later his world, to quote him, 'crumbled to pieces'. What happened is best told in his own words:

> On ~~active~~ service, Deal, 20 August 1945
>
> My darling Elly,
>
> Two days ago, I started this letter, full of life and energy and now, as you are probably aware by the crossed-out 'active', things have changed, as I try, painfully, to continue with my left hand, while sitting in front of my tent.
>
> My right wrist is broken in several places. The barracks are nearly deserted, the rest of our troop are on a landing exercise and for me, sad to say, the world has suddenly come to an end, finito, kaput ...! The end of a career? I don't know, the whole thing came as a severe shock to the system.
>
> We were dropping from a low altitude when a sudden wind gust blew me off course and instead of landing on a marked-out soccer

pitch, I went straight into a large tree. Hitting the release button hard, as instructors had told me, I thought for a moment that a safe, if rough, landing was still possible. However, the branch I was hanging onto snapped under my weight, and, falling about five metres, I hit the ground very hard, my right arm taking the full impact.

After the drop we were supposed to move inland, cross a river, and complete the day's operation at the seashore in Deal. At that time, I didn't know my wrist was broken and, although it hurt like hell, decided to join the others boarding the landing craft. My leading sergeant, who had witnessed the incident from a distance, told me to report to the hospital, however.

Arriving there, I found a long line of young recruits waiting for their inoculations and, when I went to the front to enter the sick bay, I was told not to jump the queue, my protests falling on deaf ears!

I thought then well, 'You can all get st ...' (sorry Elly) and, joining our troop again, spent the rest of the day running and climbing, feeling the pain increasing. At five, near the target area, I fainted and ended up in that hospital after all. When I came to, the doctor scolded me for not reporting sooner!

That, my love, is what happened. So, no more war games for me, no more flying away to distant places, which should please you! Or not? It looks as if I'll become a civilian again, a retired, ex-commando ...

The change from active duty to a world of nothingness frightens me. That much I have realised since I became 'inoperative'. Only last week we celebrated the surrender of Japan, and on that day we were asked to guard the barracks. I was one of those six elected to take over the duties of the Royal Marines ...!

I am tired, trying to hold that pen with my left hand. It seems as if the summer warmth on this August day has left my heart, and a cold feeling is gripping my insides. I can't function with one arm, in a military sense anyway—have become useless in fact. Doing what I know best, being a commando, has been postponed.

Perhaps forever ...

I could go on writing like this, there is a need, a desperate need to talk to someone. It hurts, Elly, it hurts deeply, not the wrist, no, I can live with that for a while. But losing the love I felt for the green beret, becoming redundant, that is what cuts through my heart.

Part One: Pierre's Story

I'll try and explain when I'm shipped back to the Netherlands again. Till then I can only send my love, even if today it is a sad one.

Pierre.

8.   A Promise Made and Quickly Broken

Pierre returned to the Netherlands on 5 September 1945, and rejoined his unit while remaining on light duties, also finding some time for two weeks leave in Paris with one of his close friends, Joep. From his diary, this was quite a wild time, especially for someone who was engaged! (Out of respect for my parents, I will leave it at that!)

In late October, just as the annoying and itching plaster cast had come off at the local Red Cross post, Pierre received a phone call from Elly who was distraught as she had just lost her much-loved grandmother.

> Elly was crying when she rang. Her grandma had died suddenly and would I please come home to be at the funeral. Oma, as she was called, had been her best friend and, on reflection, often my friend as well. Her cups of tea were always the beginning of an advice session for young people who were in love, infatuated or lovesick! Elly and I fell into any of those categories. She had guided us through numerous ups and downs in our relationship; the ups we could handle (we thought so at that time anyway) but we always seemed to fall off the top somehow, leaving us stranded at the bottom where we became our own worst enemies, loving and hating each other in a matter of minutes.
>
> Yes, she had shown us the two sides of life, thorns and roses. Now she was gone, never reaching a ripe old age, but, then again, compared with us, anyone over forty was ancient we thought. I had no trouble getting a three-day pass, as my wrist was still useless.
>
> In church we paid respect to her grandma, lying there so peacefully in front of the altar. A few red roses the only colour in a dark coffin. Elly's hand stayed locked in mine; I had never seen her so upset before. When family and friends left after the service, we lit two candles and quietly kneeled, our mind far beyond our bodies.
>
> Perhaps it was the sadness of it all that touched me deeply, so

deeply in fact that I made a promise that surprised me. 'Elly,' and here I had to wait a few seconds, overcome with emotions, 'I will be leaving the army soon,' and adding as if to justify my reason, 'I'm not much good anyway with a broken wrist and I never could be a professional soldier.'

There was a long silence, then we had left the church behind us and were walking home, arms linked again. She stopped suddenly, turned to face me, planting a long kiss on surprised lips. 'Would you really do that, Pierre, for me?'

She stood there not quite understanding yet but hoping she had heard right. 'I could leave the VHK too, then.' Her voice trailed off, coming back after a while very softly, '… we could build a future together …'

Her vocals were faltering completely, needing time now to say those all-important words. So, I said them instead, 'Yes, and later we will get married, if you want to …?'

The question mark was replaced by a smile, the sadness of death for a moment forgotten in this new and exciting world of tomorrow. 'Oh Pierre, I wish it will come true!'

I repeated my promise, adding that first thing Monday I would fill in an application for discharge, releasing me from the army in about a month. A new Elly hung onto my arm. A transformation had taken place as she whispered, 'We could have a real engagement party on your birthday in November!'

Yes, Armistice Day would be the perfect occasion for celebration.

'Oh Pierre,' was all she said, when I nodded agreement. Her lips and eyes had taken on the moisture of liquid happiness. When I finally let go of her warm embrace, I felt like a different person, already accepting my future role in civilian life.

But a civilian Pierre was not to be—at least not for another three years, and never with Elly!

On the following Monday morning, only a few days later, Pierre obtained his discharge papers from his stunned captain, completed and signed them, and sealed them in an envelope before heading to the administration building.

A Promise Made and Quickly Broken

Passing the parade ground, I noticed that every commando from our unit had lined up for a special rollcall. As I was still off duty there was no need for me to join, but, nevertheless, being curious I took my place in the line-up. And curiosity killed the cat!

Our commanding officer introduced our unit to a visiting lieutenant of the new, currently being established, Dutch army. Introductions over, the visitor spoke about the situation in the Dutch East Indies. Since the new leader of the independence movement, Sukarno, had declared Indonesia a free state in August, drastic changes were taking place.

The surrender of the Japanese forces had left a vacuum as far as the internment camps were concerned. Dutch women and children were now under control—and he emphasised the last word—of freedom fighters, who, overall, were very anti-white. At the conclusion of his emotional speech, he asked the assembly to give serious thought to his first question. 'Would any of you join the newly formed "Strike Force 8" and use your skill to train the recruits?' Then with his next words he dropped the bombshell and became specific.

'We want volunteers to restore law and order in the East Indies for an unlimited period.' The last two words hung vibrating on the parade ground, like a time bomb with its mechanism ticking ... unlimited period, the army equivalent for endless ... one month or perhaps six? A year? Two years? Or more?

There would be no answers to those questions, so no one asked ... I raised my arm, the one with the bad wrist, and it hurt like hell in more ways than one. I don't know why I volunteered that day. The form, with my resignation filled in, was in my pocket, forgotten as it were, a thing of the past, a promise broken with an ease that surprised and angered me at the same time.

The pain in my wrist would be nothing compared with the hurt in Elly's heart, a hurt that might well shatter the dreams of yesterday, when a promise was made. I felt like a hero for volunteering, yet also a damn coward for not refusing.

There were nine more who raised their hands on that bleak autumn day of October 1945. Amongst them my friends Joep and Gerry who stood next to me. When Gerry saw my arm going up, he said, 'If you go, I go!' He was that sort of friend.

Fifteen minutes were allowed for packing and saying our farewells

Part One: Pierre's Story

to the remaining members of *Stormschool Bloemendaal*; just enough time to make a phone call and tell my mother what had happened and to leave it to her to tell Elly the news of my impending departure. The army truck with the ten volunteers reached the Van Horne barracks, in Weert, by late afternoon.

Strike Force 8 (also referred to as 8th Shock Troops Battalion)—all volunteers—was waiting. For the next seven weeks, while assembling and preparing for embarkation for the East Indies, Pierre and Elly went through an horrific turmoil, trying to keep their shaky relationship alive.

On 29 November 1945, a few hours before embarkation via England, they spent their last time together and parted as 'good friends'.

> The telegram has already arrived … Return to unit, time of embarkation at 0300 hours. Only a few hours remain to be shared by two lonely people. Enough for a walk, a talk, an embrace, and a kiss … then the emptiness, the unavoidable farewell. We feel headlines forming inside: 'Love story cancelled through lack of interest' or 'To be continued … at a later date …' There are so many nuances of saying goodbye … yet none comes with a guarantee of a 'welcome home' in the distant future.
>
> Wounds, some of them old and dangerous and laid bare again only a few weeks ago, have not healed sufficiently to be ignored. The hurt is still too raw to be talked about … so the silence remains. Two figures in khaki uniform … the only difference being the colour of their berets. The black one on chestnut, curly hair could be a sign of mourning, perhaps the death of a dream. The green beret on the other figure is supposed to be a symbol of hope … Hope for what? More time to postpone the inevitable.

And then, recording the events of later that night:

> It was past midnight, the battalion ready to march to the station and a waiting train. It would take me once more across the Channel and into England.
>
> Eight hundred pairs of steel-studded boots rumbled in a chilling and pulsating rhythm through the deserted streets of Weert. A voice

rang out from somewhere up front: '*Makkers te wapen, het vaderland is in gevaar*' and, without hesitation, all those young and eager throats took over the song of an army on the march, letting it vibrate into the dark and cold night, bringing goosebumps.

Yes, '*Comrades arm yourselves, the country is in danger,*' was the most appropriate song for this raw army on its way to the Far East. People opened windows along the route, calling farewells to their own battalion that had shared their lives for the last fifty days.

The train left at 0300 hours. Strike Force 8 was on its way …!

A few weeks later, Pierre marked New Year's Eve, the last day of such an incredible year, aboard a 22,000-ton troopship—*Alcantara*, packed with more than 3000 Dutch soldiers—on deck, and undercover from a rainstorm, watching the lights of Southampton slowly fading in the distance. Once again, he was leaving behind his long-suffering Elly, but this time for an indefinite period while he pursued adventure on the other side of the world.

A letter from his family was soon chasing him across the seas.

Helmond, 13 Jan 1946

Dear Son and Brother,

It is Sunday morning, and we are just back from Mass, where I said a special prayer for your safe return. Perhaps a bit early, as you have been away only two months, but I thought there won't be much opportunity for Pierre to find a church to pray in …

Thank you so much for the photos from Aldershot, fancy you meeting Prince Bernhard and taking a picture of him as well. The words at the back of the photo—where you posed in camouflage jacket—made me cry.

No, I won't worry too much, son; I know you've got a survival instinct. You proved that often enough in the years gone by.

What did sadden me, though, was when Elly came to say farewell after her visit to the barracks in Weert (Teddy had accompanied her).

She cried, and I realised that the decision to separate as friends was not her doing but that of her parents. It might make your future so

Part One: Pierre's Story

much harder to tackle without her support.

Let's not dwell on memories … there might be other girls coming to the rescue when times get tough. You never told me about other friendships, and the speed you travelled with probably made lasting relations impossible.

Some customers in the shop said the other day, 'Mrs de Haas, it must be quiet now that Pierre has left.'

I put up both hands and replied, 'This is sufficient to count the days that he could stay at home since early 1943!' They had no answer to that!

9. ISLAND HOPPING AND AUSSIES

If 1945 had been a year of constant movement and upheaval (Pierre notes that he was posted to seventeen different places), the first half of 1946 was even more intense, this time in a very active combat zone in the steaming jungles of what was the Dutch East Indies (now Indonesia). Mostly it was counter-insurgency warfare against Sukarno's militia and small groups of Japanese troops who had not heard of the surrender or, if they had, didn't care anyway.

March of that year found Pierre's unit landed at Manado, a town on the northern part of Celebes (now Sulawesi). His diary (now as Corporal de Haas) indicates the delicate nature of their presence, in the minds of the locals just another occupation, perhaps?

> Had we come as friends or intruders? Infiltrating their lives again as enemies in an occupation force? Or would we restore the peaceful, unhurried way of life from before 1942? All questions and no answers ... yet!! The children made up the minds for their elders. Running alongside the marching column, one brave naked boy (hardly old enough to keep pace), took the hand of a soldier. Others followed and it wasn't long before an excited throng of youngsters were hanging on for dear life, holding hands with the strange white men while shouting 'SOLDADU'. It brought the first shy smiles to the stern-looking features of the local people. The ice was broken ...
>
> In the following weeks, our battalion was spread out over the top of this beautiful island, an area roughly 300 by 60 kilometres between the Molucca Sea to the south and Celebes Sea to the north. Of course, five hundred soldiers could hardly cover such a vast complex of jungle, plantations, and small villages. So, goodwill missions and show-the-flag patrols were the best possible ways to spread the message that we had come in peace.
>
> There were also many Japanese prisoners in holding camps to be

Part One: Pierre's Story

guarded and kept busy on roads and buildings, repairing damage they themselves had caused.

Then, in May 1946, Pierre found himself as one of only forty Dutch soldiers 'guarding' 38,000 Japanese POWs on Halmaheira Island. These POWs were awaiting repatriation to Japan and were not contained in any sort of camp or secure area but could roam about, the confines of the island itself being sufficient for containment.

After all POWs had left the island on liberty ships, Pierre's unit then continued the 'island hopping' nature of their operations, firstly to Morotai then Bali, where the battalion regrouped for sustained counter-guerrilla operations against Sukarno's militia, often strengthened by fanatical Japanese troops who had not surrendered.

On active service, MOROTAI, Wednesday, 19-6-'46

Dear Mam, Dad, brothers and friends,

Thanks for all your letters with news about family and that our business is picking up at long last, which will be a relief for Dad and of course you, Mam, as well.

Sorry for not writing sooner; it is unbelievable how much we move around. Often, I don't even know where I will be sleeping next day and, although exciting in many ways, it doesn't leave much time for letters.

Since arriving at Manando (Celebes), we crossed the top of that island and later went to Biak, followed by New Guinea, then on to Halmaheira where we guarded 38,000 Japanese POWs.

There was a time when our Strike Force was spread out over 2000 kilometres, just imagine trying to keep contact. No wonder mail often takes so long.

Morotai is not large, roughly forty by sixty kilometres, with areas of coral beaches and coco palms. We live in tents, which are very hot in the glaring heat of the sun, so we only use them for sleeping.

At night we can watch the latest American movies in an open-air cinema. We saw Betty Grable, Carmen Miranda and many more show films. They probably won't be seen in Helmond for a while.

We also had quite an experience with the Aussies, as the soldiers from Australia are called. There are about 600 of them left, waiting to go home. They look after the many stores, as this island is one vast dump for so much war material; one could supply an army with it!

Anyway, before the main movie started, we were shown news from around the globe, including a scene where the wharfies in Sydney refused to handle or supply two Dutch destroyers (on their way to the Dutch Indies).

As those wharfies must be all commie bastards (sorry Mam) to refuse a former ally assistance, we were very surprised to see the Australians stand up and start to applaud. We didn't take too kindly to that and, picking up the small iron seats we were sitting on, started bashing in some of those ignorant heads, in the process of which blood was spilt all around …

A funny thing, to finish this letter, also happened during our stay. At night we guard the food stores. Australians do the front, where the doors are, and we, the unworthy, patrol one hour on, one off, at the back. We managed to gain entry by removing the louvre windows and presto: canned fruit, condensed milk and other nearly forgotten luxuries were right in front of us …!

Over the weeks we have managed to eat our way through quite a substantial amount of food, to the extent even of refusing the daily grub, which often enough is not edible anyway.

To make a long story short, unless we leave this island within a week, a catastrophe will happen! I can see it all very clearly: an Aussie proudly telling his CO how much stock there is, while leaning against the stack of boxes somewhere in the middle. Then, still talking he falls in the abyss of no-man's land! Collapse and surprise …!

I better start packing my kitbag, just in case …

From Morotai, love to all and for you, Mam, don't worry!
Pierre.

From the diary records of his time in Bali, Pierre writes a piece that gives deep insight into the combat life of a soldier, probably any soldier in any theatre:

It became a lonely war. Even amidst the men in uniform, where I was equal amongst equals, I still felt an outsider sometimes. In so many ways, I had my own private war as well, even at that point.

I tried to cope with the different aspects of day-to-day patrols—or the waiting—with the help of elusive dreams. Often an hour spent in the tranquillity of no-man's land from within gave enough substance to tackle the ugliness of a cruel outside world.

Often, deep inside, I had to ask for time-out, to give me a chance to recoup, to gather the fragments that were destroying my soul. Putting them on hold was one solution.

It was not an easy war; even without action on certain days, death was often so near, so close in fact that it stuck to our uniforms. In the end, our fatigues smelled like a freshly dug grave, the earthy dampness—combined with our sweat and fear—felt like an old friend: the more you used them the more you could trust them.

When someone told us it would come out in the wash, there were men who believed it. Of course, the smell stayed. The camouflage overalls rotted away in the daily routine through jungle, streams, and tangled undergrowth. Constant washing only accelerated the process.

Also, there were times when looking at each other's faces became a really frightening experience. We were in our early twenties, but the lines we saw shouldn't be there at all. They belonged to old men.

It hardly ever occurred that a single letter dropped in. They always came in great quantities together, as if the field post office waited for long enough to fill all the available bags.

Still, one should not complain; each letter was devoured as if life depended on it, and perhaps that too had a certain ring of truth. When in combat, one doesn't need mail. There just isn't time. But once returned to base and the adrenaline has evaporated, the need is there to read about loved ones. Or when loneliness creeps in, boredom, depression, then written words take on an importance that often wasn't fully understood by sweethearts back home.

Nevertheless, amidst all the patrolling and hardships, it does seem that some of the magic of Bali, that so many people have come to appreciate today, was already very real and present and able to be enjoyed by Pierre and his fellow soldiers. In a letter to his family, dated 15 August 1946, he writes:

> But let's for a moment forget the empty shelves in the Netherlands and the ugliness of war here. Because the prettiness of Bali is manifold and, even as we leave our checkpoint 'WILMA', overlooking the rice fields deep below, it becomes like a dream.
>
> There are many vantage points from this large mountain range, sitting across the centre of this island. Here, in Penebel, we guard the slopes into the lower fields. Breathtaking is the only word that comes to mind. The tiny settlements, surrounded by mud or stone walls, with entrances in the form of a temple or offering place, look so picturesque. You feel an intruder when you must search for guerrillas and you come across an old man, sitting in a creaky chair, asking: 'Apa itu tuan?' How are you, sir?
>
> The kampongs, where people live and work, are all so clean and tidy. Sometimes, patrolling near one of those villages, one can see a market in progress. Dozens of girls, dressed in colourful sarongs, sit beside the road, displaying fruit and vegetables on freshly cut banana leaves. Little charcoal burners keep the satays hot.
>
> The girls, young as they are, have a bouncy figure and, with their bare chests on full display, often distract our roving eyes as we come closer. 'Makanan bagus, di sini tuan,' is their everyday greeting. 'Nice food, sir.'
>
> Well, with such an ample show and food to buy, it becomes rather confusing, but normally I stick to 'satay ajer', leaving the girls' charms for sightseeing only! The food is packed in leaves, a bit of string goes around the bundle and VOILA, instant cafeteria at the roadside. The people overall are very friendly and generous and when they notice that we are trying to speak their language, the rapid-firing dialect slows down somewhat.
>
> One night last week, we were invited to a dance-theatre-show, performing in the market square in front of the local temple. Their gamelan music (instruments are made from bamboo) accompanied the gracious moves of the dancers, mostly girls in their early teens. It was quite an experience, and although we couldn't understand the meaning of the words, it was remarkable how smooth it flowed together.

Part One: Pierre's Story

The music and dancing were a sight for sore eyes, as the saying goes, but the dresses, Mam, that would have been something for you to watch, the way you're always making carnival outfits: all those colours and real flowers, head ornaments with many glittering sequins, form-hugging silk on lithesome bodies. Yes, one feels out of place dressed in combat fatigues, sweaty, smelling and dirty!

10. 'ANYONE WHO CAME *THAT* CLOSE, DESERVES TO KNOW *HOW* CLOSE!'

Strike Force 8 remained in Bali till late October and then was redeployed to Sumatra, which Pierre notes was his seventh island in not quite as many months!

And it was here, in late November, that Pierre became critically ill from malaria and paratyphoid fever. For several days beforehand he had been feeling very tired and feverish, dragging himself through the unrelenting grind of patrols, guard duties and the like, until, suddenly, he collapsed.

> When I regained consciousness, I was in a field hospital run by Strike Force 7. Strangers everywhere ... but I felt too weak to care. My diaries so faithfully kept ever since I joined the army stayed empty day after lonely day.
>
> I started on a letter to Elly. I wanted so desperately to restore some sort of contact. I knew I was clutching at straws, but, in my delirium, I went for the impossible ... Before the letter was completed, I suffered another attack, received a thousand units of penicillin, recovered ... wrote some more, struggling with words ... and myself.
>
> A nurse who took pity on me finished my feeble attempts, and the envelope addressed to Suez found its way into a mailbag. Time lost all meaning; I drifted somewhere in no-man's land, dreamt about a different world, one I had never seen before!
>
> Until one day a doctor—newly arrived from the Netherlands—asked a rather silly question. 'Corporal,' he said in an urgent voice, 'how long have you had those spots?'
>
> I looked at him in amazement. 'What spots, Doctor?'
>
> 'Oh my God!' and, pointing at my chest, 'THESE ... Can you remember when they first appeared?'
>
> I looked down, saw a rash all over my body and shook my head,

Part One: Pierre's Story

too far gone to understand the real meaning behind the worried look on his face. Within a few minutes I was unceremoniously wrapped in my own sheet, carried to a waiting jeep and propped up next to the driver. Someone pushed a stengun in my hands.

'Before you reach Charitas hospital you will be going through enemy lines. You might need a weapon ... understand?'

An officer appeared. 'Sorry, Corporal, we are short of men, but you'll make it. The driver will see to it.'

A nurse tied my bedsheet in such a way around the seat that the danger of falling out was somewhat lessened.

'Go ... go ... and for God's sake, don't stop for anything,' and the jeep roared away. It must have arrived safely, but my diary showed only empty pages as I went into a coma.

Paratyphoid and malaria had taken control!

For ten long and frightening days, I drifted along the narrow ledge between life and death: weaving in and out, succumbing to eternity briefly and then returning for a short while to the reality of a nurse standing next to my bed. A smile and a question. 'How are you feeling, Pierre?' But I was off again into no-man's land where dreams took on the hazy quality of a faded postcard.

Sometimes, I met a marching column of girls, their black berets just floating above their heads, moving in unison but making no progress at all. It was a bizarre world of shades and shadows of light and darkness amidst a swirling fog. All colours on hold, contours like dotted lines.

The nurse was there again, her eyes on a thermometer, shaking her head, the smile replaced by a worried look. 'You have to fight, son ... fight with all you have got, otherwise ...' Her shoulder raised slightly as if she knew what otherwise meant.

'Fight,' I thought, trying to concentrate on that difficult word. 'Fight, but what and why?'

It was so peaceful in my dreams. I could float through a world over which I had no control and no desire, either, to end it.

'Nurse, where am I?'

'Am I dying nurse?'

There was no reply. The endless row of tents in the Scottish Highlands was silent, only a sliver of an uncaring moon whispering, 'Not yet, my friend ... not yet!'

Pierre did recover shortly before Christmas Day, and when visited by the unit's padre was told, 'Anyone who came THAT close has a right to know HOW close.'

One of the first things he did, once his mind could focus reasonably well again, was to write home, and it is in this letter that Pierre outlines an idea that would prove to be pivotal for not only his future, but also that of a teenage girl living with her parents in a small village in the Netherlands. Isn't it astonishing how often something so innocent and innocuous, and certainly without any definite expectations, can be so life-changing ... but that story is yet to unfold.

Palembang, December '46.

Dear Mam and family,

It seems such a long time ago since that letter from Bali where I tried to describe the beauty of the local scene there. We left at the end of October and, although it was a hard island for body and soul, I felt a touch of sadness, saying goodbye.

We all had that same feeling when we climbed aboard the troopship, knowing that we probably would never return. There is so much you leave behind, even a piece of yourself.

It seemed at one stage that Bali had grown on us, that special something created by a sense of belonging, even if it took the people a long time before they felt the same towards us. It was a twenty-four-hour-a-day job, yet at the very end the achievement of restoring law and order (at least partly) and bringing life for the villagers back to normal again, was a victory.

Yes, Bali in many ways became unforgettable and, one day perhaps, in the peaceful atmosphere at home, we shall recall what happened there. Now, writing from my sick bed in Charitas Hospital, it has faded to the past, but like all memories, clinging in my mind.

Because of the tropical diseases I picked up after landing in Palembang, I was not allowed to write or receive visitors. The doctors isolated me in case I was spreading the germs. Feeling a lot better now, although still weak, I can try to restore contact with the outside world.

Your letters for my birthday and Christmas were more than welcome, especially when I have all day to read, and think, and read some more. Another year is nearly gone but 1946 was a long one for all of us. So much happened, so many different places seen since that last look at England on New Year's Eve.

As I said before, when you are involved day and night, time comes to a standstill. A week often takes on the proportion of an endless month. Yet, in that particular way of mine, I loved it all, laughed a lot, cried a little, lived to the full and survived!

Now that Christmas is near and 1947 just around the corner, I can't help reflecting on what has eventuated since I said goodbye in November '45. Many events have faded, and little things were imprinted on my mind, never to be erased again. In Bali, when we were on a patrol near a small kampong, some children walked up to us and a little girl grabbed my hand and skipped along. Suddenly, she said, 'Tuan, why are you here?' looking at me with those dark eyes, expecting a quick answer perhaps. Her local dialect was hard to understand. It took me a long time before I could find a reply.

Yes, what does one say to a five-year-old naked girl holding my hand and asking a difficult question? 'To give you some sweets,' I said at last in my best Malayan tongue, giving her a packet of chewing gum. She ran away, joined the other kids and vaguely I could hear her 'Trima Kasih' from the distance.

A couple of hours later, we killed two guerrillas and the answer to her simple question lay at our feet. Perhaps one day, when grown up, she will understand, perhaps not.

The weeks in hospital without visitors have made me aware how fragile a human being is, how lonely you become when you don't see anyone all day, bar a few nurses. There was so much time to think once the delirium had passed. So much time …

For a while I lost all track of where I was and what day it would be. I lived in a vacuum and only after the first visitors were allowed did I realise that the army was still part of me. There is no denying, though, the changes that have taken place as if the past was trying to remove itself. Which might be as well. One can't dwell too long on what once seemed so important and a year later can hardly be

'Anyone who came that close deserves to know how close!'

remembered.

I was thinking, Mam, of putting an advertisement for a penfriend as old ties have been cut and new contacts might be the best cure for old memories that often won't die.

PENGUN, the army newspaper, has thousands of those ads, but perhaps I would get lost in that type of paper. However, one of the nurses here gave me a magazine called TUNEY TUNES, a monthly, with information about music etc. That contained only a handful of requests for penfriends, so on a separate paper you'll find the contents of the ad and the address of the magazine. If you can forward that please, it will probably make the Feb. issue and I'll send the money when I get paid again.

Well, this is a different kind of letter, more thoughtful. Not being used to inactivity and Christmas so close, this is the way I feel.

Wishing you all the best for the festive season and 1947 will see us together again in good old the Netherlands, I hope.

Take care, Mam, and love to all
PIERRE

The earliest surviving photo of Pierre with his mother

Pierre (R) with Jan (seated in his birthday chair) and Koos

His own bike?

The de Haas family business, and home

Pierre, at about 12 years old, on completing primary school

With his unicycle and wearing his 'drollenvanger' trousers, Dutch for 'turd catchers'!

Pierre (L) with a fellow forced labourer next to one of the buses

Found in his album and simply captioned: 'Forced labour Germany 1943, 4 French, 3 Russian, 2 Dutch.' Pierre is in the front row, second from the left.

Pierre's mum

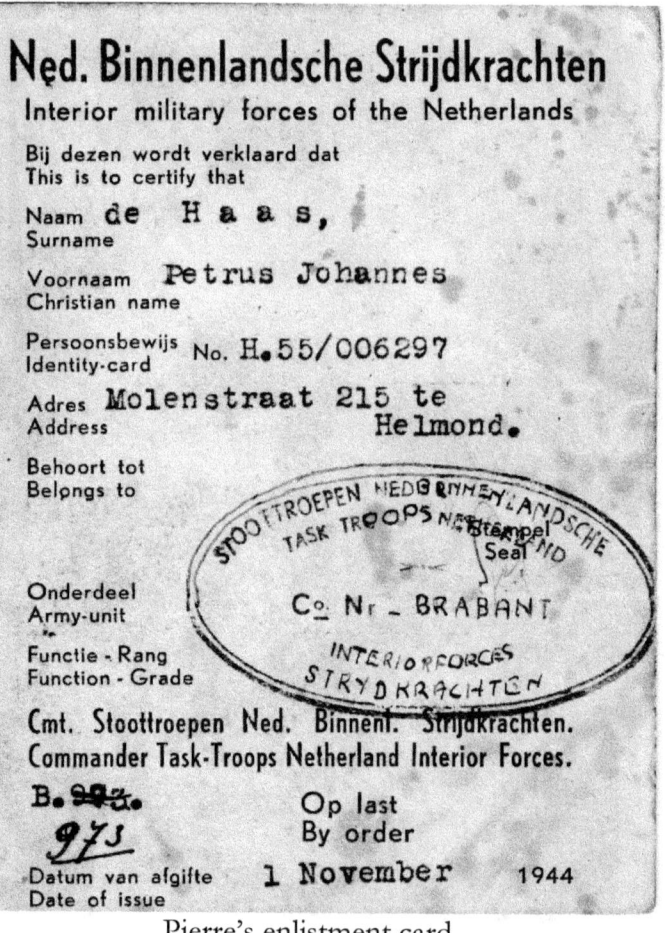

Pierre's enlistment card

Commando training in Achnacarry

Land, sea or air... Pierre grinning from the second row

Those who made it; Pierre on the far right, front row

Commando!

Portrait by unknown SS POW; annotated 'Lager Recklinghausen, 26 July 45'

A photo Pierre sent to his mother from Aldershot in December 45, with the following message (translated) on the reverse: 'End Dec 45. For my lovely mum in memory of Christmas 1945. My last photo in Europe. See you Mum. Your son will not forget you. Goodbye whether for a short or long time. A big kiss of farewell from Pierre in the Commandos. Till we meet again, goodbye.' She cried when she received it.

On operations in Bali

PART TWO: CORRY'S STORY

11. HER EARLY YEARS

Cornelia 'Corry' Catharina Siemons was born to Cornelis Siemons and Catharina Siemons (nee Van Loon) in the small rural village of Oudenbosch on 24 June 1928, the youngest of five children, in order: Nell, the eldest sister, Kees her brother, and sisters Betty and Leny.

There was a fourteen-year age gap between oldest and youngest, and Leny was already six years old when Corry was born. Family folklore had it that Leny wasn't all that impressed when Corry arrived into this tight-knit Catholic family—after all, she had been the baby all that time. Still, for many years afterwards, Corry was consistently assured that they were all delighted with their new baby sister.

Corry writes, with that wonderful touch of humour that came to the fore so often:

> It was a lucky year to be born. It was the year Walt Disney released his first cartoons. From a quite different perspective, it was also the year *Lady Chatterley's Lover* was first published. There was nothing Lady Chatterley-like in my life, but there were plenty of cartoons.

Her father was a builder-carpenter who had his workshop at the rear of the house, with access from a cobblestone laneway or driveway which opened to a small courtyard on the side, leading to the back door of the

Part Two: Corry's Story

house.

> The workshop was made of wood, and the outer walls were painted with tar to make it waterproof. The interior had two long workbenches, and along the walls were tool racks and shelves with carton boxes in different sizes which held nails and screws. The floor was always covered with a thick layer of sawdust and beautiful wooden curls. At the back stood a wooden vice on which he sharpened his saws, and a whetting stone, a big sandstone wheel, for sharpening chisels. We girls were often called upon to turn this wheel which was a hard job as Dad leaned his whole weight on the tool while water ran down its side.

In later life, Corry frequently spoke about her father having a very joyous and playful sense of humour and how the family home was often filled with gales of laughter. She emphasised that this humour 'gene' was very definitely passed on to her brother Kees, and, indeed, there is strong evidence that it has also been passed on to succeeding generations, including this editor.

She recalled many happy hours in the workshop with her dad. Being young, she wasn't allowed to touch the larger tools in the workshop; however:

> Dad also had some miniature ones for very fine work. On rainy days and as a special treat, I could play with these: a small hammer, a plane and a pair of pliers; I still treasure 'my pliers' as a memento to my youth. Usually, my masterpieces fell apart in the end, but this did not deter me from trying again.

Corry continues to describe the surrounding environment:

> My first recollection was of standing at the window in the lounge, my nose just above the windowsill, and looking out at the highway. Highway is perhaps a misnomer—it was far from the size of the four or six-lane highways we know today. The road was flanked by old chestnut trees which were so tall and broad that the branches touched

across the road, creating a green tunnel of leaves. In spring the trees grew pink 'candles'. This was a beautiful sight and fascinated me. It often seemed like a fairy-tale road, where fairies and dwarfs played at night.

Opposite our home lay the hospital gardens. This was quite a big area, planted with a variety of flowers, and in the early months of spring the air was fragrant with the heady scent of crocus, hyacinths and daffodils, a sure sign summer was not far away. The hospital owned two proud peacocks, who, on sundown, paced the enclosure, shouting their dismay at being locked up.

I have never forgotten that eerie sound and, on the rare occasion I hear it now, it takes me back many years. Strange how sounds and sights take you home. In winter, the dreamy long shadows of a fading afternoon take me back to my childhood and, in a flash, I walk that road again. I call this my 'dreaming light', and it usually sets the creative juices flowing.

Her account continues into a dramatic—and very painful—memory:

Our house was the last one built on that side of the road, but soon other houses followed, and I lost that beautiful secret view. Our new neighbours planted a hedge between our two properties, but this did not deter me from exploring my environment. Why do people leave gaps in between if they don't use them? There were plenty of meadows left for me to discover, so I used to crawl through my favourite exits, walked the length of the neighbour's garden, opened the gate, slipped through and was free to wander. Doll in my arms, 'we' used to venture out, to only go home when I heard Mum call me for lunch.

From the ladder at the workshop, Dad had a good vantage point to check where I was, and I'm sure he didn't let me out of his sight for long. One day, however, my adventurous spirit surprised them all, and I will never forget that experience.

Country children had a wealth of freedom and, at times, I couldn't be bothered to go home to use the toilet, or I would know I couldn't make it back in time. Too impatient to lose playtime on this occasion, I was caught as well and quickly squatted behind a tree which stood at the edge of a small stream. Its banks were overgrown with nettles and weeds and these reached far into the water. On that fateful day I lost my balance and slipped into the water in between the nettles. The pain was excruciating and, the more I tried to get out, the more it hurt.

I panicked and frantically tried to pull myself up onto the grass, but each time I slipped back again. Finally, I managed to grab hold of a solid clump which held, and I slowly crawled back up onto the bank. Oh, the terrible pain! My bottom felt as if it were on fire, and, worse still, what would Mum say? Panties around my ankles and howling with shock and pain, I struggled home, wriggled through the gap in the hedge, where Mum stood waiting for me, seven days of bad weather on her face.

Other than this very embarrassing 'nettle episode', Corry's earliest years had a gentle and quite stable rhythm of life within a very loving and supportive (albeit strict) family. Her recollections of this time reflect this gentle rhythm, containing mostly happy times and milestones.

Of these, and for all children in the Netherlands—then and now—Saint Nicolas' Day is one of the most special days of the year.

The weeks leading up to St Nicolas Day (celebrated on 6 December) were extremely exciting. Shops displayed fantastic toys, and the shop windows were a delight to every child. When I went out shopping with Mum, it took her twice as long, for every bakery had a unique and special window display with chocolate, marzipan and figurines, chocolate letters, and letters made of pastry with a lovely almond filling.

But before the great day arrived, we also celebrated St Maarten's day, which fell in the beginning of November and was the start of the St Nicolas season. St Maarten was St Nicolas' helper. He listened at the doors whether the children were good and well-behaved. If he was convinced they'd been good that day, he sometimes came and visited, announcing his presence by a loud banging on the door, to then open it quickly and throw a handful of lollies into the room, which of course went all over the place.

Strangely, Mum (or Dad) had, just then, gone upstairs for something.

I was usually frightened out of my skin, but called out a quick,

'Thank you!' then was on all fours to quickly gather the lollies, upon which the absent parent would come down and I'd say, 'Mum, St Maarten was here. You just missed him!'

'Here?' would be the answer. 'I didn't see him.'

'But he was here, look,' and, showing her the lollies, 'Look what he brought.'

'Well, now, fancy that and me not seeing him. You must've been good.'

In the weeks leading up to 6 December, 'St Maarten' visited the children at least once a week, and it was one of the nicest customs of this period.

On the day of the holy man's arrival, we stood waiting on the quay and, with us, most of the population of Oudenbosch. Eagerly we looked across the small harbour to see whether we could spot his boat, which was decorated by colourful bunting and flags, St Nicolas standing on the prow, holding his golden crosier, his snow-white horse beside him. As soon as the boat rounded the bend, a loud cheer went up in greeting. Dressed in red cape and mitre, his snow-white beard moving gently in the wind, he started waving to the crowd, while the band started up and young and old sang the much-loved traditional song: 'Zie ginds komt de stoomboot uit Spanje weer aan.' ('See in the distance the steamboat from Spain arriving again.')

In the weeks following his arrival, he visited every class in the schools, and here too he knew exactly who had been naughty or played up in class. He had a big ledger book, and it was all (supposedly) written there.

We all lived this wonderful fairy tale, and our parents kept the magic alive for us, for which I will always feel grateful. We could be children, and I'll always look back on those precious years, when my parents made magic happen.

Also, at this time of the year, in an age long before sprawling grocery shops and supermarkets, Dutch families prepared for the winter months by ensuring enough food would be available by stocking food for when snow abounded and farming activities were reduced, or even curtailed altogether. This was a very 'hands-on' experience which is still the norm in many less-developed places across the globe. Corry writes about one episode of a pig being slaughtered on the cobblestone path right next to the family home:

> On the chosen day, our butcher arrived nice and early, the tools of his trade hanging from a wide leather belt around his ample stomach, his black-rimmed glasses on the tip his nose.
>
> He came in through the kitchen, as most people did at the time. Dad took out the bottle of gin from the cupboard and poured him a glass, which was customary before work could start. Pete appreciated this gesture. He threw it back in one gulp, rubbed his hands and said to Dad, 'Ha, Kees, that took the ice out of my belly. Now all we have to do is wait for my job to arrive.'
>
> They didn't have to wait long. Soon a farmer's cart came clattering down the cobblestones beside the house, and the pig made his grand entrance, quite unaware of its fate. Its owner, rubbing his hands to get the circulation going again, came in to settle the financial side of things and, when business was completed, gratefully accepted his tot of gin. Pete, not to be left out, held up his glass as well, saying, 'Well, Kees, I need two steady hands and a keen eye to do the job.'
>
> They finished their drinks and went outside. I was all eyes, following the proceedings. The farmer lowered the back of the cart, and the men tried to push the poor animal out and into the side path that ran alongside the house. Perhaps this pig was a smart one; it had a will of its own, and maybe had an inkling of what was going to happen. It certainly didn't want to come off the cart!
>
> Pete took it by the tail and, with Dad pushing on one side and the farmer on the other, they steered it in the right direction. What followed next saw me flee into the parlour, hands over my ears, so I wouldn't hear the poor animal's death throes. Mum found me there later and suggested I play there for the rest of the day. I didn't need any convincing.
>
> Only later, when the porker was hung in the workshop to cure and it was all nice and clean, I had a quick peek under the sheet which covered it. Now it looked like the ones in the butcher shops, and I didn't mind so much.
>
> Pete went home in a very jolly mood and Mum worked till late that night and again the next day when Pete returned to cut out the meat and make sausages. Mum salted some, prepared cuts which had to be

Her Early Years

preserved in bottling jars; hams and sausages later went into the 'smoking room' where they stayed until properly cured. And life returned to normal.

I often think of Mum, who never owned a washing machine, vacuum cleaner, dish washer, toaster or any electrical appliance. People of my parents' generation were used to hard work and thrived on it; they were pleased to have work, for the alternative was gruesome.

During the years of the Depression, life for many people in the Netherlands was horrific, although it seems that the Siemons family fared better than most, given that they had a family business. Often the payment for carpentry or building work or repairs was made in food so the family was able to struggle through.

Stemming from their strongly held Catholic faith, from a sense of being blessed, and from the life and love so freely shared in their own home, the Siemons family was generous in reaching out to and supporting those who were less fortunate, struggling to survive during this terrible time. Corry writes about one visit to an impoverished and desperate family to deliver some food:

> Mum knocked on the door, which hung from its hinges in odd angles. It swung open into a dark hole of a room, the only light coming from the dirty window in front. Mrs B—ers was a small woman, her thin frame held together by a thin frock and tiny apron. Her once black hair was streaked with grey, which matched her sunken grey face.
>
> 'Mrs Siemons, come in, and Corry.' She smiled at me and we stepped down the two steps which led into the room, and the stench of poverty hit us. The walls were green with mildew, the red-tiled floor dirty with grime-imprinted weird patterns. Mrs B—ers cleared a variety of clothing from a chair and invited Mum to sit down, then joined her at the linoleum-covered table on which stood a few chipped cups and plates.
>
> A baby, its feet blue with the cold, sat on the floor in a filthy nappy, its little face a map of scabs and sores, playing with an empty cotton

reel. A small boy, who would have been around my age, went to his mother's side, bared her breast and started to suckle. I looked on, and I'm sure my eyes must have been as big as the saucers on the table. I looked up at Mum, whether she had noticed, but she was busy putting the crockery to one side. She placed the parcel on the table, saying, 'I've brought you some groceries, Mrs B—ers.'

The woman pushed the boy away, who immediately started to cry, a high wailing sound which turned my stomach, and earned him a box on his ear. She covered up her breast and started to unpack the groceries, to put them in a cupboard above the concrete tub and old water pump which went for a sink.

There was no 'thank-you', even some resentment, judging by the expression on her face, while she pumped some water in a battered kettle and asked, 'Would you like a cup of tea?'

To my intense relief Mum declined. 'No, thank you; I still have to do some shopping before the shops close.'

A flood of misery then washed from the woman's lips, a river of lost hope, lost illusions, no work, and no future. Apparently, they lived on hand-outs from the church and alms, and there were a lot of mouths to feed. A lot of what she said went over my head, of course, but I understood enough, and little girls pick up more information than adults think they can comprehend.

Soon however it was time to go, as Mum said, 'Well, it's time to do my shopping.' Mrs B—ers showed us to the door, still talking non-stop, and we were outside.

I took a deep breath of crisp winter air, trying to dislodge the stench of poverty from my nose. Mum was quiet, but I was bursting with questions I found hard to put into words. Life had opened a window and I had no hope of dealing with this; this sober photograph of the have-nots.

12.   SOME MEMORABLE FIRSTS

Corry's first day of school was on 1 September 1934, a day she had been looking forward to for months, driving her family mad in asking, 'Is it September yet?' It all started well and with lots of excitement.

After being too excited to have a decent breakfast, it was off to school where she met her teacher, a Sr Felicia, for the first time. She looked like a giant to five-year-old Corry! With all the new impressions and experiences, the morning went amazingly fast, and soon it was time to go home for lunch. Corry writes about what happened during the lunch break at home as they were discussing what she had done at school that very first morning of her education:

> Mum didn't know yet, but I had decided I'd had enough schooling already.
> 'I'm not going to school this afternoon, but.'
> 'Oh, yes you are. I can't keep you home now. You wanted to go for ages, didn't you?'
> 'But I learned enough already.'
> Dad came in a little later. 'How was it, Corry?'
> I threw Dad a dark look. 'Sister Felicia is very strict, Papa. I don't like her very much. She's too bossy. She was bossing us around all morning.'
> Dad hid a smile. 'Well, she has a lot of children in her class, so she must be very busy keeping you all occupied. Come on, Corry,' Dad admonished, 'eat up, or you'll be late and that wouldn't do on your first day.'
> I put my fork down. 'I'm not hungry and I'm not going back to school.' There was no comment, not from Mum or Dad, while Leny and my brother exchanged glances.
> With lunch over, Mum fetched her coat. 'Come, Corry, wash your hands and let me comb your hair.'

Had Mum forgotten I was done with schooling? I started to cry; big angry tears rolled down my face. Disregarding tears and dark looks, Mum washed my face, combed my hair and took me to the hall.

I decided on a tantrum. I took the coat and threw it on the floor. Stamping my feet, I wailed, 'No, I don't want to go to school anymore.' I sobbed. 'I don't like school.' I threw myself on the floor, but Dad dragged me up. Mum and Dad put me on the back of the bike, and, with Mum on one side and Leny on the other, they took me to school, and I'm sure my screams could have been heard on the other side of town.

So much for education …

There was another 'first' which was altogether different and celebrated in every sense of the word, a day which for Corry (and for any young Catholic child in the 1930s) was both momentous and unforgettable. It was the day she made her first Holy Communion, on 30 May 1935.

A date to which I had looked forward with eager and excited anticipation. It was the day I would make my first Holy Communion. Months before the big event, we practised and practised, first at school and closer to the date in church: how to kneel in the pews, how to go in line to the altar, how to kneel at the altar rail, how far to poke out your tongue to receive the host etc.

It was all a very serious business.

When the big day arrived, I was awake with the birds. It was a lovely day, with a gentle sun putting a shine on nature. Dad had made a trestle table which stretched the length of the lounge and sitting room, so the whole family—plus our visitors—would be able to find a seat. The day before, the baker's son had delivered several boxes of cakes and bread rolls that made my mouth water in anticipation. No visitor would go hungry that day or would leave the house without having something to eat and drink.

All this excitement was almost too much.

My proud parents escorted me to church, I watching my beautiful new shoes, a little handbag on my arm, which held a new children's missal, new rosary beads and a nice clean hanky.

Some Memorable Firsts

The church was packed. Mum took me to the section where the communicants were sitting. Strange as it may sound now, seating was such that the men and boys sat on one side of the church and the women and girls on the opposite side; it seems to be another strange custom in the world of today, but those were the rules and people didn't question them.

We little girls looked beautiful. I waved to a few of my classmates and friends, while Mum sought her seat. I must say we were perfect angels. No one talked, and since we had been drilled for so many hours, there were no mistakes. I still look back on this day as an unforgettable episode. I think I came closest to being a perfect angel that day, and those days were rare!

It was a very tired little girl that tumbled into bed that night. I had selected some of the nicest statues to put up in my bedroom, while Mum carefully wrapped up the rest. I'm sure they would make a less fortunate boy or girl happy on their big day.

Corry's account touches on the centrality of the Catholic faith in the life of the Siemons family, as it was for most Catholics in the Netherlands at that time. In Oudenbosch, this was greatly assisted by the presence within the parish of a convent school for girls supported by the nuns, a boarding school (St Louis) for the boys run by religious brothers, and a majestic basilica.

The church is a replica of St Peter's in Rome, although built on a smaller scale. This basilica was the culmination of a dream by an early parish priest, and it is one of the most beautiful and ornate churches in the Netherlands. Tourists from all over Europe travel to Oudenbosch, or 'Little Rome,' as it is called. It is no wonder, therefore, that people of the neighbouring towns often accused us of 'walking with the dome on our noses'.

From an early age pride in our magnificent basilica was deeply instilled in us. Our lives revolved around the church, first at school, later at different youth groups. The population of Oudenbosch consisted nearly entirely of Roman Catholics who were hard working and devout people.

Part Two: Corry's Story

When Corry was five years old, and for many years afterwards, the customs and practices of the Church were quite different, some might even say quaint. Today, many people often like to sit in the same place in church on every Sunday when they come to Mass. In the 1930s, to sit in someone else's seat could create some serious problems!

> One other strange custom in our parish was the leasing of chairs. Our church did not have pews, but chairs. The only pews were red-cushioned ones, placed on either side of the altar, and reserved for the church committee.
>
> Parishioners could 'rent' or 'lease' a chair for a certain period. I cannot remember whether it was for one year or more. This way you were always sure of your own seat in church as all the Masses had big congregations.
>
> The chairs were made of a dark wood with a plaited cane seat. To kneel, you had to put the seat up, but for the sermon you turned the chair around and lowered the seat which always went with a lot of clatter. If you didn't rent a chair, and sat down on someone else's, you risked the chance of being told to go and sit somewhere else. When I grew up it happened to me at times that I had to vacate a seat and make room for the lessee!
>
> We children sat on low benches in an area set aside for us, with a nun kneeling on a chair, her back to the altar, to watch us. If you talked, or giggled, you were sure to be called up in class and reprimanded.

In writing about her final visit to Oudenbosch in 1992, filled with emotion and nostalgia, she brings each of these elements of her Catholic upbringing into focus:

> The years seemed to vanish as I stood before the school, gazing at the old green gates which were open, and showed the deserted courtyard behind.
>
> The concrete paving slabs seemed to have absorbed the echoes of thousands of feet. Images, somewhat faded by absent years, tumbled through my mind like a silent movie, projecting negatives from the past. I had arrived by train, and as always on nearing my hometown,

Some Memorable Firsts

marvelled at the glorious sight of the silvery-grey twin domes on the skyline, a picture so dear to me it hurt. I tried to stem the moisture in my eyes, but still the tears spilled over, slowly trickling down to gather at the corners of my mouth.

Although alone in the compartment I quickly wiped them away, told myself not to be such a sentimental fool. It didn't help the tightness in my throat. Only through seeing this familiar landmark did I realise fully I was home once more: the domes of the basilica of Sts Agatha and Barbara, and that of the chapel behind the brothers' boarding school. My upside-down world of the antipodes had righted itself, and the greys and bronzes of Australia had made way for the lush greens of the forests and fields of the Netherlands.

It had been years ...

I entered the gates, and a mild September sun stroked the windows of the two-storey building and fired them with gold sparkles. My eyes swept over the four granite steps to the primary school. They were hollowed out in the centre, no doubt by the thousands of feet of children who had entered these doors of learning. To my right stood the pre-school, where my education began.

I walked over and peered through the windows. Brightly coloured pictures still adorned the walls, little tables and chairs stood in cosy groups of six around the room; no longer in rigid rows as was the case then, pointing perhaps to a more relaxed attitude towards training children's minds.

A tap on the window cut into my dreaming. I looked up and saw a young woman, who I guessed was in her middle thirties, beckon me as if to invite me in. She disappeared, and seconds later I heard her turn the key and the door opened.

'Would you like to have a look inside?' she asked. 'I'm Sister Mary.' It was then I noticed the small gold cross she wore on the collar of her dress.

'I'd love to, Sister,' and after I had introduced myself, she gestured, 'Come, come in ...'

She was a light person; everything about her seemed put together in pastel colours, from her blond hair to her pale-pink summer frock and bone-coloured sandals. Her rosy complexion was all smiles when she turned to me and said, 'Do you live in Oudenbosch, Mrs de Haas? I know quite a few people through the school and my youth work,

Part Two: Corry's Story

but I have never come across a "de Haas" before.'

'We couldn't have met, Sister. You see, I'm on holidays here, but I live in Australia.'

'Oh, I see, and how long have you lived there?'

'Well, for thirty years now, almost as long as in the Netherlands.'

'You must find a lot of changes here then, and I might add not always for the better.' She rambled on, but I was no longer with her, but in a private world of memories; the cosy world of a five-year-old …

13. WAR COMES TO OUR LOUNGEROOM

Life for Corry for the remainder of the 1930s continued with its gentle rhythm, both within her family and the community of Oudenbosch, marked only by the passage of regular events such as: the weekly arrival of the 'mussel man' who sold them by the bucket load from a small cart; the much loved annual fair in August; the sugar beet harvest time of October-November; and the seasonal influxes of different hawkers and vendors, one being the ice-cream man who only came in summer, whatever day that was!

However, by the time Corry was in the upper grades of primary school, dark clouds were rapidly gathering over Europe.

> As I reached the higher grades, there was unrest in the country. Rumours from beyond our eastern border raised anxiety and fear in the Netherlands. Amid all this, I, together with my parents, had to decide about my future.
>
> What did I want to do when I left school? I had always liked the idea of working in an office, and learning shorthand and typing, so it was decided I would attend the MULO (*Meer Uitgebreid Lager Onderwijs*) or, in English, 'more advanced primary education' as it was called then. I was delighted and looked forward with much anticipation to going to St Anna and furthering my education.
>
> I was to finish grade six and then go on to secondary school. But all did not go as planned. I contracted a cough that I could not shake off and was absent from school for many weeks. I had to have several tests, lacked energy and did not feel too bright. Mum and Dad were very worried. Tuberculosis was a killer at the time, and there didn't seem to be much knowledge about how best to treat this disease. Many young people spent years in sanatoriums, which had sprung up all over the country. It was a dreaded disease.
>
> Luckily, after weeks of tests and rest, I was given the 'all clear'. I

had missed so much schooling that the nuns decided I would have a better preparation for high school if I finished grade seven as well, so that's what we decided.

The rumours about war became fact when, on 1 September 1939, German troops invaded Poland and started World War II. Little did we know of the terrible consequences it would have for Europe and the world.

The Netherlands declared itself neutral, but mobilised its entire army to be prepared, just in case. The papers screamed headlines of atrocities, of annihilation of entire towns and villages in Poland, and the graphic photographs did not lie. Germany was a ruthless enemy.

Since that fateful September day, Mum, and many housewives like her, had bought non-perishable groceries and had stored these away; everybody felt there would be lean times ahead as they could well remember the severe shortages in food during the First World War. Every time Mum sent me to the shops, I had extra items on the shopping list. She also started preserving more meat and vegetables than she had other years. We didn't know what to expect, but rumours filled the newspapers, and my parents' apprehension overshadowed our daily life.

Everybody talked about war. It was a dreadful time.

Then, early in the morning on 10 May 1940, the war came to the Netherlands and nothing would ever be the same again for the Siemons family, nor indeed for any Dutch family. What follows is Corry's eyewitness account.

> May 10, 1940, 4.00 am. I woke with a start, at first not able to identify the noise that had penetrated my deep sleep. I lay and listened for a while, but it didn't stop. It sounded as if a gigantic swarm of bees was approaching the village. Strange ... it seemed to get louder. I wondered whether Leny heard it as well.
>
> I called so softly, 'Le, you awake?' No answer. It took some doing to rouse my sis.
>
> I slipped out of bed, shook her shoulder. 'Le, wake up, listen!'
>
> 'Wha ... What do you want?'
>
> 'Listen! That noise! It sounds as if there's a swarm of bees on the

move. Can you hear it?'

She nodded yes and sat up. We listened for a while longer, then heard our parents stir in the room at the back.

'I'm going to have a look.'

I opened the window, while my sister turned over and said, 'For God's sake, Corry, go to sleep. It's only four o'clock.'

I opened the window and shook her again. 'Come quickly, Le, look there in the distance.'

Wiping the sleep from her eyes, mumbling 'pest' under her breath, she stood up, leaned over my shoulder, to slowly say, 'Those are parachutes.'

'Parachutes? Those little white umbrellas coming down are parachutes? You must be joking.'

At that moment Dad entered the room. 'What was that, Corry? Let me see.' One look outside and he went as white as a sheet. 'Oh, my God, oh, God, those are paratroopers, German paratroopers, I bet. And they're near the bridges at Moerdijk and going for the airports!'

'But, but ... we couldn't see that from here, surely.' We hadn't heard Mum come in. 'Let me see. Maybe they're our troops on exercises,' she suggested.

'Don't you believe it,' Dad said harshly. He hurried down the stairs and switched on the wireless, with the rest of us traipsing in his wake.

There was no sound at first, then suddenly we heard the familiar voice of a well-known newsreader coming through: 'THE NETHERLANDS IS AT WAR. I REPEAT: THE NETHERLANDS IS AT WAR.

'Shortly after midnight German troops crossed our border. German paratroopers are trying to secure positions in the west of our country. German troops in Dutch uniforms have taken over all vital installations in the east. Keep calm. Stay indoors. There will be continuous news bulletins today. Stay tuned and follow the Government's instructions as they come to hand. Stay calm ... We repeat, stay calm.' Again, there was no further sound.

Then Kees walked in. We had not missed him yet. One look at his leaden face was enough. 'Yes, I heard. Frans told me.' Frans, our local butcher, lived opposite and had been working late when he had heard the first rumblings of trouble.

My brother looked at his father. 'What now, Dad?'

Part Two: Corry's Story

'Yeah, what now, son?' Worried and ill at ease, I looked from Mum to Dad, who for once was lost for words. What we had feared, had been preparing for, and yet could not quite comprehend, was now happening.

The Netherlands was a proud and independent nation, not known to bow to any oppressor or invader—you only had to look at the history of the country. How would we fare now?

I was scared, very, very scared.

I went over to Dad. 'What will happen to us now, Dad?'

Dad's eyes were wet. He looked down at me and stroked my hair. 'I don't know, Corry. Let's hope they'll by-pass our small town, but I think that is false hope. They'll be everywhere. We'll just have to carry on the best we can and try to stay out of trouble.'

Breakfast was a quiet affair, and it was past nine o'clock when, we suddenly realised, I should be at school, but the neighbours had come in to discuss the situation or to pass on some rumours and news. Soon breakfast stood forgotten on the table.

Around ten o' clock, my friends Corry and Ria arrived at the back door. When I went to meet them, they told me, 'Sister Eugenia sent us home; said to tell you not to come to school until further notice, Corry.'

Then as Mum came in from the lounge, 'Hello, Mrs Siemons.'

'What's this about no school?' asked Mum. 'Are the boarding schools closing as well?' She'd obviously overheard the girls.

'A lot of parents came and collected their children,' Corry answered, 'but none could get through from across the rivers, apparently. There seems to be fierce fighting where the paratroopers landed. Sister asked us to pray for the parents of those children.'

'They must be frantic with worry,' Mum said. 'I can imagine how I would feel if one of mine was boarding.'

It was an unsettling day. Dad and Kees didn't go to any outside jobs but stayed close to home. The radio was on all day. At frequent intervals we listened to the news as new bulletins were read to keep the population informed of latest developments. The news was all bad. A few hours after the invasion, the south-east city of Maastricht was in German hands, and the Dutch army had been driven back. Behind the lines of combat, chaos and uncertainty reigned and rumours of treason were rife. From Army Headquarters came the order to intern all German nationals and members of the NSB to prevent them giving help and support to enemy troops.

After a restless night we woke up to very sad news: the historic town of Nijmegen was now in German hands. In its provincial paper, *De Gelderlander,* appeared a first proclamation from the local commandant, Hauptman Wentzel. It was a lengthy edict, informing the people of Nijmegen they were now under German rule.

A curfew was imposed between the hours of 9 pm and 5 am. Nijmegen citizens were not allowed to reside out of town, and the clocks would be changed to German time—a difference of one hour and forty minutes—taking effect immediately.

Gatherings of more than three people were prohibited, and there was to be a complete black-out at night. All travel and freight transport were forbidden. The list went on and on. Possession of firearms and ammunition: 'verboten'. So, too, giving shelter to enemy troops (our own military). All communication material to be handed over, and the last humiliating order: all male citizens between the ages of twenty and thirty-five were to report at the barracks at Groesbeek, a small town near Nijmegen, on Sunday, 12 May at nine o' clock German time.

The Nazi boot had started to kick our nation into submission.

The 'grapevine' and the news bulletins on the radio kept us informed, and although Nijmegen was situated far from our western provinces, it gave a terrified population some idea what to expect. Without exception, we knew this would be our future as well. The only question was when. During this second day of war, the news was far from optimistic.

Mum and Dad carried on as best they could, but I missed Dad's quick wit, and there were no duets sung in the workshop that day. Mum's face wore a constant frown, and I spent the day shopping for emergencies; long lists she had written out and ready, and so had every housewife in the village. Some items were sold out already. It was then a matter of trying another shop, which made it hard if you were not a regular customer.

Everywhere I went there was just one topic of conversation, how far the Germans had penetrated. Confirmation of heavy fighting in the east was heartening, yet people were extremely nervous as rumours circulated of spies infiltrating the main cities in the west.

People were stopped in the streets and had to show their identifications. Civilian guards flagged down cars for the same reason.

One news item, more than any other, made me realise life as we had known it would be gone forever. The Netherlands' Military Authority ordered the owner of Ouwehands' Zoo, in the vicinity where the fiercest battles were fought—and lost—to kill all dangerous animals. This order was followed to the letter except for two newly arrived polar bears. Cages of tropical birds and monkeys were opened to release them.

On Sunday, 12 May, I was sitting in the lounge, near the window, working on an interesting project for school. Dad read the paper, headlines screaming from its pages. Mum had just poured the coffee. A tranquil scene and a familiar one, replayed countless times before. Outwardly everything seemed normal, yet there was one difference this time. Nothing stirred. An eerie silence lay like a shroud over the village. There was no traffic, no barking dogs; even the busy chatter of sparrows in the gutters had ceased. The town held its breath and waited.

Kees had gone outside a minute ago, as he said, 'To see what's happening.' He was back within seconds, his face grey with shock. 'There are two Germans with machine guns! They're crouched behind the hedge at the bicycle track!'

His words weren't cold when a shadow fell over my books. I looked up, straight into the mouth of a machine gun the German soldier aimed at me. Dad warned me, 'Sit absolutely still, Corry. Keep your hands where he can see them!'

Paralysed with fear, I nodded yes, my eyes on the weapon, then on the grim, grimy face of the young soldier. He kept his finger on the trigger. I felt sick with fear, a cold lump of dread in my stomach. Mouth dry, I watched as the camouflaged figure swept the rifle around, walked backwards, then checked the workshop and garden at the back and disappeared around the side of the house.

'My God,' Mum gasped, 'that was close!' Slow tears started to trickle down her face. 'Co.' She swallowed. 'Corry, come away from the window. There may be others with him.'

I joined them at the table and realised I had been holding my breath. I felt faint with fear. I had not imagined what it would mean—life under occupation—but I was learning fast. So, this was war ... a menace which had invaded our lives?

Dad stroked Mum's trembling hands, saying, 'We're in it this time, Mother. We missed the last war, but we're in it now. The bastards ... While the Netherlands declared itself neutral, to overrun us like this.'

'Oh, sweet Jesus, what's going to happen to us,' Mum asked the heavens. Deathly pale, she went to the kitchen, where I followed her, while she wiped her eyes. We knew this war had now ripped our well-ordered existence to shreds.

With trembling hands, she put the kettle on. 'I'll make another pot of coffee. I sure need an extra one. And I better be careful with it,' she sighed. 'I've put some by, but when there is no new supply, it will soon be gone.'

By Wednesday, 15 May 1940, it was all over. Germany had threatened that unless the Netherlands capitulated, the larger cities—such as Amsterdam, The Hague and Utrecht—would suffer the same fate as Rotterdam, which had already been heavily bombed.

Silently and subdued we sat around the table. We listened to General Winkelman (the Dutch Commander-in-Chief) as he spoke on radio in an address to the people and gave his reasons to lay down arms. At the end he spoke of trust in the future, his faith in the inner strength of our people, and urged us to work together to rebuild our broken country. He concluded with: 'Long live our Queen. Long live our country.'

We were silent. We knew what would happen: the Germans would march triumphantly into our cities and villages, like they had in trampled Poland. We would be prisoners in our own homes. They would come marching in, with their slogans and banners, their orders and threats. They would turn our safe country upside down and bleed it and our hearts dry.

No wonder we cried ...

An uneasy calm settled on the village. No one felt like working, and people gathered to discuss the events of recent days.

Before nightfall, news of a new tragedy filtered through. It seemed hundreds of Jews—Dutch nationals—on hearing the Netherlands had capitulated, had taken their own lives. The horror of their despair

Part Two: Corry's Story

clearly showed us what they already knew, and what we could expect. Then the radio news bulletins stopped abruptly and there was silence. The same cold silence that invaded my body.

A few days later a garrison contingent of about forty German soldiers marched triumphantly—and arrogantly—into Oudenbosch. German control of the day-to-day life of the town and its citizens had begun. The unit commandeered one of the boarding houses at the St Louis school for boys and remained there for the duration of the war.

Across the Netherlands, the German propaganda machine actively encouraged the Dutch population to fraternise with the occupying troops, hammering the message that Germany didn't wage war with civilians, that differences should be forgotten, and that the blood ties between the Netherlands and Germany would make it easier for them to become partners in the new Europe.

The troops meanwhile did everything possible to integrate themselves with civilians. German soldiers were polite and well mannered, so people would get the impression that occupation wasn't that bad after all. Officers were billeted in Dutch homes, while schools and halls were requisitioned to house the common soldier.

14.   LIFE UNDER OCCUPATION

So, this 'new normal' eventually settled down, despite all the initial angst and upheaval, into a more predictable, albeit different, pattern of life. From Corry's perspective, starting as an eleven-year-old, soon to turn twelve, when the Netherlands was subdued:

> ... I still had rather a carefree youth, while little changed at home or at school. We had a lovely nun in Grade 7, Sr Christina. She was strict, but she had a certain way with her, and a group of my classmates and I became the best of friends with her. Christina tried to set us some standards and we responded to this, while she prepared us as well as she could for high school and life. When we did something wrong, she always insisted we apologise, otherwise we would be totally ignored, which didn't go down well with the stubborn amongst us.
>
> At home, our kitchen garden provided us with lovely vegetables, and sometimes, when we had a glut, Mum gave some to the nuns, as they of course had no way of procuring something extra. Heaven knows, their lives were sober enough, and how the convents fared during the long years of war is still a mystery to me. Maybe they had a special SOS line to God.
>
> Dad also grew lovely gladioli, and many were the times when I took big bunches of them to the convent for their chapel, which was much appreciated. I'm sure they would offer an extra prayer for our family.
>
> At regular intervals, the Germans dictated changes, the first being the introduction of new stamps. The picture of Queen Wilhelmina disappeared, and new stamps bore the faces of Dutch national heroes and folkloristic symbols. Despite all this 'needling' everyone seemed to make a go of it, and life went on like before.

Gradually, however, the screws were tightened by the occupiers, with

Part Two: Corry's Story

new rules and dictates being issued on a regular basis to increase the level of control and intimidation. One—which proved the evillest of these—was the requirement for the entire population aged fourteen and above to always have on them an identity card. This became a requirement before the end of 1940.

These cards included a photograph, fingerprint of the right index finger, and signature, and identified the card holder's ethnic origins. As quickly became apparent, they were used, just as they had been used elsewhere in occupied Europe, to especially identify the Jews. From 1942, some 100,000 Dutch Jews were transported from the Netherlands, mostly to extermination camps at Auschwitz and Sobibor. One of these families was the Frank family, including their daughter Anne.

As the war progressed, and Germany continually expanded its frontiers across Europe, into Africa and Russia, the demands for supplies to support their military forces and operations steadily increased. Occupied countries were stripped of anything that could support the German war effort, resulting in increasingly severe shortages of food and other necessities.

> By now we used coupons for everything. Gas, electricity and fuel were rationed, and people were told to live within their means. Surrogate products appeared, such as ersatz [substitute] coffee, which wasn't too bad. However, the tea was undrinkable ... but we learned.
>
> To save on fuel, people started to soak newspapers in big tubs of water, which were then pressed firmly into balls, dried, and when dry provided some extra fuel for fires. A keen black market in coupons and goods developed for which hefty fines were imposed for those caught, followed at times by imprisonment.
>
> Equality of the sexes was still a future dream: when cigarettes and tobacco were rationed, the men were entitled to forty cigarettes per week while the women could only buy forty per month.
>
> If you wanted to eat out, you had to have the necessary coupons with you, but life was sober, and people rarely visited restaurants.

Still, there were some aspects of village life in Oudenbosch that remained very strong, providing a much-needed anchor for hope, for supporting each other and nurturing the sense of community. A we-are-all-in-this-together attitude was directed against the occupiers, who were referred to in the vernacular as 'Moffen', a bit like 'Hun' in English. Although not specifically mentioned in any of Corry's writings, the very existence of a photo of her on a spiritual retreat with other young ladies in July 1941 suggests that, at least at this stage of the long and tedious occupation, the life of the Church (and school) in Oudenbosch remained strong.

However, there are no specific writings or memoirs for the next three years, during which time Corry would have steadily progressed through high school. Other than that, there is a gap in information about any significant events in her young life from mid-1941 till late October 1944.

15. LIBERATION OF OUDENBOSCH ... TO VE DAY

Then, everything changed. As a sixteen-year-old, Corry kept a special diary to record the extraordinary events of the next few months. This diary has survived and is still held in the de Haas family archives.

This is an extract (translated in the order in which it was written):

October 30, 1944 the day of the liberation of Oudenbosch.

This wonderful, moving day will stay in our memories forever. The whole week had been a week of nervous tension, in which there were many sighs: 'When will we be liberated?'

We often asked ourselves: 'Where are they?' and: 'Will we be liberated soon?' I have to admit that we often grumbled too: 'These Tommies are good for nothing. They don't make any progress.'

Sunday, October 29

There was a heavy tank battle at Rozendaal. The relentless, ongoing exchange of heavy gunfire and explosions made us very afraid and nervous. When sitting in the living room, the ongoing rumbling and rattling of the windows was impossible to bear. That morning, our suitcases (to flee) were packed and brought to the deep cellar of the Tooten family where Kees' girlfriend, Riet, lived. We slept there that night. We were upstairs till twelve thirty, and then we moved to the cellar. We were just lying down in the cellar when suddenly there were three very loud bangs that woke us all up.

After that we heard nothing but the ongoing rumble in the distance, and the movement of the Moffen who, of course, wanted to retreat as quickly as they could. There were not many Germans moving anymore. In the afternoon we saw three Moffen busy with clearing up the telephone wire.

Monday, October 30

After a fearful night we started the day with a prayer, grateful that

Liberation of Oudenbosch ... to VE Day

we had been spared.

Quite early Mr. Tooten went to look outside, and he quickly came back with the news that shells had landed near the St Louis boys' school, near the church, and near some homes and businesses.

We went for a short look, and after that we went home for breakfast. Not that we ate much, of course. We were too nervous to do that. And shells came down during the entire morning.

Nearby, there were still five Germans waiting for the sign to blast the sluice to cut off the road.

Then, at three o'clock, those Moffen blasted the sluice. At a quarter to four the first Americans were standing here.

All of us had just been running to the cellar at the Tooten family because there was lots of shooting with machine guns. 'Listen,' Riet said, 'street fighting ...'

Mr Tooten silently went upstairs to have a look and came back soon with the message: 'Guys, the Englishmen are here!!!!'

At first, we were only allowed one-by-one to peek through a little crack at the door. But then we saw the Brothers come outside too, and that was our signal. Oh, the cheering and roaring of the crowd! What a joy about the liberation! Lena went home quickly to see if anything was damaged. Fortunately, nothing but some broken windowpanes in the door. Half an hour later Dad came to get me, and I went along with him.

The Americans were sitting and lying everywhere, wherever there was a bit of space. Lena served them coffee and handed out apples. How happy the boys were with something warm to drink.

The evening of that same day the doorbell rang at about half past seven. Kees went to look and then called, 'Corry, come over here for a minute, to speak English.' I went to the front to find I don't know how many Americans at the door, asking if we have a cellar, and if they could see it.

I said, 'Yes, of course,' and they came in with me. Afterwards even more of them came and, in the end, we had eighteen of them in the house, sixteen in the living room and the kitchen, and two of them as guards in the hallway.

Part Two: Corrie's Story

LIBERATION

These are no heroes, these tired bedraggled men.
No laurels worn in pride on victor's head.
No fanfares ringing out in welcome as they go,
Just a few flags and frightened folk instead.

They wear no well-pressed khaki battledress,
But rain-soaked, tattered camouflage;
Their rifles ready, slung lowly on the hips,
And in the netted helmets wilted foliage.

Once shining boots now sopping from the rain,
From groveling in mud and slush when under fire,
With blisters on their feet, the faces lined and grey
And lacerated hands from cutting through barbed wire.

They walk in single file along the village road,
Hugging the safety of a built-up street;
Their eyes alert—for an enemy still lurks
In quiet alleyways in panicky retreat.

And in the distance the sound of heavy cannon
Can be heard, a thunderbolt, a shell's wide trace.
The whoosh … the piercing shriek of a grenade
That sends the window-panes a-shatter in their face.

So, the town is free. How do we count the cost?
How do we justify a mother's loss?
Of a soldier left behind in foreign soil,
In the Netherlands—near a town called Oudenbosch …

Corry de Haas

At first, they sat down talking, but, around eleven o'clock, one after the other went off to go to sleep. Jack and Lorian were the two boys we had that night. They stayed till about noon the next day but were continually in and out during the morning.

Some of the boys told us their names and I also want to record these here: Irv, Steve, James, Jerry, Gorken, Haverlach, and Jeneilly.

Tuesday, October 31

It was Jeneilly's birthday! We did congratulate him, but I wonder what this man might have been thinking, being this far from home. That morning I got some little souvenirs from Irv, coins amongst other things. Kees got some cigarettes, of which I kept the package as a souvenir.

[Editor's note: the package is pasted into the diary.]

At about noon they started to leave, after Steve and some other guys had eaten some soup with us. I almost had to eat with them. We all waved them goodbye and then went to work.

A few days later …

… suddenly, I saw Irv sitting in a 'jeep'. He also saw us and came up to us immediately. 'Oh, Corry and Helen.' I was very happy to see him again. But suddenly there was Steve too and James and Jerry and Lorian and Bill *et al*. All these boys had changed so much because they were shaved! Irv the only one who wasn't!

After having talked for a while, Irv asked, 'Corry, come with me, I must show you something.'

Then we went to his own jeep and he said, 'Can I write to you and will you write to me after the war?'

I said, 'Okay, for I wanted to ask you as well. You must give me your address.'

Meanwhile Lena was talking with Steve and James and had already called to me several times that I had to hurry up. 'Yes,' I shouted, 'address.' The first time I said that in English, and she didn't understand it. Then I said, 'Adres,' and she did understand. Meanwhile we were walking back, and when we joined them again Irv asked me for a picture. I didn't have one with me but promised to give him one. Then I got a photo of him. After that James took a snapshot of us, and then Bill, Steve, Irv, James and Jerry and Lena and I went home together.

The next day Irv was off to the front and I didn't see him again in the following days.

Sunday, November 12

Approximately 700 Englishmen arrived today in Oudenbosch with their tanks. Nel, Corrie and I walked to the main road and saw them all coming from the direction of Breda. Now there's a pleasant bustle in Oudenbosch.

Sunday, November 19

Football match between VES (the local team) vs The King's Own. Went to watch of course. VES lost with 12-2. A nice match but not very exciting because the Englishmen were playing football too well.

Tuesday, November 21

Around eight o'clock this evening the doorbell rang. Lena opened the door and there were two Tommies, asking her for 'candles'. Of course, she doesn't understand a thing, but she manages to explain that she 'has a zister die English speakt.' The boys came asking for candles because they had no light in the evening.

They were given a chair and a cup of coffee and then left at nine o'clock. I told them they were quite welcome to stay but they said it would be better manners to go. I asked them to come back the next evening and they said, 'Yes, please.'

Wednesday, November 22

They came back. Already at half past six they were standing here. Their names are Tommy and Jimmy. They are nice guys. We spent the night talking and asking questions etc. Tommy has no father nor a mother anymore. And he misses a finger. His mum and dad were killed by an air-raid by the Moffen on England. He lives in Preston and Jim in Liverpool.

By the end of that same week, the unit was moving out and Tommy was given a blessing, a sign of the cross on his forehead by Corry's dad, such blessings being a Siemons' family tradition that survived into the next generations.

Tuesday, December 5

Frank and Sid at our home for the first evening. Nice guys, with whom we spent many a pleasant evening. They were with us from Dec. 5–Dec. 20. I hope we will see all of them again some time.

Although not recorded by her, there is some evidence that Frank became Corry's first love. Indeed, at some stage she revealed to one of my sisters that her first kiss was with Frank. On the back of his photo dated 11 September 1945, he wrote: *With all my love, yours, Frank xxx*. While there can be no certainty, her diary entry of many happy days between 20 May 1945—*the evening I will never forget in all my life*—and 4 November 1945, could suggest that she and Frank might have been able to spend time together during this period. After that, the album has a photo of Frank dated 26 June 1946 and two photos from 1976 with a note in the album that he died in 1977. What happened in the intervening years is now known only to Corry and Frank. However, in a listing of the highlights of her youth in the same photo album, Corry wrote: *Het verdriet om Frank*, the grief over Frank, clearly her first love.

Part Two: Corrie's Story

YOUNG LOVE – 1944

You stood before me
A young soldier,
The khaki uniform neatly pressed,
A black beret
Under the epaulet on your shoulder.
A boy, no a man,
You lost your youth
On the blood-soaked hills
Of Caen.
I was only sixteen,
But you were my whole world.
My school-English didn't make allowances
For conversation.
Yet I felt we did not need many words,
And I counted the hours until
I would see you again.
Then
That cold, dreaded November morning
You disappeared out of my life …
A new battle to be won in The Ardennes.
I saw you one more time …
And the pain of my loss
Would be part of me
For years to come.
I was so young,
But my emotions were as old
As time …

Corry de Haas

Over the next few months, there was a steady procession of units and troops in and out of Oudenbosch, and Corry records that small groups of soldiers from various units and nationalities were billeted in the family home. Her diary records a total of twenty-two soldiers staying with them: nine from the United States, eight from the United Kingdom, and five Canadians.

In late April, a Dutch commando unit (yes, the one that you, the reader, is thinking of!) found itself in Oudenbosch, being billeted at the St Louis brothers' school. Another of Corry's diary entries records:

> Rumours sprang up out of nowhere that the tank regiment was on its way for a special leave in their village. 'They are coming back,' people shouted at each other.
>
> 'Who?' came the replies.
>
> 'The Forrards, the Forrards …' and pandemonium overwhelmed the locals.
>
> Half the population—with a high percentage of young girls—roamed the streets. The grapevine was doing overtime! Stories were getting wilder and more exaggerated by the minute …
>
> Then, from the south, in the bleak fading light of a cold April afternoon, came the unmistakable sound of an army convoy.
>
> An armoured scout car, some jeeps and three canvas-covered trucks came to a halt in the market, the main thoroughfare of the village. The impatient spectators couldn't believe their eyes when the soldiers jumped down from the vehicles. Instead of the Forrards, they were looking at camouflage-clad strangers with large rucksacks, climbing ropes across their chests, tommy guns at the ready.
>
> 'Like German paratroopers,' someone volunteered. 'Green berets as well.'
>
> A young man went closer to the trucks and, coming back, he explained they were special service, called commandos. For the locals, however, they were an unexpected letdown. Disappointed, the villagers made their way home again. When I saw Leny, we linked arms and, passing close to the soldiers, we stopped dead in our tracks.
>
> 'They are speaking Dutch!' came a whisper from Leny, but her softly spoken words were heard.

'Ja, wij zijn Hollanders, hoor …!' and, laughing, the men disappeared in the school.

'Dutch commandos,' Corry and Leny said at the same time and, giggling, continued their way home.

On Sunday, 29 April 1945, there were special thanksgiving services as the 'rumour mill' was becoming more strident that the Moffen were in retreat, being steadily pushed out of the remaining Dutch provinces in the west. On the following day, the local news bulletin featured an article by an anonymous young reader. It included the following:

> Thanksgiving services were held in all the churches. Praying to God for being spared when so many millions had died. In the Catholic Church, the exact replica of St Peter's in Rome but on a smaller scale, a Benediction took place this Sunday afternoon. The church was packed, and many teenagers were present, including myself.
>
> A lonely figure stood at the back, near the heavy doors. His khaki uniform was neatly pressed. A green beret sat under the epaulet on his shoulder. Where had he come from? How far from home would he be, this Tommy? His features were hard to see in the dark recesses of the church, but he was there for a reason. I could feel it when I turned around and saw him praying: to thank God he was spared too, or was his war just beginning? I shall always wonder about that lone soldier with the green beret.

Then, finally, on 4 May 1945, the day the Netherlands had been hoping and praying for during five awfully long years had arrived. Corry records the way she experienced that extraordinary day:

> Just before nine in the morning, I was busy translating an English letter at Aunt Marie's house when suddenly radio *Herrijzend Nederland* was interrupted with the important and joyful message that the Moffen in the west had capitulated unconditionally. What a great joy that was!
>
> There was no thinking about translating a letter anymore! I jumped into my coat and asked Nel to come with me. When we arrived at the

marketplace it was as if all Oudenbosch had come out to celebrate. Flags had been put out everywhere. And everywhere handshakes and glorious, delighted faces. What a wonderful, joyous tiding.

The brass band started to play and march spontaneously. I was dancing and jumping till half past ten that night.

What joy! What happiness! We thank God for the full liberation of our dear little native country!

Between this record of her experience of the day the Netherlands was fully liberated until early 1947, Corry kept no diaries or writings of her life and experiences in post-war Oudenbosch. Probably she would have finished school during 1945 or 1946. She did, however, record that she found work *as a shorthand typist at a solicitor's office in a small village not far from here* which she described as *my first real job*.

Her writings also make no mention of the great difficulties the entire Dutch population, and the rest of liberated Europe, found itself in. In the Netherlands, just obtaining the necessities of life, especially food, was a continuing imperative and struggle over the next few years. In later years, Corry sometimes talked about how it was sometimes necessary for the family to go out into the fields and dig up turnips or swedes, intended as animal food, to have at least some nourishment.

Nevertheless, despite this ongoing hardship, it seems that in typical Dutch fashion, every effort was made to take advantage of the new freedom and peace to celebrate, to put on plays, shows and musicals and thus bring some relief and joy to the struggles of daily life. Photos of that time clearly show that Corry participated in these very enthusiastically. In fact, all the photos of this period capture a young woman full of life and vigour.

So, 1946 went by and, in June, Corry turned eighteen.

Corry at 9 months, just standing?

Corry's home as a child

In the pram, with Leny pushing

Leny and Corry

First Communion, 30 May 1935

Corry standing between her parents at their 25th wedding anniversary

Inside the basilica

Corry on retreat with her peers

> Maandag 30 Oct. 1944.
>
> 30 October, de dag van de bevrij-
> ding van Oudenbosch.
> Deze heerlijke, ontroerende dag zal ons
> nog lang in onze herinnering bij-
> blijven.
> De gehele week, was al 'n week van zenuw-
> achtige spanning geweest, waarin vele
> keren de verzuchting geslaakt werd:
> "Waren we maar bevrijd." Dikwijls
> vroegen we ons af: "Waar zouden ze
> zijn," en "zouden wij al gauw bevrijd
> worden?"
> Dikwijls ook – ik moet 't wel bekennen –
> mopperden we: "Die Tommie is hunnen
> ook niets. He schieten ook niets op."
> Maandagmorgen 29 October ± 12-1 uur

Part of Corry's diary of the day of liberation

Frank, Corry's first love

Irv, one of the soldiers who stayed at Corry's home shortly after liberation

Corry with her mother, 1947

A very relaxed Corry, 1947

TUNEY ADS

Prijs: 1 cent per letter cijfer of leesteeken bij vooruitbetaling te voldoen.
Voor advertentie's onder no. of motto geplaatst moet 25 cent worden bijgeteld voor toezending der brieven. Advertentie's moeten vóór de 17e der maand in ons bezit zijn.

2 vriendinnen 16 18 jr. wensen corresp. met d'to vrienden 18 20 jr. onder no. 0.

Te koop aangeb.: Coffergramofoon en Guitaar. Zonnebloemstraat 13, Den Haag

Sportieve R.K. jongeman uit gegoede stand leeftijd 18 jaar, liefhebberij zeilen, schaatsen en motorsport, zoekt correspondentie vriendin Brieven liefst met foto onder no. 61.

Jong kunstenaar zoekt contact m. leuk pittig meisje, houdend o.a van „rea jazz', natuur en zeilsport. Idealistisch, temperamentvol en serieus Liefst niet kunnende dansen en P.G. of G.G 18 27 j. Br. m. foto no. 62 aan T.T.

2 vlotte sportieve vrienden (beschaafd milieu) zoeken 2 leuke correspondentie vriendinnen 18 22 jaar, brieven onder no. 63 aan T T.

Rijksambtenaar zoekt correspondentie met sportief meisje 19 23 jaar, brieven met foto's onder motto „Belgium" adm v d. blad

Te koop aangeb enkele juist uit Amerika ontvangen gram. platen Woody Herman Glenn Miller etc W. K. D van der Meulen, Riouwstraat 55, Den Haag

Englishman interested in popular music wants to correspond with young man in Holland, with same hobby. Write to 'an Stuart "Medway", The Drift, Royston, Herts, England.

2 besch vlotte meisjes 17 j. dans en muziek liefh zoeken d'to corresp vrienden pl.m. 20 jaar, br: m photo, welke op eerew retour onder motto „Swing"

Jongedame 20 jr. alg. ontw. zoekt vlotte corr vriend, br liefst m foto p.a. B v. d. Brink Heerenlaan 55 Zeist

We'k sportief meisje R.K ol m 20 jaar wil correspondeeren met Muziek en Filmliefhebber die slechts zelden van radio of film kan genieten Brieven liefst met foto (welke op eerewoord retour) aan Korp P de Haas, Commando 23 111002 3 VI 1 - Reg. Stoottroepen V Brigade Veldpostkantoor Palembang.

3 sportieve jongelui wensen correspondentie met 3 charmante jongedames. Leefiijd p.m. 19 jaar Br. m foto o. motto „Hawaii" a.T.T.

R.K. Jongeman zoekt corresp met vlotte R K. Jongedame 18 20 j, Brieven met foto onder motto „Anton" aan adm. van dit blad.

2 R.K. Jongedocht 19 jr haardracht: knot met pieken, alg. ontw. liefh. kolen sjouwen en taart eten, zoek'n corr vrienden Motto: Wie

The ad as it appeared in the 6 February 1947 edition of *Tuney Tunes*, highlighted and commencing with 'W'

PART THREE: *THEIR* STORY BEGINS ...

First, some context and qualification.

What follows in this part of the story is from Pierre's writings, Book 4, and the final book of his work *Dreams and Tears for Souvenirs*. It was from this same work that *Pierre's Story*, the earlier part of this book, was drawn and extensively quoted from. In what follows, we only have his account of his correspondence with Corry and the development of their relationship while separated across the globe, Corry remaining in her quiet village of Oudenbosch, and Pierre in a whirlwind of jungle warfare in what was then the East Indies.

While the steady development of their relationship via a slow and mostly unpredictable mail service is undeniable, the actual content of the letters, and the circumstances around which they were read by Corry, may have been dramatised or embellished by Pierre for narrative effect, or perhaps 'poetic license'. Alternatively, they could also have sat down together at times while Pierre was writing so that Corry could 'fill in' the story from what she lived and experienced during the many long months while they were corresponding. Unfortunately, there is now no way of knowing ... and that is okay!

Copies of extracts of their first letters to each other have survived to this day, but they are incomplete and were also quite long. From comparing these originals to the texts below, it seems that Pierre has used direct quotes and summarised the major items of interest. No copies of any other of their original letters have survived.

16. First Letters

'What do you think, Mam?'

> Which young and attractive girl, RC aged +20, would like to correspond with music and film lover, who only seldom can listen to radio and songs. Letters, pref. with photo to: Commando Corp. P. de Haas - 231111002 - Strike Force 8 - Field P.O. PALEMBANG - SEAC

They both looked at the small advertisement in the February issue of *Tuney Tunes*, a monthly magazine, catering for the young at heart who liked music and film. It contained, amongst other things, the latest post-war songs from England and the USA. Corry read the ad aloud.

'I really don't know, dear, it says twenty. You being only eighteen, he might just throw you back into the water, like they do with undersized fish!' She laughed as she said it, turned around and went outside to get some more coal for the glowing fire.

It was a bitter cold day. The freezing wind blew at gale force, trying to take the half-opened door off its hinges. Corry held it, as her mother came back in again, a full bucket of the oval-shaped briquettes in her hand. The door was quickly latched to keep out the chilly winter.

'Brrrr ... What a temperature! Tell that chap in Palembang to send some tropical heat, will you?' She slammed her arms crosswise under her armpits to restore the circulation.

'You think it will be all right then, Mam ... I mean write to him, a stranger?'

'Well, my girl, everyone in life is a stranger, until you get to know them. You have been writing to those girls in England now for how long?'

'Yes, Mother, I know, but they are girls. This is a man, a male and a commando to boot, perhaps a hungry tiger as well!' They both laughed.

'Just tell him no nonsense, correspondence only!'

'I'll make coffee first, Mother. The ad can wait.'

Corry waited till the next day to write her first letter to Corporal de Haas:

Oudenbosch, Sunday 23 February 1947

Dear Mister De Haas,

First of all, let me introduce myself. My name is Corry Siemons, eighteen years old, blond, blue eyes. The youngest of a family of five, one brother and three sisters. I live at home with my parents and Kees, who is pestering me at the moment, trying to read over my shoulder. I work as a shorthand typist at a solicitor's office in a small village not far from here.

The reason I'm replying to your advertisement in *Tuney Tunes* is simple. The wording sounded—correct me if I'm wrong—kind of ... well, lonely, and if I can bring some light in that dark tunnel, I will do so. Although, to be quite honest, I find it hard writing to a complete stranger, but as they say in the theatre, opening night is the beginning of mistakes! I hope our correspondence won't be like that.

My sisters are all married. They are Lena, Bets and Nel and of course you've already met Kees my brother. Stop annoying me! No that is not meant for you, Corporal. I just try and write in peace.

Enclosed is a snapshot of me taken last summer. I trust you in returning it, if you decided against becoming a penfriend, you might get dozens of replies, who knows.

One other thing please. Let's keep it correspondence ONLY, no nonsense. That is if you feel like writing to me. You might well ask, what a nerve, to dictate conditions in an opening letter, but I have been hurt before when I read too much in so-called innocently phrased words. I don't want this to happen again.

Now, some more newsy items from everyday life in our village ...

Part Three: Their Story Begins ...

Corry continued for a while, completing the letter with information from the latest films, added a few titles of songs just released, and concluded with a short description of local happenings.

At last, she felt satisfied, closed the envelope and put it on the mantelpiece. Looking at her mother, she said, 'You know what, Mam, I feel like ... like little red riding hood and the wolf!'
They didn't laugh then, they roared.
Outside the temperature dropped to minus ten degrees Centigrade.

It was a different story across the world, just south of the equator, where both the heat and humidity mostly hover at oppressive levels, impossible to shake off. Pierre had started to wonder whether the advertisement in *Tuney Tunes* might be proving to be a fiasco because no letters had yet been received, even though mail was frequently interrupted for no apparent reason.
Then, one Friday evening, after returning exhausted from an extended patrol through the swamplands near Palembang, there were twenty-four letters waiting on his stretcher in the tent.

Lost for words I couldn't laugh, feeling a tear instead creeping up inside, for here, I knew, without opening any envelopes, were dreams of a new unfolding saga in my life. It took me a long time reading them all, attaching the many photos to the correct letter and most of all trying to absorb! They had reached out from across the world. Suddenly, the Netherlands was so much nearer ...
Some used sophisticated language, others short, simple sentences. All with a feeling of sharing my life and pushing the war back for the time being. There was an intimacy attached to their words, even when they did start with 'friend'. One wrote, 'to an unknown soldier,' and for a freezing moment I saw a graveyard and then the image faded ...
Others, who began with 'Hallo there' ended with lots of love, having changed tack somewhere halfway through. After a few more weeks, the total number stood at fifty-one. The very last was from a girl called Corry. She was the only one who started with 'Dear Mister'.

First Letters

I bought writing pads in the canteen for making an index, listed all the girls in order, noted their hobbies, ambitions, statistics, age, date of birth etc. Names of streets and towns I had never heard of. Others were from the main cities. The hardest part was to select those one could write to with ease. A short list of twelve remained. The rest would receive a nice thank you letter, and their pictures returned as soon as time was available.

I felt like a secretary from a lonely-hearts club. Only one more to go; the last on my alphabetical list was Siemons, age eighteen, blond, blue eyes, first name Corry. Yes ... I remembered, still I had better read her letter again. Carefully I memorised the four neatly written pages. I looked at the clock. Only two hours before night-patrol ...

I started to write ...

Palembang, 24 March 1947
On active service

Dear L.C.

Well, lucky last I guess, and to put you straight into the picture, you are the only one left (from all those girls that answered my cry for help). The other fifty, I should add, have already been replied to.

I am overwhelmed with this kind of goodwill from the home front, all of a sudden, you girls seem to be living next door. New connections have been made, links established, even if we are so far apart.

You, Corry, were the only writer who looked deeper into the why of my advertisement, but homesickness it is not. I like being on my way, between here, there, and nowhere in particular.

Forgive my bad manners, here is an introduction. P stands for Pierre. (I hate common names like Piet etc.!) I am three metres tall on many occasions but shrivel easily underneath a door on my bad days. Hard, staring eyes, a touch of green or grey, depending who's looking at me! A black circle in the centre. Misty sometimes (when it's raining) and faded of course from the harsh sunlight.

Over the years, those eyes have taken many pictures, copied them all and now that information is safely stored in a corner of my mind. I can recall them, those imprints, in a lonely moment when the need

Part Three: Their Story Begins ...

arises.

You gave your age as eighteen ... how smart of you to be so young! I? I'm old, will be around forty soon if time doesn't slow down. Just imagine, sometime next year, I might be sixty, and you, only sweet nineteen. You could be my granddaughter then!

My true age is hidden in my army number. I leave it up to you to solve that riddle. It is a test, you see, finding out how intelligent my future penfriends are!

What, my dear young lady, made you start your essay (it was more than a letter, I thought) with 'Dear Mister'? Did you recognise a gentleman when you read my ad, or is it your job at the solicitor that makes you so polite?

Only joking, Corry, only joking ... I like that name ... and your tiny photo which explains my heading L.C. (Little Corry). No, I'm not laughing at all, the blots on the paper are teardrops, you know ... the liquid coming from cloudy eyes!

I do agree with your 'no nonsense' in your letter, seeing you got hurt with careless words before. It happened to me like that, so many years ago. 'Strictly correspondence only' was another phrase you used, but at this distance there is no need to worry!

You did sound a bit like 'Achtung Minen', where you enter a minefield at your own risk. How about we keep a safe demarcation line, then, sort of a no-man's land between us!? Yes, I like that!

Reading again what I have put down so far, I came to realise that the other fifty girls have been done an injustice. All they did receive was a 'thank-you' note and their picture back (except of course those on my short list), and here I am, pouring out my secret self to an unknown teenager, when I definitely asked for a twenty-year-old lass!

So, you see, young lady, how lucky you are to be included in this most-wanted list! I'll have to finish now. Our night patrol is leaving in ten minutes time and the leading sergeant is Yours Truly. Thanks so much for writing to me, we'll talk about music and film in our next letter, that is, if you still want to continue after reading my nonsense. After all, it's only correspondence and isn't that what you asked for?!

Your Mister Sergeant, Sir!

PS. I was promoted while in hospital. Due to popular demand, I ran out of photos. Will send one next time. A girl asked, 'Are you in the war zone?' I replied, 'Through that door … you can smell it…!'

It had already been more than a month since Corry had written her first letter to Corporal de Haas and she was starting to wonder whether perhaps eighteen was too young, or perhaps he was tired of having to respond to what was probably a large number of letters to other young women. Nevertheless, in post-war Oudenbosch, life was already good, especially at this time of the year, with spring ready to blossom. She still lived at home, and it is into this stable and loving environment that the first 'on active service' letter from Pierre arrived, her mother playfully hiding it behind her back when Corry arrived home from work one evening.

After reading it upstairs in her room, Corry came down for dinner and her father noted how quiet she was, which was unusual for someone normally so bright, cheerful and carefree.

'She got a letter from Palembang,' her mum said to no one in particular.

'Isn't that where all those street fights were between Merdeka and Strike Force 8?' Kees was always well-informed, going through The News as soon as he returned from work.

'Yes, he seems to be in the middle of it,' Corry replied at last. 'His letter was cheerful enough, though.'

Dinner was finished in silence and, after washing up, she read the letter again, this time not minding her mother looking in, welcoming it in fact. She wanted to share the feelings that those written words from a complete stranger had created.

'Around forty … that seems rather old for a commando … but his true age is hidden in his army number …' Corry said aloud. They both looked at the address, containing the figure 231111002.

'Twenty third of the eleventh, 1911,' her mother said at last. 'That makes him … let me see … thirty-five and a bit.'

'Why would he ask for a twenty-year-old girl to correspond with? He is nearly twice my age.' She couldn't keep the irritation hidden.

'Because he's a dirty old man!' Kees dived in at the same time,

Part Three: Their Story Begins ...

avoiding the rolled-up newspaper thrown at him.

'The butcher across the road has a son in the army. He should know,' and before anyone could reply, she was out through the front door.

'He is twenty-three and born on Armistice Day.' Corry couldn't keep the triumph out of her voice as she entered the lounge again, and grabbing her brother Kees by his neck, shouted in his ear, 'Dirty old man, heeej!?'

But she did ask her mother, 'What is a short list?'

17.   SPARRING PARTNERS?

For the next few days, she pondered how she should reply to that commando, not quite sure what to make of his teasing way of writing. Reply in the same flippant tone, draw him out of his shell, or ... put it both ways?! Heads, you win, tails I don't lose. Then she wrote ... and wrote.

Oudenbosch, Sunday, 13 April 1947

Unknown teaser,

Seeing that you did nothing else but make fun of me—just because I wanted to be polite calling you SIR— I shall refrain from writing anything nice to you in reply to your letter. Having said all that, I'd better ask: How are you?!

Congratulations on becoming a sergeant; you must have kissed the right nurse while in hospital!

Thank you anyway for your long letter. You probably need a permanent secretary to keep up the correspondence with the crème de la crème from the Netherlands' young ladies.

See, I can play the same game as you do, tease I mean! Indeed, I feel very honoured to be included in your short list. But why me? I was the only one (your words, not mine) who said straight away, no nonsense please, correspondence only!

Poor girls, they don't know what they let themselves in for. I think I might stay incognito, a lasting secret so to speak. Enough of this bantering away, I better change the subject, otherwise Mr Sergeant will be offended, hear, hear!

We had a very cold winter but now, with a helping hand of some useful rain, spring is transforming the countryside from the bareness of December to the beautiful blossoms of April.

Do you like nature? Going for long walks through forests and meadows full of flowers, or are you a city-slicker, contented with

Part Three: Their Story Begins ...

concrete sidewalks and endless rows of streets?

What sort of music do you like? Classic, jazz, or perhaps jitterbug or maybe ... old-fashioned romantic melodies? If you let me know in your next letter, I might be able to get the correct words of some new songs you haven't heard yet.

Oh dear, I'm assuming again that you will answer this letter. How silly of me, with fifty competing film stars, clamouring for your devoted attention.

I found out how old you are, but not before some confusion in our family, who thought you were around thirty-five! Is that your character, Pierre, to talk in riddles?

Oh my gosh, I have used your Christian name, beg your pardon, Serg, it won't happen again!

Have you ever been to Oudenbosch? It's a little village in the western part of Brabant and the very proud owner of a replica of Saint Peter's in Rome, so wipe your feet if you ever get this far!

I'm looking forward to your reply and the promised photo ...

Otherwise, I could be talking to an orang-utan. Goodness me, I've done it again and getting complimentary in the process!

Bye for now ...

One of your 51 penfriends. Corry.

PS. This is not the real me, but then again, you were not the real you the way you wrote! True or false?

Pierre's promised photo arrived with his next letter in late May. When taking out the letter, Corry hadn't seen the photo also enclosed in the envelope. Luckily, it fell out before she tossed the envelope into the fire. She saw a photo of a young man, casually dressed in an open-necked shirt and wearing a strange sort of cowboy hat. On the back of the photo, she read:

To an unknown penfriend. Bali-August-1946. You like my digger's hat?
[Australian]
Kind regards, Pierre.

Suddenly, Pierre had become real. The distant stranger, who entered her young life so recently, and unexpectedly, now had a face.

9/5-1947. Palembang-Sumatra

Hallo Corry,

Well, that was quite an epistle from one so young. Not in length mind you but in quality (the letter I mean, not you!). I can stand the teasing bit. I actually like orang-utans very much, they have a thick skin too, otherwise who could survive?

As you said in your PS it is not the real you or me. So far, we are two strangers, flung together by an ad not bigger than a matchbox, cut in half. It will be up to both of us, deciding if we want to learn more about the way we are or stay in easy lane: long-distance penfriends.

First, some news from this end and then answer and question time. We took part in a guard of honour for General Kruls, the Dutch commander, and it being a sweltering day as usual, were glad when afterwards we gathered in the NCO mess for a cool beer (or 2 or 3 …)

Some new films are shown now in the rebuilt theatre. Last night we saw *Bells of St Mary* with Bing Crosby and Ingrid Bergman. Not a bad movie really, although for my taste rather sentimental. You, Corry, probably find more of Bing's music in your *Tuney Tunes*.

No, I'm not a city-slicker as you called it, more a town-crier! Where that town is where I used to live in? It is in the eastern part of Brabant, but I will leave the details for later, perhaps.

However, I do know your village. Yes, according to my diaries—faithfully recording each day of my army life—I visited that church you mentioned about two years ago; to be exact, on Sunday 29 April 1945. That was an unforgettable experience, with a thanksgiving service in progress and I standing at the rear, watching a silent congregation listening to your parish priest.

When he mentioned allied armies having liberated the village and how the population was saved from the terror of street battles, I moved deeper inside the shadows near the door, because quite a few

Part Three: Their Story Begins ...

of the mostly young congregation turned their heads for a look at that lone soldier.

That's how I will always remember Oudenbosch: the large dome-shaped church, laid out in the form of a cross, hundreds of teenagers ... and a sole commando who was I...!

On VE day, our unit returned for a couple more days and stayed in the Brothers' school, if my memory is correct, before moving on to Winterswijk, near the German border.

So, you see, Corry, our paths have already crossed, without you or I being aware of such an important happening! Yes, we nearly touched in a not-so-distant past, when you were perhaps sweet sixteen? And I also still young and innocent, hear, hear!

Sorry, I have to break off, Strike Force 8 have just been put on RED ALERT.

Take care,
PIERRE

18. WORRIED

This sudden and very abrupt end to an otherwise happy letter frightened Corry. It sounded very dangerous for Pierre, and the fact that the current newspapers were full of incidents, as the reporters called them, portraying the harsh realities of the many battles being fought in the Dutch East Indies, only increased her fears. There were also far too many death notices in the papers, each framed with a thick black line:

'Our son, age 19, died in Soerabaja. May he rest in peace …'
'Our beloved father and husband is missing in action, presumed dead.'
…and the like.

Pierre hadn't talked about war in his first two letters, except for that one line: *through that door, you can smell it!* Neither had he told her much about his stay in hospital. Was their correspondence then a camouflage for the real world he was living in, a world of war and destruction? Was he letting off steam in a joking way, hiding the ugly side of army life? Because she was a young girl, not to be touched or contaminated by a dirty war? Did he already care so much for her …?

Nevertheless, to her great surprise and joy, Pierre already knew her village and had been stationed there. His diaries wouldn't lie about dates. She told her mother, 'We have nearly met, Pierre and I, and I bet he was the one standing near the church door when we had that special Benediction.'

Corry had now promoted Pierre to something more substantial than 'penfriend'. Exactly what she didn't know yet, but her next letter was slightly more than just teasing—the beginning of a new dream?

Part Three: Their Story Begins ...

Oudenbosch, 25/5-47

D. Pierre,

(D stands for anything you like!)

Your letter, although still in that flippant style of yours, ended so abruptly, that for a frightening moment I felt a panic rising in my body. Suddenly, I realised how far apart we are, how living in such opposite worlds from each other makes our correspondence so much more important.

The way I feel at the moment is: reaching out and touching you! Please, don't laugh. I know very well you are a commando and not in need of a helping hand from an unknown teenager.

Yet, somehow, I would like to be there in person. I tried ... oh ... yes, I tried. Last year, when I turned eighteen, I wanted to join the army. It is called VHK, perhaps you've heard of them? Anyway, I collected the forms from the town hall and took them home to fill in.

Well, you should have heard my mother! I hate to repeat what she said. For the first time she actually swore at me—just imagine!

'... if you think you can join the army, you've got another think coming, Cor!' She uses Cor when she's mad at me! And that was the end of it, the papers were burnt, and her no-no was the final word. Enough said about this exercise in futility.

Back to your letter, Pierre ... haven't you noticed that you hardly ever touch the subject of film or music, the basic ingredients of your ad? Is war so close that you dare not lower your defences? Perhaps you have already penetrated mine. (They are not very strong!)

Do you have that same feeling when you receive my letters or are there minefields around your heart, supported by barbed wire? I'm bantering away with nonsense again and so be it because I am a sucker for assuming too much and trusting people I hardly know (like you!).

I can't seem to touch the right note in this letter. I want to dig and probe, ask questions, tell you about myself, the fact that we nearly met two years ago, but there is hesitation somewhere. Let's leave it at that.

Thanks so much for your photo from Bali, it nearly went up in smoke (not on purpose). I liked what I saw. See how trusting I am? Do you often play in cowboy movies or is the shape of that so-called Aussie hat to lure innocent girls like me?

Worried

The picture is pinned on my bedroom door, amidst dozens of other film stars! Back to the teasing toddler again I notice; feel better for it.

Something I really want to say is… take care, Commando.

Corry

PS. Could you describe Palembang in your next letter—that is, if you can find time—the way you see the city through the eyes of a soldier?

For Pierre and the rest of Strike Force 8, the red alert had not come as a surprise.

Many incidents were reported daily: acts of sabotage, bridges blown up, local unrest through intimidation and subversive tactics by the TNI (*Tentara Nasional Indonesia*, literally: Indonesian National Military) and other terrorist groups. It was intended to stir the population into an uprising against the Dutch and, willing or unwilling, people around Palembang became the meat in a gigantic sandwich of death and destruction.

More landing craft found their way to the harbour and, as trucks full of war material rolled down the ramps, it became obvious that sooner rather than later a breakout would take place. Our battalion was waiting for orders to launch full-scale counterinsurgency operations.

In the meantime, the alert meant increased patrols, doubling of guard duties and endless training at full battalion strength. Sport was still an essential part of keeping fit, but recreation did suffer with curfews curtailing outside activities. Writing letters was one of the first casualties, and although the one to Corry just beat the deadline, further mail had to wait until RED phase was scaled down to YELLOW and, after another week, to GREEN.

Tension then eased somewhat and even a dance was organised in our mess. Letters from overseas, although often delayed, kept coming in a regular pattern of one or two, followed by an avalanche of twenty to thirty. For some reason, I always kept Corry's letters until last.

The one thing that caused some worry was the changing tone of her words. It happened ever so gently, or perhaps I was looking for more than the usual teasing. My sensitivity picked up the differences in nuances of an expression.

Her last one sent on 25 May was a typical example. I had read it several times and understood very well what she wanted but had not dared to say. Of the many girls that corresponded with me, Corry was the only one who tried to delve deeper into my own private world.

The rest mostly cruised on the safe: 'How are you, I'm very well' platitudes. From the large cities came news about nightlife, modern dancing, theatre, etc. while village girls had their own little topics to write about.

Corry didn't fit any of the categories; she seemed to drift somewhere in between. I had to be careful in my reply, didn't want to start something that could create expectations in the receptive mind of an eighteen-year-old. Writing about Palembang would be a good idea, a protective outlet of impressions gained over a period of time. It was postponed, however, for nearly three weeks, as large manoeuvres involving our Brigade, supported by patrol boats and fighter aircraft, took place just outside the city near the airport corridor.

In continuous heavy rainfall, we slugged our way through muddy terrain; it was commando training all over again but adjusted to the tropics. The heavy rain squalls, the impregnable jungle and the oozing mud were added obstacles in an army life that had lost its former appeal! We became masters of the art of merging with nature in whatever form or colour.

Shortly after our three-day-long wargame, we had to put into practice what had been taught. I found myself leading a long-range patrol of six men which had penetrated enemy lines and, without being seen, moved behind their positions. The five men with me were the same veterans from Bali; our objective: *to bring back as much information as possible about the deployment of opposing forces.* Also, a request: *at least two prisoners for interrogation.* Finally, an order: *no firepower to be used unless in self-defence.* Silence and stealth were the words impressed upon us!

After four exhausting days and nights we returned safely with two 'Pemoedas', their hands tied behind naked backs, and a loose sling around their necks, just in case! The frightened look in those dark eyes told the humiliating story of being captured in the safety of villages, far behind the demarcation line. It must have been an experience they would not forget in a hurry.

Palembang the city, as seen through the eyes of a soldier—that was what Corry had asked. Yes, definitely easier than writing about a long-range patrol where adrenaline and often nothing else kept you on your feet. Where war became ugly and deadly … not the sort of story to tell an eighteen-year-old girl.

Perhaps later when I got to know her better. But even then, it might be too much of a gamble to tell everything!

So, in an undated letter, Pierre writes to Corry:

Palembang, as seen through the eyes of a soldier …

We leave our fortified position just before daybreak, following a narrow path, bordering the Moesi. This large, muddy lifeline stretches all the way to the Straits of Malacca. The river is high and wild. For weeks now the catchment area inland has received enormous amounts of rain due to a tropical cyclone.

Perahu (small boats) and houseboats in all shapes and sizes glide softly on the murky surface, their lights flickering like a thousand fireflies. The city—of close to a million people—is already awakening, and early fruit and vegetable vendors are on their way to the markets. The heavy loads of baskets balancing on long bamboo poles sit on naked and bronzed shoulders. The young, and old with years of practice behind them, make light work of a seemingly daunting task.

Road stalls are set up alongside the compact gravel road into the city. Sometimes our 'Selamat Pagi' is answered by the same words. Because of the scars of war, a 'Good Morning' seems in bad taste, I thought, as I lead the patrol through the narrow alleys away from the river into the Chinese quarter.

Here the open spaces, still covered with burnt-out buildings, are more noticeable. The January street fights played havoc with people and property alike, making no distinction between races. Whether Indian, Arab, Chinese or locals, they all suffered in that first week of 1947. However, through the extensive looting by Indonesian extremists, the Chinese businesspeople lost most of the goods from their warehouses.

Walking roughly ten metres apart in single file, we check papers on occasion, keeping a careful lookout for suspicious elements. A watery sun colours the eastern sky and soon trade will start in this bustling city. Some of the smaller coffee shops are opening. We reach the Moesi again as we make a wide sweep through the city centre. Palm trees stand silent, like eternal guards, near the water's edge. Far away a foghorn penetrates the mist patches, a sign of yet another hot and humid day.

Even at this early hour, our camouflage overalls are already soaking wet, they hardly ever dry out in the tropics. They cling to our bodies like a second skin and have that feeling of old friends one can trust.

A Higgins patrol boat zigzags across the open waterway, nearly one kilometre wide at this point. Their task: to keep the enemy on the opposite side, as agreed in the armistice conditions laid down after the January battle.

We enter the business section where banks and offices, built in the pre-war European style, give a more solid impression of a real city centre. There is an oriental touch to the buildings with their white, overhanging facades supported by coloured pillars.

Dead trees in an overgrown park, and neglected footpaths with uncollected rubbish, spoil the otherwise pretty sight of Palembang at dawn. As we turn away from the square, the same squalor of Singapore, Menado or Makassar is evident again: when an open sewer sends its rotten stench into the humid air, together with the overpowering smell of palm oil used for cooking in the many eating-places.

On a balmy night, when darkness hides the ugliness, there is a different atmosphere in Palembang, with people sitting in their favourite food stall, eating nasi or bami-goreng, topped with half a dozen or so sticks of satay. Sometimes, on the rare free evenings, we of Strike Force 8 join the locals for a meal, as soldiers are never averse to a generous helping of Chinese or Indonesian food.

We return via a route that takes us close to the American quarters, where modern housing built for oil company members stand in stark contrast to the seedy, dilapidated lean-to type of dwellings used by refugees, only a few hundred metres away. War is such a complicated word, but the idle thought stays deep inside. Everyone is aware of the battle scars; you don't have to be a solider to realise the full implications.

Our stronghold embraces us with her safety net—imaginary of course yet, on several instances, very real. Our stinking greens are handed to the native helpers. A cold shower, clean and faded shorts and a well-deserved rest on my stretcher. Later, a game of volleyball to keep us in shape for the inevitable!

… this, Corry dear, is a different Palembang from the one I saw in November last year, shortly after we arrived in our landing craft. There was an uneasy peace then and the city centre had not yet suffered from the ravages of war.

I did a story then, full of beauty and romance, the way one sees a picture for the very first time. I wrote the words, while recuperating from a malaria and typhoid attack; Charitas hospital was my home at that time! However, when I left my sickbed, the Palembang described in my essay was about to be destroyed in fierce street fighting.

So, Corry, even before I knew you, I was already answering one of your questions. But I tore up that article, knowing that the old familiar places would never be the same again.

This is all I have to say about the city. Hope you like it.

Until we meet again in our next letter,

AU REVOIR, MA CHERIE!
Pierre

PS. Two nuns who nursed me back to health in Charitas came from your village. Van Aken is their name. Do you know them? They helped me write that ad in *Tuney Tunes*. Now there is a good omen!

19. THE OFFENSIVE … AND A TURN IN THEIR RELATIONSHIP

After the intensive brigade level training exercises, it came as no surprise that a major offensive was launched in Sumatra on 21 July 1947, aiming to capture all the oilfields around Palembang, and to do so before the terrorists set the whole countryside on fire by breaching the pipes and installations and then setting fire to the oil. The offensive had been anticipated, however, and for the next few weeks there was an intense conflict involving running battles with guerrillas and militia who were often supported, and thus 'stiffened', by Japanese deserters. But the threat to Pierre's men wasn't always from them …

> One village was overrun, while the local militia was still doing their training in the market square. Leaving behind their weaponry, they disappeared into the nearby jungle. Few prisoners were taken in those first days of the offensive. There simply was no time or transport to accommodate the confused warriors of Soekarno. Like in Bali, however, as soon as Japanese deserters were involved, we could expect a fight, or at least a stand, against the advancing army of the Netherlands.
>
> Combat rations were all we needed to keep going, although, after three days, drinking water became a problem. One of the tankers had bogged down in a riverbed and we were rationed to a few litres per person per day …
>
> We made sweeping clearances through the adjoining village, and one very useful commodity was found behind an old school building: coils of rusted barbed wire! It improved our position to such an extent that we could spare more men for extended patrols, but the isolation became dangerous as rations and supplies were running low.
>
> That night something happened that I shall always remember. 'Sergeant,' said our CO, a young lieutenant, 'what if you post one

man—quite visible—in front of our stronghold. That would attract enemy fire and we could then counterattack!'

For a fraction of time, I was completely unable to speak. Then, very softly, but with a deadly undertone, I replied, 'I know the perfect person for just such a target ... YOU!' and stalked away. He never asked again.

Thursday 31 July, ten days after leaving Palembang and still wearing the same stinking gear, we were surprised when we heard the distant sound of a plane. A low-flying Mustang, following the road to the hilltop, spotted our position. As he made a slow approach from the opposite side, we quickly laid out the Red Cross flag, indicating wounded personnel. The plane flipped its wings and disappeared.

Less than two hours later, our friend was back and dropped supplies, including first-aid kits, ammunition and, wonder of wonders ... mail! Amazing, I reflected: here we are without any passable road link to the outside world, then comes a Mustang, and now you are reading what a young girl, somewhere in the Netherlands, has to tell you.

Corry's letter was sent a month ago, but I read the words with all the eagerness of a man receiving mail from a long-lost friend. Perhaps that's what isolation does to combat troops. A change takes place even if you are not aware of it.

That evening by candlelight, I wrote two aerograms: one to my mother and the second to Corry. I don't know why I started out by saying, 'If you receive this, I'm okay, if not, you will never know.' Morbid? Or a sense of danger? We were still surrounded by an unknown force. Later that night I wrote the third and last letter to Corry as well and wondered when, if ever, I would have the chance to mail it.

By the flickering light of that single candle, somewhere in the Sumatran jungle, with the platoon cut off and isolated, and not knowing if Corry would ever receive his note, Pierre wrote: *I would like to meet you, just the two of us.* He was only too aware that there might be no second chance to say this. The platoon had found itself in a critical situation after overshooting its target. Its supply line through the impregnable jungle had been cut off by roadblocks, and radio contact had also been lost.

Part Three: Their Story Begins ...

The next day, Pierre's platoon managed to fight through, against a mostly unseen enemy, and, after destroying several roadblocks which were booby-trapped with grenades, to join up with patrols from Strike Force 7, thus completing their offensive sweep through southern Sumatra. He records that an hour later, his platoon had their 'first hot meal in twelve days. Freshly baked bread with fried eggs and spam tasted like a gourmet meal.'

Meanwhile, back in Oudenbosch, on the very day that the offensive in Sumatra commenced, Corry had picked up the *News of the Day* and put the paper neatly on the large office desk ready for Mr van Guild, her employer. Then she saw the headlines screaming at her, touching a raw nerve deep inside:

The Netherlands have drawn the sword in Indonesia.

Underneath in smaller print came some details about fighting in Java and, as she read on, saw the line: *Strike Force 8 held up by oil fires in South Sumatra.*

Her mind travelled across oceans to Pierre, the combat soldier, who in his letters hardly ever talked about war, only implied it was close and vaguely hinted at danger. As a war volunteer (called OVW) and commando as well, they would be the first to go in—that much she realised from newspaper and radio reports.

'No mail again,' Mam told her as she arrived home at six. For the next five agonising weeks his letters were absent when she came home from work. The look in her mother's eyes said enough, day after lonely day. Meanwhile, the list of army personnel fallen in action grew steadily and, in the beginning, Corry had looked through the alphabetical order of young men who paid the ultimate price. Once she saw his name, panicked, until she read again and noticed the different initials and army number. After that, she didn't dare look at that list again.

The seven o'clock news at night from Radio Hilversum was followed with more than the usual attention. The standard bulletins, however, seemed to be: *Our forces in Indonesia are making progress on all fronts.* Details about units involved, or places captured, were rare. After a week of uncertainty, a reporter attached to Strike Force 8 started to talk about a *Blitzkrieg*. As the successes in Java were measured in a couple of kilometres, the war in Sumatra became an extensive penetration of the interior.

Another ten days went by, and the battalion Pierre belonged to vanished into the vast expanse that was South Sumatra. According to unconfirmed reports, villages were overrun with such speed that often enemy troops were caught while still doing their daily routine. Then, all news from that area stopped abruptly.

Somewhere in that vast, sparsely populated island was a green beret with his men, but still alone within himself. That much she had gathered from his letters received so far. Not a person with many close friends, but a self-contained force.

August was coming to an end; days were getting shorter, and the annual funfair with its three days of carnival atmosphere had gone. Getting a touch of influenza, Corry stayed home from work in the last week of the summer month. It was Monday 25 August, a bright sunny day. She was dozing in bed while her mother had gone shopping when she heard the letterbox in the front door rattle. Quickly, on wobbly legs because of the fever, she went downstairs.

Three letters, all marked *on active service*, were waiting …

Only one was a proper envelope. The other two, written in barely legible pencil, were *luchtpostbladen,* the grey aerograms with hardly any space for words. Upstairs she ripped them open with her nailfile. The message in the first one was short and mentally tore her apart. It was obvious that the pencilled words were written in haste and under great duress.

Then, when she read the last lines, Corry was stunned. Pierre used the exact words about meeting together that she had been tossing around in her mind. Now it was right there in front of her, in writing on that barely legible aerogramme! From the very playful, even teasing, exchanges which had been central to their letters till then, now Corry felt that their long-distance relationship was moving into a new level, a deeper level. She quickly understood that being in a very fluid and unpredictable combat situation, when one is pushed to the very limits of physical and emotional

Part Three: Their Story Begins ...

endurance and each moment can reveal new threats to one's very existence, cuts through the unnecessary and the frivolous to what is really important.

Then, in looking at the third envelope, her heart stopped. The address had been neatly typed and looked very official, very threatening. Afraid that it contained some terrible news, with shaking hands she slowly opened the envelope, and began to read.

To Corry Siemons   4/8/47

As a favour to my friend Pierre (I am Jacko by the way), a few lines to let you know we are safe and well (for the moment). He (Pierre that is), sends his love and kisses (excuse me a sec, young lady), he is gesturing at me from his bed (he's got a bandaged hand). Definitely no kisses he said, only kind regards, as you are classified: 'PENFRIEND'.

Make up your mind, Pierre (he is signalling again), the girl is waiting. 'A touch of everything' (he is smiling now, the bl...ba...) sorry dear. So, there you have it. I leave the finer points to this crazy commando when his hand (and hopefully his head) improves. By that time, I'll be out of reach!

Yours Truly,
Jacko.

PS. He is mumbling for an encore.
He just said, you are more than a penfriend. Time is too short to explain. War is waiting, we are moving out soon ...

Corry didn't know whether to laugh or cry. In the end she did both. Safe and well ... war is waiting ... love and kisses ... a touch of everything ... a bandaged hand ... moving out soon; all contradictions, her imagination said. Or perhaps not all, like 'love and kisses', she fantasised. The full truth would not be known until there was time for a long, explanatory letter.

20. Towards a Deeper Friendship

She replied two days later, using the intervening day to gather her thoughts and feelings after experiencing such an emotional rollercoaster on reading these latest writings from Pierre. She also moves away from the light-hearted banter of her earlier letters, matching Pierre's desire to explore the possibility of a deeper relationship and commitment.

Wednesday 27 – August – 1947

Pierre, oh Pierre … was I glad to hear from you after nearly five weeks of frustrating anxiety. I was in bed with a bad cold when the mailman called.

Trying to describe how I felt when I read what happened over there is a sheer impossibility. Only when I saw Jacko's letter could I laugh again as it brought me back to the sergeant I know so well!

Or do I?

The casual way we were making contact before the offensive had started seems so far removed from the actual person that you probably become when in action. I don't know you at all, do I?

Which brings me to the point I would like to make in all sincerity. What brought it on, having written to your family, to send the last of your aerograms to a girl you have never met? Perhaps in a quiet moment later, you might care to give me an honest answer. You know what I did after reading your letters? I crawled underneath the blankets, shutting out the cruel world, and had a silent cry. Didn't want anyone to hear or see me. Just to be with you, I thought, even if you are living in a combat zone.

Silly me, to assume so much and know so little! Still, a girl of nineteen is allowed some daydreams or not, Pierre? Yes, it was my birthday not so long ago, but I won't bother you with details—you having too much on your plate, I guess, to worry about maturing penfriends.

Part Three: Their Story Begins ...

Is the infected hand improving? I hope so, otherwise all your letters will be written by strangers ... meaning you couldn't even slip in some tenderness just in case you wanted to ...?!

One dumb thing I must confess. While waiting for your mail, I kept postponing my own writing, thinking (silly really), I'll answer his correspondence when it comes in. Sorry about that, Sergeant. Regretfully, it means you will be waiting for MY words of wisdom. Unless you are smart and tell me more about the battle in Sumatra before you receive this! I have followed the daily papers more mindful than ever before, but details were hard to come by and after the first couple of weeks I gave up. It was too emotional for me to read about the struggle over there.

Also, the yearly funfair in mid-August, an occasion to let your hair down and enjoy three days of merriment, never got off the ground as far as I was concerned. My friends tried to cheer me up but how can one explain the feelings deep inside? That I kept thinking about the emptiness that the absence of your letters created?

I'll leave it at that, and how else can I end this letter other than asking: please write soon!

Your favourite penfriend
CORRY

And this letter crossed in the mail with Pierre's next letter.

On Active Service, somewhere in Sumatra, 29-August-1947

My dear Corry,

At last, with an improved hand to write (I had cut it badly rolling out rusted coils of barbed wire), contact can be restored, and a more detailed report sent to my penfriend.

It will be very hard to explain how I felt while we were on the offensive and, even now, with only a couple of hours rest to recoup, I realise that the impact of what has happened is still sinking in. Slowly, ever so slowly, life is returning to normal, if one can call it by that name. We travelled over 600 km. We overran cities and villages too numerous to recall, and only my diaries, which tried to keep up

Towards a Deeper Friendship

with our advance, give an indication where we went.

Prabamoeli and Muara-Enim are the only two that stood out, as we stayed there overnight and found a large amount of equipment that the fleeing enemy had left behind. The place we are in now is called Lahat—sitting near one of the many rivers flowing into the Moesie—and, after guarding a 200-metre span of railway bridge, we are ready to move out again at short notice.

That's why I'm trying to get this letter posted asap to erase that worried look in your eyes (no need to blush now!); after all, I did tell you who my favourite girl was ... or not? Can't remember! I am very tired, and so is everyone else. We all have that ghost-like look that seems to line our faces; sunken eyes as well, and a dirty smell, like a festering wound, hangs around us.

I never knew that a person could be so totally exhausted and feel that tendency to collapse alongside the road. Sometimes, however, when I fall asleep in a moving vehicle, I get an all-overpowering desire to call it a day and just die all by myself. Probably that's what we are doing now ... dying a little every day ...!

I better change the subject. It is not the sort of talk that a young girl wants to know about, or do you, Corry?

I hope you received my last three letters. I simply can't recall when or where I dropped them in the mailbag. I do remember that Jacko, our driver, wrote one when my hand was still bandaged. Hopefully, he was polite to you. He never gave me a chance even to read the letter! The last thing I want is to make a bad impression on you, even if there is a war on!

The trucks are waiting ... Sorry, I can't tell you more about the battle in South Sumatra, but seeing it's such a deadly game, perhaps my silence is the better description ...

From somewhere in LAHAT, Pierre sends a touch of everything.

Till we meet again ... in our next letter.

Then, a few weeks later, while his platoon was guarding a vital railway bridge along the main supply lines for the Dutch forces, Pierre received Corry's letter and replied:

Part Three: Their Story Begins ...

Perdjito 12-9-47

Hallo there, my lost friend Corry ...

For a couple of uneasy weeks, I was getting the impression that one of my most trusted pen pals had deserted me. However, your letter from 27 August explained it all.

I laughed when I read, quote: 'I was in bed with a cold when the mailman called?' unquote. No comment from this side of the world, you did say it, not me. I'm innocent, back to tongue-in-cheek!

Your coloured envelope was one of twenty-five delivered that day, as if the mailman was taking revenge for you being sick. I kept your epistle till last. I read somewhere that Christ did the same with the wine he was pouring, kept the best for later. So, I held on for the warmest of words till the end.

You see, Corry, I get a lot of mail, and whenever I have time, I try and answer them all. Some of the correspondence is from way back—before your time—others are like yours, answering my advertisement in the *Tuney Tunes*. Then there are old school friends, relatives, my four brothers and, of course, my parents. Dad never writes, he leaves that to Mam, whom I love very much. There is actually a saying in the family about me being her favourite ... the reason: I'm never home!

Why am I telling you all this? Well, in your last letter, you asked for an honest answer to the question: 'What brought it on, sending my last aerogram to you when we were surrounded?' In all honesty, I don't know myself! Perhaps you are different from other penfriends, the way you communicate with me. Like when you wrote: 'crawled underneath the blankets and had a silent cry.'

That, in turn, filled me up and, although I haven't cried for many years, I'm still a very sensitive person at heart. I picked up those vibes coming from you. Not being a man's man, as they call it, I can feel very lonely on certain occasions, and, somehow, your words fill in a gap in my life.

At the moment, I am in charge of ten to twenty men, depending on the situation. We have a railway station as outpost, roughly 200 km from Palembang. A large steel bridge across a swollen creek is our main object for protection as all supplies to the interior follow this route. The soldiers of this section are all trusted men and their lives

Towards a Deeper Friendship

and well-being depend partly on the decisions I make when alarming intelligence reports put us on full alert.

Ever since we entered the tropics—some twenty months ago—I have shared the night-guard duties with my men and, although as an NCO I don't have to, I feel better for it. Only when we patrol the outside perimeter at night, and I stand sentry with one of the soldiers, camouflaged behind trees, comes the time that some men want to unburden the enormous pressure they live under.

Over the many months of being in an army I have learned to be a listener, rather than a talker (except after a few beers!). So, in consequence, my section feels confident enough to open up. As long as they know that no one is overhearing their words, they relate to me about their hopes and dreams for the future.

Needless to say, the touchiest subject is female relationships. Often the incoming mail creates more tension than relief, more uncertainty than hope … Just having me listen to them can ease the pain somewhat. I can't stop the war, but at least I can try to put a bandage on wounds that fester on the inside. Wounds that get worse as time goes by …

Of course, emptiness can overcome me as well, and in your last letter you mentioned that word too. Also, when I'm listening to the problems that my men experience, it often happens that a raw nerve inside me gets touched.

Last week, when we buried a corporal killed in an ambush not far from here, I realised how remote we have become, how the words of our padre seemed to fall on deaf ears as he spoke of resurrection and eternal life.

Which brings me to a question I want to ask. Do you accept the fact that my letters to you have grown into more than just chit-chat, that, in actual fact, you are an outlet for my feelings from deep down? That I can freely talk about life and death, or war and destruction instead of promised music and films, that, so far, have hardly been mentioned?

But, if you are uncomfortable with that mysterious mind of mine, please let me know in your next letter. We can then return to easy street, where your replies are just part of the mail being delivered, instead of being something special that, so far, has put you in a class of your own.

Part Three: Their Story Begins ...

I leave this up to you, but perhaps you already answered my question when you wrote: 'just to be with you ...!'

Reading that you are all of nineteen now (why didn't you tell me your birthday was coming up?) I assume wisdom has been upgraded to double A!

My hand is completely healed and, to prove it, here is some of my tenderness, sneaking in through enemy lines ... Can you feel it? Good! It's very hard to come by these days, especially from me.

Reading through this letter again, I see what a serious tone has crept in; probably the heat and exhaustion are taking their toll, better stop this nonsense before I slip in something silly like Jacko did with his 'love and kisses!'

Crazy boy—but he is a good driver—that's why I didn't kill him after he wrote that letter to you. Pretending he was writing on my behalf, knowing all the time I couldn't stop him with my bandaged hand. Still, it was meant as a goodwill gesture.

No harm in 'love and kisses', so long as they are sent to special friends only! Like a girl, just turned nineteen, who wanted correspondence only ... When was that again? Sometime a decade ago?

I might go on patrol and disappear in the jungle, probably safer than talking to teenagers who I don't know at all.

Don't catch another cold, Corry dear, 'cause the postman always rings twice ...!

With that riddle, I say over and out.
Write soon please!

A friendly hug,
Pierre

By now, it was becoming apparent to Corry's parents that her relationship with her faraway commando might be becoming much more serious. Every day on arriving home from work she asked her mother, 'Any mail for me?'. Once, when an unthinking comment was made about buying stamps for Pierre, that 'he won't die if the mail was late', Corry's reaction left no one, least of all her mother, in any doubt that she was

Towards a Deeper Friendship

already caring a great deal about him. 'Don't you dare talk about dying, Mother, because that is exactly what those soldiers are doing every day!'

Nevertheless, Corry's parents were rightly concerned about her being hurt once again, given the very unhappy episode of Frank's letters stopping so abruptly in the last months of the war in Europe, without any further news about him at any time afterwards. He had just disappeared from Corry's life. Now they saw their youngest daughter developing another serious relationship, but this time with a soldier who remained a complete stranger to them—Corry always remained very private about the content of their letters, which were only read and kept in her bedroom upstairs.

Sometime in late September 1947, she wrote:

'Peterle ... was hast du nun mit mir gemach ...'
I don't know if you remember all the words from this German wartime song, because if you do, I have said too much already!
'What have you done to me ...'
I like that word Peterle, an endearment for the more solid Petrus the rock where I'm supposed to build a castle on?!

It took me a long time absorbing the letter from Perdjito. I would like to continue our penfriend relationship in that jocular style, first adopted by a certain Mister Sergeant in Palembang! Because only then could I never be hurt if something happened, either to you or our friendship.

I am afraid I can't do that. You involved me, an eighteen-year-old stranger, right from the very start, Pierre. It is the way you write ...! I can't turn back the pages of history anymore, your letters, every word of them, have become part of my life as well as yours!

No, I'm not uncomfortable with that mysterious mind of yours, on the contrary, I like to know more about what goes on inside, and, if that means revealing the dark side of war, so be it.

Carrying the burden of your men as well as the loneliness that overwhelms you on certain days seems to be reason enough to confess there is an outlet available to you ... me!

Not pretending to be a solution to problems, Pierre, but a back-up when need arises. If I can become a long-distance support, I will be very happy to oblige. The fact that Mam said something today

Part Three: Their Story Begins ...

upsetting me deeply might be the cause behind all these serious words. Basically, I am a very joyous person. Not that my parents or brother always agree with such a statement, but that is the privilege of being a teenager!

Your letter from that post you and your squad are protecting touched me in many ways. For the first time you talked about yourself: what you feel, the pain, isolation, the endless nights when you share the guard with your men ...

You never mention any specific friend, Pierre, and apart from Jacko, who was kind enough to send me that lovely note (yes with love and kisses!), I have no idea what the soldiers there are like. But you do seem to care very much for their well-being and safety. Perhaps a time might come when you would like to transfer that concern to somebody else?!

Thanks so much for the tenderness you managed to smuggle in! It was in every word, and between the lines. I like it. Keep it coming.

Autumn is upon us. It's getting cooler. Some warmth from your part of the world will be more than welcome.

My hands are cold from writing ...
But my heart is glowing
Corry

And Pierre responds:

Sumatra, 20 October 1947

Dear Corry,

A while back you asked why I never talked about friends. I'll try to explain. In all fairness, they have been part of my life since my early youth. The only trouble is, they seem to vanish ...

Let's start with the first one, while still at school, sometime in grade four. He lived across the road from us and, as The Great Depression was causing havoc, he helped his parents in the butcher shop. I was doing the same in our bicycle-repair business after classes finished at four.

Towards a Deeper Friendship

We had one thing in common: we both liked playing chess and, on the weekends (when free), Gerard and I went through hundreds of quick games. Suddenly, he was transferred to boarding school way out of town, and I had, at least temporarily, lost my first real playmate.

I was doing well at classes—my best subject being languages—and made numerous friends, without having a special one. Exams and school behind us, relationships evaporated and, having lost track of most of them, I returned to my own self.

Next to the butcher was a small menswear shop, Jewish people being the owners. Their daughter, a raven-haired beauty even at twelve, used to come over and together we went through difficult subjects while still at school. She had a fierce temper, and it was quite common to see Ellie and me charging away at each other in the playground next door. Then, the Germans invaded the Netherlands and neither she nor her parents were ever seen again.

As I was the middle one of five sons, my Mam and Dad seemed to use the two above me in the business, spoil the two below me and somewhere in that process I got lost! I ended up doing slave-labour in Germany (although not in camps), got bombed without mercy and, finally, after seven months of document manipulations, made it safely back to the Netherlands.

Home, of course, was out of the question, too dangerous a place to stay, so I became a fugitive, going underground to survive. Later, when my older brother was called up to work on the Atlantic Wall, I took his place. Hardly anyone noticed, least of all the authorities!

Still no friends around. It was hard to trust people, so I never did. Safer too that way! I joined the Interior Forces, ending up along the river Meuse, facing the German army on the opposite side. Before I had a chance of getting close to any of my fellow warriors, I volunteered for a special services snit to be formed in England. We started out with a hundred and twenty men. Three months and a green beret later, there were only seventy-nine left, the rest had fallen somewhere along that hard road that was our training. You see, Corry, no matter how many one starts with, in the end there is always only one left ... yourself!

When war ended, we were stationed near your village and from there via several other postings moved to Germany. Army HQ selected twenty-eight men of our unit for special training with the

Part Three: Their Story Begins ...

Royal Marine Commandos in England. I was one of them. So, you leave your colleagues behind once more.

August 1945 came and a bright, windy day I broke my wrist when an exercise went wrong. Goodbye comrades, never to be seen again. I crossed the Channel and spent a few weeks leave in my hometown and The Hague, where an Uncle and Aunt lived. Met the remainder of No2 Dutch Troop which had left Germany. For the first time I formed a closer bond with Joep, a professional boxer, and together we had a memorable week in the City of Light, Paris. Gerry also became a good friend, having already spent some leave with me while in England, and we managed to get hold of one-day passes.

Again, we moved. This time to establish a storm-school at Wildhof, close to the North Sea dunes near Bloemendaal. One misty day in October an officer called asking for volunteers for the Dutch East Indies. Out of thirty-six present on the parade ground at that time, nine put up their hands. Joep was one of those who volunteered, and when Gerry saw my arm moving, he simply said, 'If you go, I go!' confirming to be a special friend. He is still around in another platoon nearby.

When you replied to my advert and your first letter arrived, there was also an envelope marked RETURN TO SENDER. Underneath, neatly typed, 'Killed in action'. Joep died in New Guinea. He had joined the Paras, the same unit I had applied for earlier. My request was denied by my company commander ...

That's why I am here, writing to a girl called Corry, trying to explain that, yes, I have made friends in my life. So few, however, remain! I moved too often and too far ... Permanent relationships never had a chance of survival!

The only reason you and I are on such good terms (close friends even) is our correspondence. Letters keep following me wherever I go and, if you don't stop this nonsense, one day you might catch me.

I hope you do!
Pierre

This letter was not received by Corry till early January 1948. In the meantime, further letters were exchanged.

Towards a Deeper Friendship

Gunung Megang, Wednesday 12 Nov 1947

My Dear Corry

Sorry the 'my' slipped in without realising it, means you belong to me. How silly can you get?!

Lately, our letters seem to cross each other in sequence. I'm answering questions that you have asked months ago and vice versa. Today, then, just a report how my birthday went yesterday. (Yes, it was my birthday, where were your red roses, all twenty-four of them?). Shame on you! Anyway, firstly, thanks for your best wishes, I hope they all come true! Being home at Christmas, well that's been delayed for an unspecified period!

A lot of mail came in which, after all these years of separation, is a welcome sign that old acquaintances never die, they just fade away somewhat. When I woke up at six, straight away I remembered the date. The reason? Very simple, as I will explain. I must go back a few years, otherwise you wouldn't know what I'm talking about.

1943 ... when I escaped from Germany and went underground. Even my own mother was so surprised when I phoned her, that she forgot to say Happy Birthday, Pierre!

1944 ... somewhere in the trenches near the river Meuse ... my twenty-first was completely forgotten, and not until I went to bed late that night did it dawn on me what an important day it was. Twenty-one, and all by my lonely self, shocking, I thought, and shed a tear for every year of my life.

1945 ... being stationed in the Van Horne Barracks in Weert, where Strike Force 8 was assembling before departure for the Far East. 11 November came and went without a whimper. Everyone remembers Armistice Day, no one, however, wanted to connect such an important event with a forlorn soldier, trying desperately to attract attention ... still NO birthday cake!

Last year ... being in coma in Charitas hospital, 11 November must have slid away without my permission. Even my diary, so faithfully kept updated, was empty for several weeks. When I came back to life, all I could remember were the scars of yesteryear, scars I had been dreaming about in my delirium.

So, 1947, I told myself, was to be the year of revenge! Before

Part Three: Their Story Begins …

finishing my guard duties at two in the morning I scribbled on a piece of paper, 'Lest we forget,' and put it next to my stretcher. Aha, I thought, after waking up, the day of reckoning has arrived. A couple of days ago, a surprise parcel from my parents was received with great joy, as it contained, amongst other goodies, two bottles of BOLS genever, the liquid that brings fire to the most experienced of drinkers (which I am not)!

Around six in the evening, after our usual meal of mashed potatoes and spam, topped up with baked beans, I made an announcement: party at seven. Those on patrol or night duties excluded of course. And the lieutenant …? Well, we didn't want to waste good Dutch Gin on a shallow character. As there were just the six of us, the tinned fruit and meat from the Netherlands soon disappeared, and the serious business of some solid drinking got underway. Near midnight we had become a jolly bunch of singing, shouting, arguing half-drunks, toasting to all and sundry.

If you want to stop reading, Corry, I fully understand … What did happen next could have turned into a nightmare (with hindsight). Our beloved lieutenant marched into the room shortly after twelve and said, without so much as a flicker of understanding in what condition we were in, 'Sergeant, why don't you take your men on patrol through the kampong,' and then, as an afterthought, '… the fresh air will do you good!'

Just because we didn't invite him, he showed the spoiled brat he really was. But orders are orders … We armed ourselves and moved out in single file, a zigzag one at that, into the humid darkness of a tropical night.

Fortunately, there was a full moon, because we needed all the help in the world to make it safely through the maze of narrow tracks and dirt roads before we even reached the village. To show we were still a force to be reckoned with, we let off a stream of bullets in an ear-splitting blast, shattering coconuts and palm leaves. Yes, we were aiming high, very high … at the stars!

I got seven days house arrest for endangering my men and the local population. But confinement to a house is a laugh, where would I go in the evenings: the local dancing, theatre, window-shopping? My word, the last time I had R&R leave was in Bali and that only because I had malaria and a forty-degree fever!

Next year (if there is such a thing!) I hope to celebrate the eleventh of the eleventh somewhere near the Rhine River, holding a girl perhaps, instead of a gun. She might even look like you, who knows. We could drink a glass of Moselle, sing a song… 'Warum ist es am Rhein so Schon?!'

Still, I don't regret this birthday. At least for one mad moment war was forgotten!

I hope you won't stop writing to me. Life is too short!

Pierre

This letter clearly travelled by air because only nine days later Corry penned this reply:

Oudenbosch
23-11-1947

Dear Pierre,

Thanks so much for your birthday exploits. It saddened me to read how this special day in the year turned out in such a bizarre fashion. I don't like alcohol myself, yet I can quite easily imagine how sometimes you crave for something stronger than tea or whatever the field kitchen can supply.

What did upset me more than anything else was your description of days gone by, when 11 November must have appeared like just another day, yet in your heart there probably was the pain of being alone.

You talk about Germany, trenches, barracks and finally a hospital where your advancing years went unnoticed. Letters like these always fill me up, make me aware how far apart we are, which in turn brings on that feeling again of reaching out … I realise this has been said before by me—and perhaps others—yet somehow, I can't see you as a person freeing his deeper thoughts just to receive sympathy in return. Compared with your birthdays over the last four or five years, mine are simple affairs of having a friend over for a cup of coffee, a few presents, if money is available, and a home-made cake from Mam.

This year, 24 June, I got three hankies and a piece of material for a blouse, while my girlfriend surprised me with writing paper, knowing how I like to keep in touch with a certain penfriend!

The theatre has re-opened too in our village and we are busy practising for our first performance in Fidei-et-Arti (a beautiful name for an old building). *White Horse Inn*, an operetta from Vienna, is scheduled for late December and, surprise, surprise … I landed myself the leading role of Otillie. Suddenly, Sergeant Pierre, your favourite girlfriend (that has to read penfriend of course!) has become a celebrity.

So, for a month: rehearsal three times weekly, and as the bus from work doesn't get me home till 5.30, it will be hectic to fit it all in. Ah … to be famous one day, adored by millions, the dreams of a nineteen-year-old should be allowed to be cherished.

Thank God the dark and often sombre days of November are nearly over. I hate them; can't wait till St Nicolas arrives on his horse in December—you being young at heart probably still believe in him—although it might be a meagre affair this year with shop windows mostly empty. Dad always says, 'It took the Germans five days to overrun the Netherlands, but it will be a decade at least, to put the country back on its feet.'

How right he is. I'm not complaining though. I usually get a bit cranky on days when my chocolate allowance runs out and having a sweet tooth doesn't help! Sometimes I swap my cigarette rations with Kees who is a heavy smoker. That way my coupons last longer. So you see, young man, it is not only the army that suffers from hunger pains on occasion, but also poor little girls like me, here on the home front!

Only kidding, Pierre. I'd hate to see what you soldiers over there are eating while on patrol, or at your base for that matter. Unfortunately, I can't send food parcels like your mother did for your birthday. What I do have to spare is understanding and warmth, on special days even 'leftover tenderness …!' Feel free … help yourself! But in moderation and on one condition: only if you need these free gifts. You never had a better offer, Sergeant, be quick before I change my mind.

1947 is closing fast. I feel nervous. Could it be opening-night approaching? Or the dawn of a new year? When perhaps I might have to face a new challenge, someone from across the ocean, caring enough to visit a village, tucked away in the woods somewhere in the western Netherlands?

Where so many moons ago, a commando stood in the shadow near the entrance of our church ... Just a passing echo? Or was he on a fact-finding mission, known only to himself? The answer to all these question marks is: 'Opening night nerves.' Of course!

How silly of me to think otherwise.

Seeing we are in the festive season ... something extra from Corry!

PS. Sergeant, will you look after Pierre for me and wish him a MERRY CHRISTMAS?

21. ANOTHER CHRISTMAS ... GIFTS OF DISAPPOINTMENT, AND HOPE

A merry Christmas it was not! There had been eager but, as it turned out, unfounded, anticipation that Strike Force 8 might have been back in the Netherlands by Christmas 1947, given that would then have been two years since they set out on their Far Eastern adventure. As the year dragged itself to an end, with no let-up in counter-insurgency operations, it was steadily becoming more obvious that they were not going home.

> There comes a certain period in the life of a field army when rot slowly oozes to the surface. When grumbling noises are heard ... faintly at first. Then louder until finally it explodes. We called it 'Time Disease'. The reasons for it were simple—so we thought, if it affected only a few—yet complex when more and more men showed signs of suffering from this deadly sickness.
>
> Having spent so many months on duty overseas gave us a light-hearted feeling of entitlement for being home at Christmas. This happened in the latter part of 1947, when two years had passed since leaving the Netherlands. War volunteers, of course, signed up for an unspecified period of service anywhere in the world! Here then lay the danger, and when the first symptoms of 'time disease' became noticeable, we tried to blame the system—whatever that was—for failing to send us home.
>
> The fact that so many conscripts were arriving gave us the impression (wrong, of course) that enough new troops were available to take over our positions. We could not, however, see the overall strategic picture and that, even with over 100,000 men involved at certain times, we still lacked power.
>
> Married or engaged personnel suffered most from home sickness, but there was no exact line to be drawn. Many events taking place on

the other side of the world could trigger a depression, or, worse, total collapse. The 'Dear John' letters had mostly happened in the first six months or so of our tour of duty, as our impulsive war-hunger was sometimes called in the beginning. Later, the unwelcome letters of goodbye seemed to lessen in quantity; their effect, however, never varied: a devastating lasting impact in most cases.

Death in families back home also caused havoc amongst men in the field. All too often, combat soldiers were spread out to such an extent that the padre—after receiving first-hand information from HQ—came too late to comfort the victim. Mail sometimes arrived, notifying of the death of a loved one or dear friend, while the letter, with news of that person being sick, was still in transit!

I had no problem as far as home sickness was concerned. Looking back at the last fifty months, I had spent less than one of them in my own bed!

The loss of Elly, although spread out over a lengthy period, had left me with a long-lasting sense of emptiness and uncertainty surrounding her. Now, after writing to many new penfriends, especially Corry, for most of 1947, the sad memories had faded somewhat, and it was often hard to recall what had happened in another world, when I was a different person altogether.

Yes, Corry had picked up a vibe that there was more to my life than the teasing, joking chatter that I often used for correspondence. Yet I didn't know her well enough to feel sure that she would become more than a passing dream. Perhaps she could stem the restlessness that had controlled my moves for so many years.

At least I didn't suffer from the symptoms that were spreading so rapidly throughout Strike Force 8.

'Home by Christmas', the slogan that had penetrated the furthest outpost, was gradually losing its credibility as the year came to an end. In one of the army newspapers a new slogan was published. A hard-hitting, no nonsense quote:

War volunteers ... prolonged ... due to enormous success!

Across the oceans, far away from Sumatra, it was such a different story. The village of Oudenbosch was gradually being transformed into fairyland as gentle snowflakes drifted down, making for an early white

Part Three: Their Story Begins ...

Christmas. It was Saturday, 20 December, opening night at the local theatre only a few hours away.

As Corry was nervously preparing at home, under the supportive gaze and care of her Mam, the letterbox rattled ... and all the preparations stopped immediately. Corry was quickly in the hall and found a card and a padded envelope from Sumatra.

On the card, 'Season's greetings from Y-Brigade-Sumatra', Pierre had written on the back: 'Hope you have a lovely Christmas.' Corry then sat down at the table and opened the large letter with a penknife. In surprise she looked at pieces of coloured paper and cardboard, forming a rough outline of a theatre. FIDEI-ET-ARTI was written on the top triangle, at the bottom the words OTILLIE in large capital letters. Taking out some cotton wool forming the centre-part, she dropped it on the floor, then read his tiny words: 'To someone special.'

'There is no message, Mam. Perhaps it's *his* way of saying good luck for opening night.' A slight disappointment echoed in her voice.

Suddenly, her mother bent down and put the cotton wool back on the table.

'Here, look here! This is his message.' Great excitement in her outburst.

Corry froze, staring in utter disbelief at a sparkling golden filigree ring, winking at her from its protective packing. Tears filled her eyes as she gently slid the intricate piece of craftsmanship on her finger. A perfect fit, as if that mysterious stranger in the jungle had known all along the size of her ring finger. She grabbed hold of her mother in an emotional embrace.

Later that evening, Corry wrote this letter, and there was a not-so-subtle change in her salutation:

Another Christmas ... Gifts of Disappointment and Hope

Christmas, 1947

My dearest Pierre,

'Silent Night, Holy Night' ... the sounds of this eternal song drift through the house ...

Next to our fireplace stands a small tree, its candles are twinkling, some shiny decorations reflecting a play of lights and shadows. Underneath leans a crib, an overhanging branch as roof, tiny statues gathered on straw covering the stable floor.

Peace on earth ... at least in this part of the world.

Where you are, Pierre, it might be a different story, I don't know.

This afternoon our matinee went smoothly, and we played for a full house. One more performance on Boxing Day and your Otillie will cease to exist, except for one all important factor ... a golden souvenir from Sumatra! I still have trouble accepting that it belongs to me, that it isn't part of my role in *The White Horse Inn*.

Why, Pierre, why ...? I keep asking myself this question. 'Does he care so much? Is he trying to tell me something or was his answer in that short sentence: 'To someone special'?

I find it extremely hard to simply say, 'Thank you, Pierre.' Because, right now, there is so much more than words flowing through my heart. When the ring arrived (Mam discovered it), I was getting ready for opening night, nervous and very tense. Putting that precious present on my finger seemed like an omen. Nerves disappeared, and when later in the evening I sang: 'Im Weiszen Rossel Am Wolga Meer', I held my hands together, gently stroking the filigree pattern, knowing I was singing for a faraway commando!

Afterwards there was a glass of champagne to celebrate our success. It was then that many questions were asked. The main one being: 'Where on earth did you get that beautiful ring?' 'Inheritance, boyfriend, parents'?

'From a secret admirer,' I finally managed to whisper. Two of my friends, in whom I have confided about you, Pierre, smiled knowingly. The rest were just a teeny bit jealous. Who would have believed anyway that a distant penfriend sends a twenty-two-carat piece of jewellery to a girl he has never met!

You have become a thief, stealing heart and soul from an

Part Three: Their Story Begins ...

unsuspecting teenager. Don't let it happen again! One surprise is all I can handle ...

Have a safe New Year, Pierre, and YES, thank you SO much!

A happy Corry

PS. Can I give you a kiss? I'll do it anyway ... like it or not! Where will you be next Christmas? You DON'T know!? I DO!

It is more than likely that the letter crossed in the mail with Pierre's next despatch:

Sunday 28-12-1947
On Active Service

My Dearest Corry

Well, I sure hope your Christmas was a brighter one than mine. What a mess! It all started so promisingly. A passing convoy from the Palembang harbour on its way to HQ stopped briefly at our outpost and became an inviting means of celebrating the festive season in more luxurious fashion—meaning a Midnight Mass with carols, early breakfast with fresh bread and a special dinner later that day. As I was free of duties for 24 glorious hours, I hopped in one of the jeeps and was on my way.

In less than two hours we reached Battalion HQ and met many friends from bygone days. It was then that I realised that mail for our platoon was waiting to be delivered on Boxing Day. Going through the bags I found a dozen or so letters addressed to me, including two from a girl called Corry (I'm starting to like that name!).

Asking a simple question like, 'Why not deliver the mail today in time for Christmas,' I got a stupid, and to my way of thinking, cruel answer from the administration officer. 'Two more days won't make that much difference. Anyway, no convoy is going that way.'

Before this heartless response, I had often wondered how far HQ was removed from everyday soldiers, who, by doing the dirty work, became the innocent victims of neglect or apathy. His uncaring answer said enough. HQ had their letters from home, or wherever,

Another Christmas ... Gifts of Disappointment and Hope

and the frontline where the combat troops were stationed could wait. From personal experience over a long period of time, I know the impact mail has on a field army; especially on days like Christmas when loved ones seem a lifetime away.

It didn't take long to find me a bodyguard, and together we roared back to Gunung Megang, three bags full of letters and parcels in the rear of a commandeered jeep. It wasn't the first time I had 'borrowed' from the army!

We made it in record time, delighting the platoon on arrival with the unexpected mail from overseas. Three more men decided to join us for the return trip, and, after changing into their 'pakean best', off we went.

I must explain here, Corry, that December is part of the wet monsoon, when cloud bursts with torrential rain can hit you at short notice. It was nearly dark when we left. The equator being next door means the sun sets at 5.30 every day of the year.

Protected by canvas covers, we tried to outrun the approaching rain, knowing full well how roads, mostly gravel and clay, would turn into nightmares without warning. To no avail.

Nearing the halfway mark, we suddenly slewed sideways on the slippery surface, only retaining any control through the determined efforts of our driver. Again we skidded, this time we landed in the oozing mud at the edge of the dark jungle track, in the full blast of a tropical downpour.

Our Christmas present had arrived ...!

Our jeep's headlights were like two solemn candles pointing up at the green Sumatran undergrowth surrounding us, with the rain furiously pelting down. An hour later we managed to get mobile again, but the jeep had made up its own mind in which direction we were heading. It was facing our outpost, where we had come from! Anyway, we were too tired and filthy to try again for HQ.

It was past midnight before we finally reached our platoon, having bogged down with monotonous regularity. Carols by candlelight and those five dirty, stinking men were a dream and world apart!

Late on Christmas Day, the weather being fine for a change, we placed a dozen cans around our perimeter, filled them with petrol and set them on fire. From our Red Cross supplies, we had taken cotton wool, rolls of bandage and, with the help of some branches, decorated

Part Three: Their Story Begins ...

our outpost. Someone had received rum in his Christmas parcel and, lacing our coffee, we drank a silent salute to our loved ones in the Netherlands. Gathering in a circle, we sang 'Silent Night, Holy Night'. Emotions penetrated the darkness within the ring of petrol cans.

Not the sort of Christmas one remembers from younger years, but it came close to that experience in Scotland where a thousand voices in five languages vibrated through the mountains. No that's a lie, it didn't come close at all ... but, under the circumstances, the best we could do.

On days like these, my thoughts travel across the oceans to the people left behind. People I love ... there is also a girl there somewhere, a girl I hardly know, one I have never met. She is called Corry and writes letters that embrace me in lonely moments. Who formulates words into tender sentences? Perhaps she takes me in gentle arms in between her lines ...?

Still a dream and world apart ...

As I say goodbye to 1947, I do the same to you.

Goodbye for now, see you in 1948, in my next letter.

From somewhere in South Sumatra, over but not out.

Happy New Year ... darling!
Pierre

PS. Yes, I know, I promised once not to use silly words; words like darling, but I do like breaking silly promises ...!

Oudenbosch, 17 Jan 1948

My dearest Pierre,

It's getting harder by the week, Sergeant, to write letters to you, because something is happening between us and I don't mean correspondence! Perhaps the gold ring was a secret signal ... or else the way your words have changed. Even the beginning of a new year has caused a tremor, like a 5 or 6 on the Richter scale.

We are not playing games anymore, young man. A serious tone is creeping into your dialogue, like the one you used, when saying farewell to 1947. 'Still a dream and world apart,' what a beautiful expression!

Are we really, Pierre? What if we have the same dream?

A frightening prospect, or intriguing possibility?

I realise that our worlds are far apart, you being in a warzone and I in the safety of a family home, but that won't last forever, will it? You DO intend returning this year, or not?

What did disturb me deeply was your letter about disappearing friends. It must have come by sea mail, took nearly two months to get here. It also took my breath away, reading over and over about the turmoil in your life.

So dreadfully bare, the simple way you describe your bygone years, so hurtfully true the way I felt it.

Sometimes at a party or evening out, I meet boys who, in great detail, describe one of those experiences. I have yet to meet anyone who went through the same emotions as you did. Your mother was right when she said, 'Pierre is my favourite, because he is never home!' How true! No wonder friends couldn't keep up with you. Perhaps not even girlfriends, at least you never mentioned any!

One thing I do know, and it gives me strength when I read about the mounting death toll in the Indies. You are a survivor! Have you ever thought of standing still, Pierre? Reflect on what is happening to you and turn back? Of course, you can't do such a thing in a combat force. I mean inside you, deep, very deep, where no one can see or touch you, free to move, think, build your own private kingdom?

I would like to be part of that process if ever there comes a chance of terminating that bizarre cross-country run of yours! To play a role in erasing the hurt your eyes so far have encountered.

Yes, we are still 'a dream and world apart'. How much longer? We are already on the same wavelength, I can feel it in my bones, even if we hardly ever talk about music and film. What a sneaky way of entangling an innocent girl like me and offering light-hearted comedy, when all the time it was a soulmate you wanted!

With 1948 upon us, the road back must be priority number one. For you, Pierre, when it finally comes it will be a hard one. I can feel it with every word you write (or ... omit!).

I think you are tired, letting your camouflage and armour slip, exposing the real man behind all the bantering, unaware that a certain penfriend is looking in: NOT to find weakness, but to discover a

Part Three: Their Story Begins ...

gentle touch that somehow survived your restless years.

Our letters are getting more honest as months fly away. It won't be long before you or I surrender. Or both! To say those three words that count. You are only allowed one guess!

Your Corry

PS. Who said DARLING was a silly word? I know an even sillier one!

22. THE FIGHT GOES ON

After these heartfelt and revealing exchanges of letters over the Christmas and New Year period, there are no surviving copies of any correspondence between Corry and Pierre for the next few months. In the meantime, the threat of attack or involvement in offensive operations such as fighting patrols and night ambushes—the substance of counter-insurgency warfare—was never far away. Pierre writes about one incident where, without the prior work of winning at least one heart and mind, the outcome could have been disastrous:

> The attack when it came caught us in the worst possible situation. Through increased enemy activities, our manpower was stretched to the very limit and although several divisions of army conscripts had recently arrived from the Netherlands, most of the raw recruits were diverted to Java. In Sumatra, only small groups of newly formed units came to our assistance. Each company received a token number of '*aanvulling*', replacements, to bring Strike Force 8 to capacity strength.
>
> That night we had two patrols out to nearby hamlets. Their return not expected until daybreak which left us with three men outside and seven, including myself, asleep. Fortunately for us, at 4 am the last of the nightly guard changes took place, making for six men on alert.
>
> It was a miracle that Joessoef—an old villager who we had befriended and became our informer—was not killed when he stumbled into one of our sentries in the dark. Luckily, the old man's gait, more like a trot, was immediately recognised and, sensing danger, our sentry quickly alerted the rest of us.
>
> In tears, Joessoef had difficulty explaining what was happening. A large force was on its way, that much we did understand from his words, coming from a heaving chest. Apparently, he had run all the way from his village to warn us.
>
> '*Berapa Joessoef? Tidak tahu?*' How many, he didn't know.

Part Three: Their Story Begins ...

'Weapons?' Again, the same reply. I told him to disappear and, for his own safety, never to come back again. I shook hands with the old, tired villager before he faded in the protective darkness.

Whenever there was an unknown number poised for attack, we followed a set pattern of defence, twice proven successful in Perdjito. 'Leave the post' was part of the plan.

First, we switched on the radio transmitter to receive, put up the volume as if constant communications were maintained. Then we would light at least three hurricane lamps inside, go down through the trapdoor in the wooden floor and vanish. Two 'soldiers', sitting in rattan chairs, would be clearly visible on the veranda. Being mere uniforms held up by tree branches and straw, covered by a steel helmet, they were included in the deadly game we were playing. Away from our post, in camouflaged trenches, dug deep into the red earth roughly ten metres apart, each holding two men, we waited. Our trenches had a solid wooden cover with grass tufts and bushes nailed to the outside, blending with the surroundings both day and night.

To our left was the fast-running river, up front our deserted house, to the right a tiny village with friendly people, who shared our everyday life, doing trade, paying polite visits, even organising an occasional feast of local food for us. Behind us the hostile jungle forcing any intruder to the only path available, its exit dead centre between two of our covered trenches. Even Joessoef, passing them twice daily, had never become aware of the death-traps, awaiting the enemy.

We heard their footsteps on the muddy track before we could see them coming out of the darkness in front of our positions. Silhouetting themselves sharply against the lights from inside our strong hold, they very carefully moved out into the open, satisfied perhaps with the garbled radio traffic and the two soldiers, seemingly asleep on the veranda. Slowly our camouflaged covers were moved further backwards, enabling us to extend our cramped bodies. Weapons came up, grenades laid outside, ready to start their destruction.

A deadly silence covered the area, making the voices coming from the radio sound like a macabre interlude. Even the crickets had gone quiet, as if in waiting. One trench further to the right and close to the house contained our only Bren gun. Its objective: to stop any terrorist

The Fight Goes On

from reaching the village with its friendly inhabitants. Some of the infiltrators wore uniforms, others had dark-coloured sarongs and a black cap, like the fanatical Muslim Hizboelah in Palambang, I thought, waiting for the signal to open fire.

The booby-trap wire, strung low across the grass fronting the house, would—when touched—release a spring that plunged a lever into a 303 bullet. It was that explosion we were waiting for ... In the split second of panic that followed, of enemy soldiers running for cover or firing at the two silent figures on the veranda, we released a concentrated barrage of death.

In confusion, with bullets coming from behind them, they darted forward and were met by crossfire from the right. The first grenades were already in the air, their seven-second timers giving us enough scope to pull our heads down then up again for another salvo. The Bren gun, firing in continuous bursts, gradually drove them back towards us ... and annihilation. Some dived into the fast-flowing river and were swept away. Others tried for the jungle, but no one got that far. It was all over in thirty seconds, and if anyone had wanted to surrender during the onslaught, it went unnoticed.

The only remarkable thing was that one of the helmets of the make-believe soldiers on our front veranda had fallen off. Perhaps a lucky shot I wondered, heaving myself out of the slime that had gathered in the trench.

Life went on and death followed closely behind ...
Letters were sent, answers received.
Old ties broken, new relationships established, by mail only.
One soldier managed to get married by proxy ... we all joined him on his honeymoon to nowhere!

My brother Jan, whose place I took nearly four years ago, married the girl who told me that war wasn't over for me yet. How right she was then, how right she still was! I sent them a telegram and wished the bride and groom all the happiness in the world.

We moved constantly. More reinforcements arrived, fresh from the Netherlands, and once again our battalion was at full strength. There were also some occasions for a laugh ... I decided to tell Corry about one of them ...

Part Three: Their Story Begins ...

S.E.A.C. – AREA, On active service, Sunday 4-4-48

Hello darling,

Guess what happened? War can have its lighter sides as well, which was proven earlier this week; but before the BBC gets hold of the details for inclusion in their bulletins, here is the story:

Our platoon commander, the baby-faced lieutenant, was absent—as happens quite frequently—leaving me in charge of stronghold GM. One of the recently arrived reinforcements, Eddy, was cleaning the officer's room when he called out, 'Hey, Sergeant, have a look at this!' Everything was quiet on our part of the front, so I sauntered over, wondering what could be important in a nondescript office of an even more nondescript person.

'A diary,' Eddy exclaimed, 'and wait for this, a statement about you; and don't look for compliments!'

I read the lines underneath his grubby finger, pointing at a certain page. My name first and then: 'Not a likeable person; tends to enjoy arguing with me. Determined; causing friction in my command. Would request transfer, but can't spare him, due to his commando training.'

So, you see, young lady, how popular I am with the Officer Corps?

'Now hear this,' I said, reading his neatly written words aloud to the men who had gathered out of pure boredom. Laughing and catcalls surrounded me.

'I knew all along, you were a bl- b-,' a voice in the rear.

'Write him a thank you note,' came another.

'Send it to Army HQ, please explain,' somebody laughed.

Advice and abusive remarks about the absent officer kept coming.

I put the diary away where Eddy said he had found it. End of part one! At that moment, someone pointed to a large cluster of yellow bananas hanging near the high ceiling. 'Where the hell did he get those?' an angry voice shouted. No pisang (banana) plantations existed in our region, only rubber trees or jungle.

One of the younger platoon members was already lowering the fruit ... within a few moments only one bunch remained, the rest of the delicacy greedily devoured by nearly two dozen men. End of part two!

Early yesterday morning, His Majesty returned. Everyone not on duty made himself suspiciously invisible. 'Sergeant, get the men together for parade,' a degree of sharpness in his voice I didn't even know existed.

'Who of you people has stolen my fruit?' You never address an army as 'you people', but he wouldn't know! 'One more time, who?'

That was as far as he got. A young recruit, fresh from overseas, stepped forward. 'I had one, lieutenant.' A soft snigger went through the platoon.

'Anyone else?' was met with more silence. 'Sergeant, take these men on patrol right now.'

'Yes sir,' the sir extended beyond recall.

With an icy, barely controlled anger in his voice, he supplied the coordinates and a few minutes later we were on our way. A thirty-kilometre route march along narrow, dark jungle roads. What happened in the five hours it took us to cover the distance became the most hilarious event I have ever encountered; and yet in those long hours of heat and blistering feet, something totally different came to the surface: a long pent-up emotion.

We started our march with a collection of songs, some to keep us in step, others to dance on. English, German, French, Dutch, even the old Transvaal was there. Indonesian words, to add spice, extra spice. From the First War, or the Second, it didn't matter.

'Lily Marlene' or 'Till we meet again.' The further we advanced, the louder our voices, like a rising crescendo, vibrating through the encroaching jungle, where under normal conditions our patrols moved silently and secretly. No enemy would have dared to attack us, such was the volume of an army on the march, as if Strike Force 8 had gathered for a last show of force. I felt goose bumps all over, as I headed this proud bunch of veterans, who showed their sergeant where their basic loyalties belonged!

A shame we had only one spectator, our beloved leader, following in his jeep, just to make sure we did the required thirty kilometres. That he had left our outpost behind, protected by only three men and one lonely recruit, probably never dawned on him.

That same lieutenant must have felt very lonely too, when his platoon, dog-tired as they were, started to play volleyball as soon as they returned; a last insulting defiance to an officer, who never became one of us. The new conscript, who had stepped forward earlier that day, walked slowly up to me as I watched the game. 'I'm sorry, Sergeant, about this morning! I mean ... I thought ... well one should always tell the truth.'

'You did, son, you did.' (I felt like a father saying this). 'You told the truth, and we didn't tell any lies either!' Looking into those innocent eighteen-year-old eyes I added in a confidential tone: 'You are one of us anyway.'

His face lit up like a Christmas tree and, saluting smartly, he said in a strong voice, 'Thank you, sir!' I had made another friend.

After the volleyball, we had a swim in the nearby river and, refreshed after that long and memorable day, sat down for our meal. Shortly after, the CO asked me for a patrol report. I looked up, staring him out and then said politely, 'Nothing ever happens on Pisang Patrols, sir.' The 'sir' as an afterthought.

Enemies are never far away in this part of the world, but who said war was such a serious business.

Take care and lots of love
PIERRE

PS. When we were singing Vera Lynn's words 'I don't know where, don't know when' ... I thought of you.

There are persistent rumours that Strike Force 8 might return home before August. Tell your Mam to get the coffee ready ...

23. CONFUSION

When this letter arrived in Oudenbosch, Corry could not contain her excitement. Only her father was home, in the workshop out the back. 'Calm down, Corke.' His soft voice was hardly ever raised. When her mother said *Cor* it was an order, but her Dad's *Corke* was a caress, an endearment. 'Who is coming home then?'

She pushed his shoulder, the letter still clutched in her hand. 'You know *who*, my penfriend Pierre!'

'Oh ... the stormtrooper,' he said laughingly.

'Don't use that word, Dad, he is a commando.'

She looked at her father again, waiting for his reply. 'Well, I'd better start making some barricades then. Don't want to make it too easy for him to storm the house do we now!'

'Oh Dad, you *are* impossible,' and as she came closer to embrace him (she had to hug somebody to share the news), he warned her back.

'Not too close to the saw, dear,' raising his left hand at the same time. Half his index finger was missing. 'We don't want this to happen again.'

Corry was silent then, only remembering vaguely; she was still quite young when it occurred. He switched off the fast-rotating timber saw and said, 'Will you do me a favour, girl, and clean the workshop a bit? With Kees out on a job, I'm rather short-handed today.'

She picked up a broom and swept the shavings and sawdust to one corner, then wiped the bench clean. She didn't mind doing little jobs for him because she loved her father. He had such a gentle personality, often sensing more than asking how things were going. Where mother was strict and of the no-nonsense type, he always seemed to look for compromises. 'Opposite poles attract each other,' she had often reflected when seeing her mam and dad so contented together.

She would answer the *Pisang Patrol* letter tomorrow. It was postponed,

Part Three: Their Story Begins ...

however, for several days. Either the sawdust or a virus had infected her, and although she went to work next morning, by the time evening came around, she had a high fever. 'Better stay in bed, Corry. The doctor will have a look at you later.' Her mother always worried so much about colds and other ills! Not that she minded. It was nice and warm in her bed and dreamworld only a thought away!

Hello there, dear Commando

Help! Please help. I don't know any more if I am coming or going; lost the date of the month, forgot what year it is! And ... it's all YOUR fault! There!

Tore up several letters over the last couple of weeks, some were too much too soon (I thought). Others too little, too late (am afraid). Confused is the word. Wanted to laugh with your hilarious Pisang-Patrol letter and ended up crying when you said to that young recruit, 'You are one of us anyway.' Am I one of yours, Sergeant?

I am in bed with flu!

No, it stands for influenza, definitely not a boy's name. Knowing you, you would try the postman's bid on me again! I'm not a tart! Perhaps delicious French pastry to munch away on a rainy day! But only for real connoisseurs, and you, living in jungle territory, probably don't understand the refinements I'm surrounded with.

You read too many lewd novels, sing too often those bawdy army songs to appreciate how delicate a friend you're writing to!

See ... how confused I am, but please bear with me. Tearing this letter up as well means you'll never get any more mail. Except from those two or three dozen other girls who write love-letters to you!?

Oh Pierre, why don't you just come home and tell me what I want to hear most! That one PS in your last letter, 'home by August', might have caused all the commotion in my heart.

I had better change the subject as goose bumps are appearing ... The other day, my girlfriend Cora and I went to the local bookshop and, trying to keep a straight face, asked for, 'How to Handle a Young Commando, Returning from Combat'. The girl behind the counter referred us to the library. Outside we burst out laughing.

It being a sunny spring Saturday, we decided on a brisk walk to the outlying fields. 'To clear the cobwebs of my mind,' I thought. For the first time, your homecoming, Pierre, came up in our conversation. Cora is a long-standing friend and, at least with her, I am assured that confidential talk doesn't travel. She understands what goes on inside me, that is how close we are.

As to your plans, Sergeant, she was groping as much in the dark as I. She suggested asking you (without delay) the following questions:

But first a warning ... have you something handy to hold on to?!

One: Do you, my friend, intend visiting me?

Two: If yes, are your intentions honourable?

Three: If not, will you come back for a second try!?

While talking away on the subject, we came to a roadside café and, still being in that flippant mood, sat down on the terrace and ordered a glass of Moselle. So, if those three questions sound strange to you, then perhaps they were born after the second glass of wine. Born with giggles, I should add!

No wonder I got a cold. Punishment my mother would say for being naughty! But nice, hey Sergeant? Are you listening over there? Will you please hurry up with your embarkation? Just ask for compassionate leave! Tell them you and I are running out of paper and patience.

Write soon, answer all questions honestly and forgive me if I sound delirious... I am! Have you found those three words yet (re my letter from Jan.)? or do I have to wait for an answer until you arrive home? It doesn't matter anymore. Sooner or later (but rather sooner) I'll squeeze them out of you. Even if you have experience in unarmed combat...!

Tell me when you learned those deadly movements with your bare hands, did you use real girls (sorry, I mean men of course) or dummies? Why do I ask, you wonder? Ah well, just in case...! It might make it all worthwhile... I often fight with my brother Kees, you see. Perhaps it is time I changed partners... I wouldn't mind doing battle with you. Even losing ... I still might win the war!

See you later?!
Yours, with happiness.
Corry.

Part Three: Their Story Begins ...

PS. Home by August? I'm not ready yet! Have to do my hair, paint my toenails, polish the floor, roll out the red carpet etcetera (you follow?). Here is a poem, made especially for you, Pierre.

Oh, idle hope ...
Oh ... Do tell me dear ... Far away from me
Please ... Have no fear, waiting at the quay ...
For a ship is a-coming ... I can hear ...
While I wait for yee ... And shed an idle tear ...
For thee ...!!

Corry Siemons

To Pierre with ...!

'Confused' was the word Corry used to describe her state of mind in her little village, across the oceans. However, her muddle, although very real, was dwarfed by that caused by the often conflicting and unfounded rumours then flying across the Brigade through the 'bush telegraph' after someone, somewhere, heard a very simple radio broadcast simply stating: *Infantry division landed in Palembang, to replace long-serving Strike Force 7 & 8, presently deployed in South Sumatra;* end of bulletin and the beginning of much confusion and questioning, without clear answers being given.

At Brigade HQ, where daily incoming reports were analysed, news items like those quoted above hardly raised an eyebrow. Personnel there lived so much closer to reality. In the far distant outposts (often a day's journey away), life was not so simple. We only received faint rumblings, like garbled, declassified leftovers, ready to boil on the cooking pot of loneliness.

Nothing foments and ferments so easily and with such devastating effect as rumours. Just a gentle stir, aided by a sprinkling of naivety and delusion. Whatever is available on any given day will hasten the process. The resulting taste of the local brew is exhilarating. It takes you on a high—like a drug overdose—then when fresh, negative tidings deny all substance of an early withdrawal, drop you in the abyss of total despair. It gets repeated, over and over again, and the deadly time disease claims victims through all ranks. You know—and everyone else does—that somewhere in those news reports is a hidden message.

Had to be, we thought in desperation, when 1947 dragged to a close. What we were hoping for again in the new year and weeks turned into months, and then April appeared on our calendars. But life went on regardless of our feelings: patrols, enemy infiltration, someone close dying, guard duties, restless nights, love-letters unanswered ... endless days, another friend disappearing ...

We moved positions frequently, dashing hopes once more even when new recruits kept pouring in. Our strongholds were taken over by fresh-faced youngsters from the Netherlands, and we shifted to yet another lonely and deserted village. An unrelenting operation, sapping our endurance. Patience was often shot to pieces ...

Discipline, always a true barometer of the quality of combat troops, suffered as well. We had to wear armbands when we crossed the demarcation line—an elusive dream of some negotiators in Europe to keep the warring armies apart. Our armband had VP on it. *Vredes Patrouille*—Peace Patrol! What a farce: the bullets coming our way were as deadly as before the fruitless talks had started. Such is life ... or death!

When the bombshell landed, it still took us by surprise. The encoded dispatch, when it reached us, contained a single line: Strike Force 7 due to leave 27 April-1948. No mention of our battalion, but that was a minor detail yet to be worked out by army headquarters.

It came as an anti-climax. We couldn't believe it at first, even thought it was another cruel twist in the long line of disappointments. When we saw the large convoy on its way to Palembang, passing our stronghold, we, at last, believed! There was no mistaking those waving, singing members of Strike Force 7, the dedicated soldiers who had supported us in the street battles in January 1947 and later in the vast areas of South Sumatra.

We paid them a silent, saluting farewell, a goodbye to comrades in arms. More vanishing friends on the long road back to civilisation. Time to send Corry a letter, I reflected, as dust settled behind the disappearing trucks. She would be the first to know.

We walked back to our compound, had a game of volleyball, but somehow my mind drifted away across oceans. I smiled, that inward

Part Three: Their Story Begins ...

smile of knowing ...

The long-awaited rendezvous with a stranger was no longer a mirage!

24. PREPARING TO LEAVE

Then, at last, a few weeks later in mid-May, Strike Force 8 was advised that their departure from Sumatra would be on 11 June 1948. As part of the preparations for their departure, stores and weapons were cleaned and returned to 'the system' ready to be reissued to the replacement units. Pierre also did some cleaning out: of all the letters from the many penfriends and others he had received while on active service, except for one set of letters, those from Corry. These were travelling home with him together with his diaries.

> I stared at my diaries neatly stacked in an old biscuit tin. Records of endless days and nights … intimate scribblings, sometimes hardly legible because of stains, like spilt tea or perhaps a lonesome tear …
>
> There had been many lies over those restless years, yet this rusty container held only truth. Faithful details about girls I had met, often leaving behind a bitter-sweet taste, interwoven with hard accurate facts of death and destruction as war took over.
>
> Made love to a stranger … it said.
> Guard of honour at a friend's funeral … I read.
> Met Elly again after many a day.
> Goodbye to Ann and hello to Mam.
>
> Letters to and from, their details written down for later reference. Years that came and went. A lonely Christmas trying desperately to stand out as a special day and failing, so often failing.
>
> Forgotten birthdays, the dates were there but space behind empty …
>
> How many days now? After each month, I had added the total since joining the forces. It stood at 1333. An awesome collection of twenty-four-hour periods flying away from me, and yet some of those hours had the capacity of lasting a lifetime. Either with a girl you loved or waiting in an ambush, they felt like eternity.

Part Three: Their Story Begins ...

So many highlights went into those journals, often terribly important when you wrote them down. Years later you wondered why. There were times when you wanted to fill whole foolscaps with tender feelings of love and happiness. Later, you were glad you didn't! Also, weeks went by when it was near impossible to keep track of your thoughts. Jotting down words, while in combat or on the run, is an art in itself. I never tried. Left that job to the war reporters. Tropical nights in the 'off' period from guard duties were ideal for filling in the missing links, when only crickets kept you company.

The little books in different colours and sizes were the only proof that I lived through those turbulent years. Where a camouflage overall would literally rot on your body, where army jungle boots were torn to pieces and friends fell along the merciless road, only memories remained.

I wanted to close the old tin containing the memoirs, but there was still a hesitation. Would I ever have the courage to open those books again and show them to the world or even read them myself? They had followed me from the Rhine to the Moesi River ... London to Scotland ... Paris ... Germany ... Palembang ... Bali ... Morotai ... an endless list; a million steps from autobahn to jungle tracks; meeting up with thousands of strangers, making hundreds of friends ... and now sitting alone on a stretcher, feeling deflated, deflated like our volleyball used in too many games!

One more book to be started. I mark the cover: 'Leaving Sumatra—Arrival Rotterdam.'

No more combat reports, no more bloodshed or disappearing friends. Only the winding-down process, then back to Palembang Harbour, a short trip to Java, embarkation and the long journey home. A matter of three months at the most.

...

For the first time in many years, there could be spare days to go through accumulated letters. Ready to destroy. Could I do that? Destroy, I mean, killing part of myself? Severing connections so carefully built over a long period of time? I sorted through the box, picking up a special one here and there. From some I recognised the handwriting, read lines that once had meant so much.

Sitting on my stretcher I let the words, like fine sand, slip through my fingers, making a fist only once or twice as a particular note strikes more than the surface of my mind.

But one can't keep memories forever. Some, knife-sharp, cutting open barely healed wounds. Others had the feeling of the soft contour of a female breast ...

I started to tear them up, page by page, tearing myself apart as well, so I took the lot outside. At least burning would be quicker and less painful.

Lying in the grass near the river's edge, I lit a match setting the box and contents alight, then tipped over the carton again. To let them all vanish in one unmarked grave ...? No, impossible. It had taken years to collect those words. At least they deserved a fitting requiem.

Slowly, one by one, they burned to ashes. A farewell to friends—Anny and Josje, Agnes and Nancy, Mia, Nelly, Mona—even a few left from when Elly still wrote, now so long ago. The Netherlands, England and Suez, flames made no exceptions!

Piece by painful piece, correspondence was taken away from me. Like old friends, never to return, clinging to my fingers as in a helpless cry: Why me, Pierre, why me of all people? I had no answer.

So many words, supporting me in time of need.

Some had loved me, others thought they did. I ...? I had loved them all. If not in reality, at least on patient paper. One thread and only one was a common factor in all those epistles: they cared, because of me.

The pain was still there as flames died down.

For a long time, I sat near the river, my mind floating away with the gentle moving water. I gathered Corry's letters, the only ones travelling home with me. Better close the windows to the past and open the blinds on the other side, where a new sun would rise on the horizon of a hesitant future—perhaps called Corry—whose words of fantasy had touched ... touched! Would she be waiting at a station, her mother getting coffee ready? Was I ready? I got pen and paper and started to write ... to a dream!

Still on active service ... but not much longer, 8 June 1948

My dearest long-distance girl,

This might well be a farewell to Sumatra, but NOT to you! We are

Part Three: Their Story Begins ...

now in a holding position, meaning 'Move out at short notice'. Isn't that wonderful news for both of us? And for more than 700 men of our battalion.

Strike Force 7, which left the Netherlands one month ahead of us in 1945, is already in Java. Only a few more days now. Sounds unbelievable doesn't it, after two and a half years of absence. How long ago was it that you first wrote to me? Remember? DEAR MISTER, you'll never live THAT down! It feels like a lifetime and yet that was last year in February.

So much has happened since then, so much ... never to return again ... Regrets? Yes, I have a few, and you, Corry, sorry you answered my ad?

One gets tired of low pay and long hours, no breakfast in bed, often not even a proper bed to sleep on. A stretcher, a concrete floor, or jungle tracks ... Yes, I'm used to the little inconveniences of army life, but to say I still like it, that would be a lie.

Time to return to civilisation. To hold something soft in my arms again (I do miss my teddy bear!) and have a sleep-in till 9 or 10. Real sheets and pillows to rest my weary body on, oh such luxury ... Did I ever tell you the last period I slept at home? I was still a teenager and look at me now! An old man!

I'm finding it extremely difficult to tell you in simple words what goes on inside me at this moment. Perhaps I don't know myself. I was updating my diary this morning when something caught my eye. You want to know? It said there, 'Corry and I have reached the point of no return!' Entered the very day we were told of our coming departure. Does that frighten you? I can't turn back anymore, made too many retreats in my life already. I would like very much meeting you, say hello, shake hands, perhaps exchange a friendly kiss, seeing we are still strangers.

And you, Meisje?

I should have opened up to you before, instead of waiting until the last moment, knowing all too well your reply won't reach me in time. But I have been hurt before when I DID open up. I was afraid it might happen again. Yes, I am a coward dreading what a young girl might say when we meet ...!

I'm trying to think of a fitting conclusion to our correspondence. Something about the danger we encountered here and, also, the

Preparing to Leave

awakening of a new feeling, for which I can only thank YOU!
Here it comes …

Straight away I was 'ware,
So, weeping, how a mystic shape did move behind me,
And drew me backward by the hair
And a voice said in mastery while I strove …
'Guess now who holds thee? '-----'Death', I said,
But there the silver answer rang 'not death, but l o v e'.

I nearly forgot …
24 June, HAPPY BIRTHDAY, CORRY. We'll be (probably) at sea by then but will drink to your health. Funny really, the poem was supposed to be the ending of this letter yet feel a reluctance to stop talking to you.

Perhaps the fine print will have to wait until we meet.
An artistic member of our platoon coloured the enclosed photo, taken a couple of months ago. It sure makes it more realistic, I would say, and what a handsome chap you have been writing to! That's the trouble, not having any mirror to speak of you don't get to know yourself, until one day when you look at a stranger on a postcard …
Our weapons have been collected, heavy gear and equipment is all packed, boxes with personal belongings are ready for the shipment. Only our kitbags and the men in uniform remain.
Countdown is beginning … the date: Tuesday 8 June 1948.
Tomorrow, the last day for overseas mail from Sumatra.
I'd better get this letter finished.
Once again, from under the equator to a special girl in the Netherlands,
LOVE … SUN … and … WARMTH … all in the right proportions.

Pierre

PS. After arrival in Batavia I will send details of embarkation, name of ship and estimated time of crashing into Rotterdam!

Part Three: Their Story Begins ...

Pierre reflected on this letter:

I didn't seal the envelope immediately, instead pondered for a while if enough was included; the testing time of probing and teasing, the convoluted way of delving below the surface, belonged to the past.
This was NOW.
Expressions, so matter-of-fact in the beginning, had changed ever so gently. The long-distance dialogue had become intimate, like a phone call, without voices.
The skirmish of words, made into a special art by both of us, had not brought winners or losers, only equals! That's how I saw her. First as a good friend, then a girl, a lovely dream ... a future companion? Wait, wait ... my mind is getting ahead of me. Too far ... too fast ... I had been hurt before when that happened.
Love was hardly ever cited in our letters, yet, in between the lines, the abundance of warm feelings was overwhelming. But we never admitted; we played with words and with each other, on paper, always on paper!
As I put my mouth to the envelope to moisten the flap, I felt the taste of lips meeting me: a mirage, a dream, or was it her? I smiled, closing the last episode from Sumatra. It was up to Corry now to find every little word that mattered. To look through the camouflage and smoke screens I had used for so many months. Yes, she would succeed—she had been practising since February last year!
Only a few more months before we would meet in a long-awaited rendezvous. Two strangers, letters and photos the only tangible proof that, indeed, we existed for each other.
It felt good to be alive ... and in love? The question mark would remain in place until we met.
As I left the old building—our home for the last couple of weeks—the rays of a watery sun touched my green beret. My jungle fatigues were damp with sweat.
Yes ... it felt good to be alive ...!

25. Departure

Strike Force 8 arrived in Batavia, Java, on 12 June and were granted a whole week of R&R, their first 'downtime' in two and half years! They did what most soldiers would do after such a long, unbroken stint of combat operations: drinking sessions, cinemas, soccer matches, daytrips into the coolness of Java's countryside, eating in tiny restaurants, chatting up bar girls, playing volleyball games, and most found the time to write that final letter telling loved ones the day of departure and estimated arrival in Rotterdam. Pierre also found time to pay his final respects to some of his comrades.

> When I passed the cathedral in Japan Lapangan, I went in and lit a candle, thinking the least I can do is to say thank you. I also paid a farewell to those staying behind forever.
> At the field of honour, Menteng Poeloe, I laid some flowers on a grave with a familiar inscription. The corporal from our company had died in the street battles of Palembang. This was his final resting place. I stayed there for a long time, the hot afternoon sun shimmering between rows of wooden crosses. I thought I was crying but my eyes stayed dry. Perhaps there were no tears left. It would have been a relief to go to pieces, just once, just once, to break down, open the floodgates; but, as had happened before, they had to come from too deep inside, too bloody deep.
> My old *Voigtlander*, years ago, had taken a picture of someone playing volleyball. Now it had the sad task of capturing his name on a simple monument of death. Even the fragrances of the frangipani flower, lying at my feet, could not erase the smell of a graveyard.
> I saluted, not just him but all those friends resting there.
> Time to find a friend who could last the distance ...
> Time to write a letter to Corry ... the distant dream ...

Part Three: Their Story Begins ...

Sunday 20 June 1948
CURTAIN CALL TODAY, BATAVIA

Darling,

Tomorrow afternoon MS *Indrapoera* will take me homewards, and weather and wind permitting should deliver me at your doorstep (read ... station) roughly four weeks later.

How does that grab you? I still can't comprehend that at long last it is happening. Can you?

A hectic week is behind us. Exploring Batavia mostly by Becak, the tricycle you can rent for a few guilders. Met up with old friends who had been transferred to the capital; saw some good movies, including *Casablanca*; did a lot of sightseeing; and, apart from one day as duty NCO, was free to do what I liked (to a certain extent!).

A lot of delayed mail came in during the week, including two from you. They had quite some intriguing questions which I prefer not to answer. Rather leave that for when we meet. By then the need for any answers might be smothered by a friendly kiss.

But what happens when you don't like what you see when I stumble out of the train, all nervy and frightened? Does your stationmaster sell instant return tickets as well? I sure hope so! Do tell your mother I like my coffee strong and sweet (same as my girl[s]). The S slipped in by mistake!

I wrote nearly thirty letters of farewell and thanks, not only for the memories, but also a token of affection for the many people who saw me through these dark years in Indonesia. Without their help in many letters, life here would have been so much harder. But no matter how I tried not to show emotion, in the end there is still the hurt of a final goodbye.

I have never mentioned the girls I have been writing to. Some perhaps read between the lines and felt the pain afterwards when they realised there was nothing to read there. Others didn't understand my wording at all and lost interest a long time ago, becoming strangers again after being friends for a while.

Only ONE letter was started with DARLING ...!

My parents will be pleased too about our embarkation and, although Mam never wrote about feeling worried, I know her too well, not to believe otherwise. I also met a nephew who had just arrived from the Netherlands. He seemed so fresh, so young, and so vulnerable. Looking at him made me feel old. Still, I wouldn't swap places, the newcomers have their tasks cut out for them for the next couple of years.

By the time we see Rotterdam again, a thousand days will have passed since we left the Netherlands. Unbelievably long and yet, looking back now, they feel as if my mind is flipping through a mental atlas of faraway places.

Only my diaries and your letters remain, as a reminder that those bygone years were not dreams. I'll take them with me and, perhaps one day in the future, somewhere quiet, you and I might read again what was written in my restless years.

All the distant thoughts, of a young girl called Corry, are neatly tied together with a coloured string. On top of that bundle is your first 'no nonsense, correspondence only!'

In words, if nothing else yet, we have advanced from former 'just friends' to the more eloquent sphere of 'loving strangers'.

For one more month we will be asking ourselves, 'What are we for each other?' At that station in Oudenbosch, there will be the answer! Until then, Corry, a tender goodbye kiss from Insulinde.

PIERRE

PS. You might have to follow the radio news about our exact time of arrival. My phone number in Helmond is 2509. Please call after disembarkation as I can't contact you.

I didn't tell her about the poem she had sent. It was so beautiful, a personal 'thank you' would be more appropriate. I read it again. She had understood exactly what I felt now that departure was close.

Neither Corry nor Pierre could know how prophetic this poem would ultimately prove to be!

Selamat tinggal (goodbye)

It won't be long; the time has come
To leave this land behind;
Looking back, 't went far too fast
Though life was oft' a grind
These lush, green islands of the east
Held me as in a spell;
't is only through a war that raged, I have to say farewell!

I'll miss the folk at the 'pasar'
Their faces, so serene;
Who would exchange a friendly word
Amid a bustling scene.
And I'll miss the naked children, that frolicked in the stream;
Their voices high, calling 'tuan', it seems almost like a dream!

For in a country such as this,
So close to the Netherlands' heart
The roads that once went side by side,
Now, have been wrenched apart.
So many of the Dutch brave sons
Died ... so that they could live.
And is there any sacrifice
Greater than this, to give?

'Selamat tinggal', pearl of the east,
I'll have to leave you now!
But one day I'll return, I know!
I'll manage it, somehow
I gave you three years of my life
And I'll leave my heart behind;
But I'll claim it—when we meet again
To strengthen th' age-old bind!

Corry de Haas

26.   Homeward Bound

Perhaps the length of the homeward journey by sea was a genuine blessing, not only for Pierre, but for the whole contingent, enabling them to not only rest those battle-weary bodies, but, perhaps more importantly, to prepare themselves emotionally for returning to their families, friends, and especially 'civvy street', separating from their comrades-in-arms who they had trusted with their very lives. Pierre writes about this in his description of the journey home.

> Everyone aboard ship wanted the old lady of the sea—MS *Indrapoera*—to hurry along on our final voyage home. However, like all old people, she had developed some hard-to-cure habits, as was the case now. One motor had already given up and the half-speed we were able to maintain had dampened somewhat the euphoria of our first week at sea.
> Standing alone at the railing, I wondered (as I had done over the last couple of days) if I felt the same as the majority who wanted speed more than anything else. Farewelling Indonesia and its people had touched me deeper than I first realised. As if something had been left behind; perhaps in a sense that was true. Part of myself with every footstep—millions of them—as they had criss-crossed so many islands.
> Leaving is dying a little, and it had been done frequently over the nearly 1000 days since we left on that cold November night in 1945. Yet, here I was, reluctant to accept the fact that with every turn of the mighty screws, this troopship was closing the distance to the Netherlands and ...?
> '*Wieder einmal unterwegs,*' on my way once again. How often had I heard that before? The past already out of sight, the future still on hold. Travelling in a vacuum. Another intermezzo in four years of army life. No ties, no bonds with anyone, free to move after so many months of war service.

Except for one, all-important factor! Corry, turning twenty today, 24 June 1948.

The unknown … still … even with letters and photos to bring her closer … she remained a mystery. A lovely girl, judging by the snapshots. An intriguing smile across her face and a pleasant way of putting words to paper when she sensed the need had arisen in that faraway commando.

Yes, I had never touched the texture of her skin or put my hands through that flowing hair. Never met her eyes or embraced that slender body. A long-distance love affair? Impossible!

Perhaps I was afraid of falling in love when the word itself was hardly ever used in our letters.

Did I want this voyage to last forever? To postpone the moment of a rendezvous with a penfriend, who had become much more than just that? Afraid in a real sense—not of the girl, but of the aftermath? Had I lost that feeling of belonging, that perception of attachment that was so close to the surface in my earlier times in the army?

Time to switch off and laze away the endless days of sunshine …

Tuesday 29 June, Colombo in sight, my diary said.

Supplies were loaded aboard. Then, surprise, surprise, a contingent of ATS girls, marching smartly to the farewell music of an army band, joined the bronzed veterans. Many whistles of approval pierced the air when they were welcomed by our CO.

Spare parts for the ship's antiquated engines were hoisted onto the deck and, by nightfall, we lifted anchor.

Early next day we organised a long-distance quiz with *Grote Beer*, another troopship on its way to the Indies. We lost by a narrow margin, perhaps due to the years of tropical sun having affected our brains!

Friday 9 July, 'We enter ADEN,' I wrote in my booklet. The last of diaries was easily kept up to date with so much spare time. Hundreds of small boats surrounded our ship. The Arabs, desperately trying to clinch a deal, showed their wares: cigarettes, rugs or other types of souvenirs.

I bought five cartons of Camel, and, as I wanted to buy Corry a leather handbag, I realised my money had run out. No problem, the merchant yelled out, anything to trade would do. I lowered an old pair of shoes in a basket, together with Dutch coins. He looked at the

Homeward Bound

Dubbeltjes (dimes)—hardly worth bargaining with—and the black leather shoes, and the deal was made. The side of our ship became a gigantic lucky dip with hundreds of tiny baskets going up and down like yo-yos!

As we moved into the Red Sea later the MS *Indrapoera* developed another malfunction. The heat became unbearable as the ship stopped and the anchor was lowered. We drifted in a restricted circle. The sun, up until then a pleasant companion, turned into a ruthless enemy.

When we attended Holy Mass, our padre thanked us for being there. 'Men,' he said, 'the fact that you joined me in this terrible heat proves that you care for what we believe in; also, that those hard years in combat have not destroyed your souls.' It was the shortest sermon I had ever heard from him.

… and the longest and hottest week to cover a mere 1800 kilometres of blazing Red Sea …

Finally, reaching the Suez Canal, our reluctant transport seemed to shake off her lethargy and managed to drop anchor at Port Said. A pleasant surprise awaited us: mail from the Netherlands, including a dozen letters for me. One was from Corry, written on 20 June. I read it several times, letting it all sink in, and felt a longing for a girl I still had to meet for the very first time. One line in her letter touched me deeply.

Yet, a day earlier when I saw Suez and remembered the girl whose written words had become vague and finally disappeared completely, a certain pain of lost memories had filled my eyes.

We entered the Mediterranean Sea, the blue, smooth and cooler surface a welcome change from the last couple of weeks. Several troopships, including the SS *Waterman* [Editor's note: you, the reader, might like to remember this name!] approached at close range, and the contrast between our tanned bodies and the whiteness of the raw recruits going the opposite way was a weird experience.

As we closed the distance and neared Gibraltar, people became quieter. One would have expected a carnival atmosphere, and in some cases that was true. Yet, there came an undertone of seriousness in our conversation. The banter was gradually disappearing as if the realisation of that final week at sea became clear.

'Let it last,' I often said in those last days. 'It will never come our way again!' Friends I was talking to looked at me in surprise, not understanding what I was on about. 'That moment of arrival,' I tried to explain, 'will never be repeated in your life!'

'Don't you want to see your family and friends, then?' Gerry asked, then, adding after some hesitation … 'Or Elly… or Corry…?'

'Of course I do, but the leading-up time is as much part of our homecoming as the actual arrival!' But I was only fooling myself …

I failed to convince anyone. They were all impatient to cover those last 1000 kilometres, especially when a dense fog covered the Atlantic Ocean, slowing us down even more.

We were issued with our European uniforms when temperatures dropped. Finally, on Monday, 26 July, the English coast appeared on the horizon, the fog cleared, a watery sun came out and all was ready for our last day at sea.

Later that evening, the lights of Eastbourne were visible to our left. The Beachy Head beacon put pinpricks of fluorescence across the Channel. The Strait of Dover was choppy as usual, and the MS *Indrapoera* bucked so violently that seasickness sprang up again.

I did not go to sleep that night …

Even seeing Eastbourne in the far distant world of yesteryear had brought on a nostalgic feeling I could hardly control. How long ago was it that the landlady's daughter said to me, 'Pierre, when the war is over and you get married, would you like to spend your honeymoon with us?' At that time there was only a girl in uniform wearing a black beret I could have asked to marry me; that was 1945, not 1948!

The war was over—at least the combat part—but inside it was just beginning: the battle between the old and the new!

Shortly before entering the English Channel we received the following goodbye message from the captain of MS *Indrapoera*.

Homeward Bound

> ### *A word of farewell to all military personnel.*
>
> *Now that the end of our long journey home is near, I would like to express on behalf of myself and the crew a great sense of satisfaction the way you have behaved aboard ship.*
>
> *There was always a good atmosphere of happiness and a strict discipline. You have held the best traditions of Dutch Forces to your utmost ability. I hope therefore, that the return to your Fatherland and the reunion with your loved ones will make an everlasting impression on your life.*
>
> *We wish you strength for an easy transformation into a civilian world.*
>
> *There have been warnings in some newspapers, not to expect gratitude from the majority of the Dutch population. But please be convinced that amongst us, seamen of the East-Indies route, a great understanding exists for what you have achieved in the Dutch East Indies.*
>
> *All the best for your future.*
>
> THE CAPTAIN

That night, as I stood at the railing as I had done so often before, I felt the tug-of-war taking place in my heart. I cried silently, stars being the only witnesses.

At last, I sat down on a forgotten kitbag, felt extremely tired and lonely and dozed off.

When I woke up shivering, we were entering the Hoek of the Netherlands. Three hours later we touched the quay in Rotterdam. Strike Force 8 had returned home.

27. HOMECOMING

In the end there were only four of us left.

The chartered bus—one of many waiting at the Rotterdam docks when MS *Indrapoera* berthed early that morning—had already travelled through half a dozen cities.

Checking his list carefully, the driver would stop at each selected address, where enthusiastic family and friends were patiently waiting. Front doors were decorated, flags flying. It was a grandiose welcome on this warm, sunny day of late July 1948.

At last, our hometown, Helmond, came in sight.

We were sitting together near the driver, pointing out the different buildings and landmarks as we approached the centre. Our voices, rising with excitement, yelled a 'See you around', when the first (after a quick handshake) left the bus. We all lived in adjoining streets and, seeing them depart one by one, the last of Strike Force 8, brought a tight feeling to my chest; a shiver travelled across my spine and goose pimples appeared on my tanned arms.

I was on my own, only one more street to go!

'This is it,' I said to the driver. 'Thanks for looking after us,' and I stepped down onto the pavement.

I was blinded by a flashbulb as eager arms embraced me, and soft hands stroked my face. Words of welcome came from so many sides that I had trouble recognising anyone at all. Nearly choking on my own emotions, I saw through the throng of people the flowers and decorations above the shop's entrance. Three red, white and blue flags unfolded from upstairs windows. A line of potted palm trees forming a guard of honour …

Mam was holding me tight. One of her hairpins scratched my skin, making me bleed. 'He is wounded as well,' someone called out. A boy was pumping my one free hand. Repeatedly he kept saying, 'I'm Will, your brother!' I hardly understood what he meant—he was a kid when I left, now as tall as I.

Dad, my other brothers, neighbours, uncles, aunts, friends … they

Homecoming

were all jostling me as if a long-lost son had finally been found. Probably, that was the way everyone looked at these homecomings. Their sons at last back in the safety of the family, unharmed, at least on the outside.

When I entered the shop, Mam let go of me to give other people a chance to give me a warm welcome. 'Gerard, how are you? Long time no see!' Our handshake firm and sincere. He was that kind of friend who would gladly have given up a career to follow me to the end of the world. He said so anyway. 'You have changed, Pierre: older, wiser perhaps?' He smiled, leaving the implications hanging in the air.

I moved along, shaking hands, kissing more cheeks or lips—depending—and pleasantries went back and forth. Yes, it felt good to be home again.

It soon became obvious that the carefully planned strategy my parents had in mind was doomed. Tonight, they had decided earlier that day, only close family. Tomorrow, the neighbours, and the rest of our relations the day after! But people were still coming, and nobody was leaving; so, by 6 pm, over eighty well-wishers were spread throughout the house.

Dad, using his black-market connections, had bought two boxes of first-class Bols Jonge Genever, and those twenty-four bottles of superb liquid, together with some three hundred Heineken, would guarantee an unending party. It was heart-warming to watch the goings on, the toasting with all my friends and relations.

Here and there, while mingling with the crowd, I could overhear part of the conversations: '... the war has put many a hard year on his face ...'; or, '... he must have gone through a lot, no wonder he has such a staring ...'; and, '... did you see his eyes ... like coal fires...!'

I took it all in, accepting them as compliments if nothing else. They forgot to ask how I really felt and only saw the surface. No one noticed the scars on the inside, and I had no intention at all to delve into the why or how. Of course, my mother, with that sharp, observing instinct of hers, came awfully close to the truth. 'Did it happen to you, son? Did you get hurt inside?' She handed me a glass of crème de menthe, my favourite liqueur.

'Yes,' I said at last, after sipping from the green fluid. 'In many ways it did.' I thought about the twenty-eight men of our Strike Force who stayed behind. But talking about it doesn't always work, even if,

Part Three: Their Story Begins ...

sometimes, you remember things that tear you apart.

Seeing my eyes narrow, she quickly added, 'But now is not the time for sad reminiscence. Tonight, we celebrate, eh Pierre?' As she moved on, she called one of the girls who were helping us out to bring me another drink.

I stood there for a long time, deep in thought, the music of the sound system drifting through the shop. I was born in this house, rode a push-bike before I could hardly walk, grew up, helped in the business at an early age, became a teenager, and fell in love. Then the leaving started, always the leaving; until today; perhaps this was the final homecoming!

There was a nagging feeling inside me, nothing to do with logic. It was something deep asking for a solution. I had grown old too fast. Youth had faded with every passing day. Yet, if I did not stop the process now, it might be too late, forever. There had been times on this long journey home that the whole of my young years beckoned me as if there was a magic somewhere. As if they wanted to be called 'The Good Old Days'.

Many memories still had a nice ring to them, and just as many were associated with sadness, or death even. I tried hard not to think about my first love, Elly, the girl I last saw in her black beret, replacing it instead with the image of another girl I had never met. I wanted to feel at home again and carry on where I left off so many years ago, when one was so young and in love.

Now, the change had taken place. This was 1948, not the heady 44/45. Disillusioned? No, that was too strong a word. I had not made the long trek home to repair. A fresh start was needed. Could Corry supply that requirement? The girl in the picture? The distant dream?

Footsteps coming down on the staircase woke me up from my fantasies. It was Gerard carrying two large beer mugs and obviously looking for me. I gave him a curious look and, for a long, silent moment, I was lost for words, remembering what was said earlier that evening.

'I have always wondered, Pierre, what would have happened if I had followed you that day when you joined the forces and my father called out, "If you leave with him, don't bother to come back!"'

We walked into the near-empty shop and, leaning on one of the counters, drank from our mugs. 'Prosit ... Good to see old friends again.'

'A votre santé.' His French, still with the beautiful intonation of an expensive boarding school. 'I still envy you all those places you have seen, all the people you have met, all ...' and his voice trailed off.

'Aren't you forgetting something, Gerard, like danger and death, the loneliness, the endless waiting?'

After a pause, 'Yes, those as well!'

Here then was a successful shopkeeper, already taking over a thriving business from his ailing father, and yet having a hunger for the life of an adventurer. Of course, in hindsight, reliving someone else's war becomes easy. Yet, he meant every word he said.

'It seems like yesterday that you left for the East Indies, but it must be at least two years, I guess.'

I took my time answering. 'A thousand days, Gerard, a thousand long, hot, often frightening days, not to forget the nights, especially the nights.' He sipped his beer, looking at me with eyes full of questions. I answered them before they were asked.

'There were periods in those years that each felt like a lifetime, nights in ambush that ticked away, second by lonely second; also, weeks that drifted lazily as if time had lost all meaning.'

'Would you do it again?'

I looked at him in surprise. Where for God's sake was the answer? 'You fall in love once, and you volunteer once. You can repeat the first but hardly the second, not when the best years of your life are involved. Or the worst ... It depends which way you look at those times.'

'And Elly?' he asked softly.

I took two bottles of Heineken from a crate behind the counter, poured us some beer, taking my time. I tried to make up my mind how much would be true and how much wishful thinking, if I replied to that question. 'She became a casualty sometime in those three years. While I was in hospital, we lost contact!

'I'll be meeting a penfriend in Oudenbosch ... We liked what we saw in our letters, so perhaps ...?' and left it to Gerard to form his own conclusion.

'Pierre ... telephone,' someone yelled, trying to reach me through the smoke and noise. That cry had been coming all evening as if everyone I knew wanted to say 'Hallo' to the home-coming

Part Three: Their Story Begins ...

commando.

'Pierre speaking.'

'This is Corry from Oudenbosch.'

'Corry, what a lovely surprise! How did you know about the arrival, the *Indrapoera* was several days late!'

'I heard it on the radio this morning. Disembarkation starting at noon, they said, so I figured by now you would have settled in.'

'How are you, *meisje*? I mean, how does it feel being so close now?'

The line stayed silent. At last, a whisper of a sound.

'It's been so long, Pierre, I wanted ... I ...' A tear travelled long-distance, touching my sensitive ear.

'Don't cry, Corry... please. I will be there soon.'

'I know, *jongen*, I know, but just thinking about it makes me all shaky.'

'I'll hold you tight then when we meet, okay?'

'I'm so happy, Pierre, that you are safely home. So happy for you, and me. I can't wait till I see you at the station!'

There was such an honest innocence in that voice. It made my eyes moist. After all these months of letters, this was the real Corry, the distant dream. 'My mother scolded me for not inviting you to the party, but I told her I didn't want to put you on show with eighty people asking who that girl was! I also said we would meet somewhere quiet, just the two of us.'

'She must be glad to see you back again, Pierre.'

'Well, actually several people have already asked when I am leaving again, so there can be another party.'

She laughed, a sparkling sound of happiness and something else, like a promise perhaps for later. 'I must go now. All my small change has gone, *dag jongen*. See you at the station.'

'Yes, the 14.55 train, remember? I love you ...' The line was already dead, the last words still in transit.

The unending party swallowed me up once more.

Gerard and I joined the dancing throng of young people. Mieps' younger sister, Tonny, grabbed my arm. 'Come on, Pierre, let's swing and don't look so serious. You did come back in one piece. Enjoy yourself!' She was an expert flirt and used her charms to capacity. Suddenly, while cavorting through the room, I laughed out loud. 'That's better,' she giggled and held me closer.

Suddenly I heard somebody (I can't recall who) whisper, 'Wouldn't that be lovely, two brothers and two sisters?' They were referring, of course, to my brother Jan and Mieps—married while I was in Sumatra—and Tonny and I.

I had news for them, I thought, smiling on the inside; my mind was already travelling ahead to a station, some hundred kilometres from where we were having a party. A girl would be waiting there; letters would be replaced by an embrace, a kiss would hold us together, even for the briefest of moments! I felt the top pocket of my uniform. Yes, Corry's last letter, received in Suez was still there; it contained one special sentence. But it was enough. The waiting time was nearly over ...

28. FIRST MEETING

Near five in the morning, Gerard and I helped the last two survivors on a pushbike. One uncle across the handlebars, the other planted in the saddle. As they zigzagged on the pavement, they just managed to avoid an early morning police patrol.

'A bit late for a party, De Haas!'

'Never too late, Constable, never too late!' And I went back inside. But sleep was far away. I re-read the last letter from Corry:

20 June 1948
OUDENBOSCH

My dearest Commando Pierre,

It is a quiet Sunday evening, just past eight, a warm summer day coming to a close. Memories of Glen Miller drift through the house, 'Moonlight Serenade', the haunting melody ... Mam, knitting as usual, sits in her easy armchair, the men are playing billiards at the local.

I ...? Well, trying to write this last letter to Indonesia seems as difficult as that first one, already so long ago, the 'no nonsense' episode, that in hindsight was a waste of well-meant advice. Or perhaps it was not a waste. In one of your letters, you said that my letter caught your attention because of it. More than fifteen months have passed since that hesitant beginning and look what you have done to me!

Waiting anxiously time and time again for mail from Sumatra, to read that you came through another day 'INTACT'!

Now you will be embarking on a troopship again for the voyage home to a warm welcome from family and friends. Somewhere, backstage, a girl will be waiting. She will turn twenty this week and should now qualify for inclusion in your 'most wanted list'! Your advertisement read: ... lovely, pretty girl, age 20 ...!

More than ever before, I feel convinced that, somehow, I have

First Meeting

graduated to the top of the class and that all the other penfriends of yours have faded away, as departure time is approaching. Presumptuous? Yes, I know, but your last letter, before leaving Sumatra, gave you away, Pierre. Your armour came down when you wrote that beautiful quotation, ending with: 'not death ... but love.'

I like that very much; even made me cry.

Also, the enclosed photo, coloured in for more reality, showed me a new person for the very first time. Before, all those black-and-white snapshots of you—however welcome they were—portrayed you in a different way, kind of remote, even untouchable!

Now, my young man, you have come alive!

If only I could hold that face in my hands, feel the texture of your skin, let those hard, penetrating eyes enter my mind, share their feelings and dissolve the hurt they encountered.

I realise full well how long a wait it will be because patient I am not! There is so much I want to tell you and even more I would love to ask, but our correspondence will close with this letter, so, alas, all the questions will have to wait until you arrive.

In all honesty, thinking of the coming meeting, sometime next month, frightens me, for although in your letters you have become very real, perhaps I don't know you at all!

However, we have a month before the big day, time to prepare ourselves for a rendezvous that, hopefully, shall never end!

I will be thinking of you, mister Sergeant, sir!

It is nearly ten, the last rays of that glorious sun have disappeared, twilight is fading ... and I think I love you ...

Tomorrow is the longest day of the year and the longest month in my life is about to start!

Goodnight, Pierre, wherever you are, may your dreams be as sweet as mine. Kiss Insulinde a farewell from me ...

Your Corry, forever?! I hope so ...

PS. As yet, not many trains come this way. Every three hours is the schedule. Mam said, 'Take the 14.55.' The coffee and I will be waiting ...!

... and I think I love you ...

Part Three: Their Story Begins …

Early that afternoon, in Oudenbosch:

'Cor, stop looking in that mirror. It will crack in a minute!'

How she hated that word 'Cor' instead of Corry, and Mam always used it when short-tempered.

'No harm in making myself pretty, is there?'

'Well, it's not the queen who's coming, only a penfriend.'

'That's what you think. He's much more than just a friend you write letters to.'

'How would you know? You've never met!'

'I know, Mam, I just know.'

'What, from a few words sent in an envelope? Paper is patient, they say.'

'We wrote a million words to each other and there are no secrets between us, and Mam, stop teasing me. You are as nervous as I am. I'll be off then, Mam.'

'Wait a minute, my girl, it's still half an hour before the train is due. You could give me a hand with the spuds, seeing we have a guest tonight.'

'I want to be there early. Pierre wrote me once: always arrive ahead of schedule. That way you can reconnoitre the situation.' *Well said*, she thought. *You will be a great actress one day!*

'What's this? A military exercise? It's only an old station!'

Corry slipped into the hallway, had a last look in the full-length mirror, adjusted her shoulder straps slightly and opened the front door.

'Tell him we've got spare ribs for dinner. That will hurry him along,' her mother called out.

'What if he likes my ribs better?!' she yelled back and, closing the door, she giggled, the nervousness of this first meeting with him at least temporarily subdued.

It was only a ten-minute walk from their side of the village to the station. She took her time, enjoying every step and every second in anticipation of something new, something daring, born nearly eighteen months ago. There was no thought of possible disappointment, no negative feelings that it wouldn't work out.

That phone call at his homecoming party confirmed what she felt now. In that split second before the line went dead, she had heard very distinctly 'I lov', and then came the click. It was enough. Her ears were as sensitive as his, the way he picked up that escaping tear.

She continued slowly and, when reaching the church, she crossed the road on impulse, entered the dark basilica and said a silent prayer: for our future, she reflected and, after the sign of the cross, closed the massive oak doors behind her. The large clock showed there was still ten minutes to spare when she reached the near-empty station.

Sitting down on one of the wooden benches with the bright afternoon sun warming her face, Corry felt a thrill in her body: a desire so all-consuming that for a fleeting moment the thought of a distant dream entered her mind. She closed her eyes, feeling herself drifting to another world, where reality had no entry.

Floating across a sea of letters, she saw a village with palm trees and bamboo huts, an army of green berets marching along the dusty road. A face materialised—only ONE —and then came the recognition, just as a faint whistle brought her back to the station. She stood up, facing the direction from where Pierre would be coming. The heat haze shimmered where, faraway, the rails met.

The time of waiting was nearly over …

She was the only one on Platform 2. Meanwhile, on the train, Pierre was just as nervous.

'Why don't you sit down, Sergeant? You make the place look untidy.' The voice startled me.

'Sorry, er, madam, I was far away,' and taking the seat opposite her, carefully hiked up my trousers, letting my fingers glide over the perfect crease in my uniform.

She followed my movements with bright eyes. 'I'll bet you are meeting a penfriend in Rotterdam?' she said, still with that intriguing smile on her face.

I wondered how she had guessed, at least partly, but then the answer dawned: with so many veterans returning from war, many penfriends might be waiting. 'Correct with the first, but not in that city. I'm changing trains at the next stop.'

She was smartly dressed, late thirties, an eager, open city face, sharp features. Sharp mind too, I thought. 'My eldest daughter used to write to a corporal in Sumatra. He came home last month.' She had that easy, fluent conversation, like most city dwellers have.

'He must have been from Strike Force 7.'

She looked at me in surprise. 'You fought together?'

I nodded.

There was a long silence then. 'No one returning from that war seems to be keen to talk about it,' she said at last, giving me another inquiring look.

'War is never easy to translate into words, madam; perhaps the sun also affected the grey matter, here,' pointing at my head. We both laughed.

I felt the train slowing down, got up, took my overnight bag from the rack and planted the green beret on my head. When I adjusted it, she said, 'You don't see many of them around. Your girlfriend won't have any trouble finding you in a crowd.' The train stopped. 'I hope she'll be as happy as my daughter.'

'I hope so too, madam. Nice talking to you,' and stepped outside.

The south-bound was waiting at the opposite platform. As we moved again, I looked at the passing scenery, the green of the fields, the dark cattle, a distant farm on a narrow country road. So peaceful after Indonesia and so full of hope for the future, I thought.

... 'I think I love you...' The words danced in front of me, moving to the rhythm of the train. I took the letter, received in Suez, and read it yet again.

'No nonsense, correspondence only'. That is how she had started as a penfriend, and 'I think I love you...' how she had finished. Within a few minutes I would know who the true Corry was, who had written those lines.

The train entered the outskirts of Oudenbosch and, looking outside, I could see the church with its large dome. April 1945—if my memory was correct—a Sunday afternoon when I, together with the congregation, had prayed there. Perhaps, without knowing, Corry had already become part of my life, as we thanked God for being spared.

We slowed down, crossed the main thoroughfare of the village,

First Meeting

and came to a shuddering halt. I grabbed my bag, put on my green beret and exited from the train, not sure if I was remembering to breathe. There was only one girl waiting. The photos received so many months ago did not do justice at all to this sparkling picture of twenty years of youth!

I walked up to her, saluted and said softly, 'If you are Corry ... I am Pierre.'

We met in a gentle kiss, as this was only the beginning! The old station clock looked at us, winked with its hand, and moved it to twelve. It was three in the afternoon of 29 July 1948. The sun embraced us; a welcoming breeze sprang up from behind the large oak trees surrounding the station square. We linked arms as young people do, close ... intimate. A smile travelled between us, the waiting time over now.

Our first walk through Oudenbosch, the first of many more to come!

First photos

Pierre in a slouch hat...a premonition of things to come?

Observation post ... Pierre kneeling in front

The hasty, Aerogram sent to Corry while Pierre's patrol was cut off. It concludes with *One day I would like to meet you, just the two of us.*

Pierre with some unknow comrades, photo captioned: *The Three Musketeers*

Taken during a village clearance operation, Pierre (L)

Homecoming in Helmond

First photo together

PART FOUR: BUILDING OUR LIFE TOGETHER ... AND OUR FAMILY.

29. 'THE BEST YEARS OF OUR LIVES'

From this time until some eleven years later, there are no surviving diaries or letters, just photo albums with some scattered labels of places and times. What we do know, however, is that their relationship not only blossomed but also became very fruitful in that, by 1959, the de Haas family included five children, aged seven and under, of which this editor is the eldest. But I am getting ahead of Corry and Pierre's unfolding story ...

To mark the first years they spent together, Corry kept a photo album titled *The Beste Jaaren Van Ons Leven* (The Best Years of Our Lives), and the date on the cover is 30 July 1948, the day after their first meeting at Oudenbosch railway station. Corry dedicated the album: 'In memory of the wonderful days after our first meeting; if the same sun keeps shining into our hearts, then everything will be well.' Photos taken the next day—a rare sunny day in the Netherlands—on a trip into the nearby Liesbosch park, clearly capture the happiness she was feeling.

Interestingly, in those same photos, Pierre is still wearing his uniform, even though he would have been on leave. The photos suggest that he is a little formal and restrained. This is perhaps to be expected; servicemen and women who have returned from tours of duty in combat situations would well understand how difficult the initial adjustment back to 'normal' life might have been for Pierre. Only a few days earlier, he was still on a

Part Four: Building Our Life Together ... And Our Family

troopship, and, for the past five and a half years before that, his life had been both turbulent and completely unpredictable.

For the next few weeks, Corry and Pierre enjoyed extended bicycle trips, movies, dining out together, activities that allowed them to share the simple pleasure of life and get to know one another a little better. Then, on 7 September 1948, Pierre was discharged from the army, and on that day he wrote these words, later preserved in the same photo album:

> So, this is the farewell, not between us two, but from a piece of my life. Perhaps I am the only one of all those young men who is thinking about these things this evening, but I do want to mark this hour because it brings to an end a time full of adventure, things that a normal person would never have experienced, but which also brought the start of another period filled with a new happiness and hope for a much better life.
>
> I am dragging these words out of myself, with the help of my girl, Corry, who is sitting next to me, so that, later, she can think back on this last hour, in which I am also feeling so very, very good about what she already means for me.
>
> We will keep these words because they signal the beginning of a new and better life.
>
> May God help us on this journey, till we are bonded together for all time.

One can only imagine the mixed emotions going through Pierre as he was experiencing this pivotal moment in his young life: looking forward with hope to a very different future, a much more settled and predictable life with Corry in the Netherlands; and looking back to a sustained period of wartime high adventure, shared risks and mateship, always on the move through the wide-open spaces and islands of the tropics. Time would show, however, that he could never again settle down in the Netherlands, a small, highly developed country where the weather mostly drives its citizens indoors.

Two months later, on 11 November, Pierre turned twenty-five. Finally, after the turmoil of recent years, this birthday, also a significant milestone, could be properly celebrated with his family, friends and, especially, with Corry. Perhaps those enjoying the occasion might have reflected on how much life someone just turning twenty-five had already lived, even if they didn't know how close Pierre came to dying only two years earlier.

During these first months, Corry and Pierre each continued living at home, Corry with her parents in Oudenbosch, and Pierre in Helmond. Times were different then, and given the dictates of their Catholic faith, there is no chance that they would have been living together before they were married, or even considered that as a possibility! Pierre went back to work in the family business to provide an income while Corry kept working at the solicitor's office. So, except for weekends, special occasions such as Christmas and birthdays, and for annual holidays, their relationship would have been mostly at a distance, Helmond being 100 km from Oudenbosch.

Corry writes about this period, and the adjustments she (and her parents!) needed to make:

> Until I met Pierre, I had not been away from home for any length of time. Because I had led a rather sheltered life and I grew up an innocent, I was not aware of its realities and still wore my rose-coloured glasses when I met Pierre.
>
> After his return from Indonesia, we met and fell deeply in love and a new world opened. Finally, Mum and Dad had to let me out of their sight, and out from under their wings. We took turns spending the weekends at each other's homes, which was not at all to Dad's liking, and it was Mum who initially gave the okay.
>
> I was very self-conscious. Walking into a restaurant or cafeteria I at first insisted that Pierre lead the way, which he flatly refused. His 'Don't be silly' soon cured me. Pierre was confidence personified, probably through his harsh commando training, which certainly had prepared him for any situation life threw at him. He opened many doors for me. Like all young people we loved dancing and going to the cinema. I wasn't spoiled in that regard; there was seldom a film worth seeing at the local hall, and Mum would not allow me to go to dances in the neighbouring towns.

Part Four: Building Our Life Together ... And Our Family

Pierre lived in a big industrial city; there were plenty of things to see and do and I loved being with his family. His mother was a gentle, darling woman who I soon addressed as Mama. His father, however, was a totally different character. A brusque businessman who seldom smiled, he made me feel extremely uncomfortable at the start. Later, though, when I knew him a little better and found he did not bite, I started to relax around him.

Pierre had four brothers. When I came onto the scene, two were married and both owned shops. The youngest, Will, was away studying, and Pierre and his younger brother, Ted, managed the family business. It was a real men's household and vastly different from mine, so it took quite some time to get used to this.

Their 'Best Years' album carefully records the joy of Corry and Pierre's first Christmas together, an occasion which, from that time on, would always be a special celebration for them, and subsequently for their growing family. Pierre, learning from his Mam, always took great pains to set up a beautiful nativity scene and a brightly lit Christmas tree.

Another event which became a 'first' for Corry and Pierre to celebrate together was *Carnaval* (Dutch for Carnival), in February 1949. These festivities are still held annually in the Netherlands in the days leading up to Lent, which is a period of fasting and prayer leading up to the celebration of Easter. *Carnaval* is a time for fun and going a little bit crazy, including dressing up in extravagant costumes. On their first outing as a couple, Corry and Pierre won first prize for their costumes, probably prepared under the experienced eye of Pierre's mother.

Apart from an extended bicycle holiday in the summer of that year, with the photos now showing a much more relaxed Pierre than in the first weeks of their time together, 1949 came and went unremarked and unrecorded.

30. ENGAGEMENT AND MARRIAGE

Some may be surprised at the length of time between Pierre's return to the Netherlands and the date of their engagement on 10 April 1950. However, such a delay was neither unusual for that period, nor should it be unexpected given their vastly different backgrounds and life experiences until the time Pierre stepped off the train in Oudenbosch for the first time. There would have been many aspects of their vastly different personalities to understand and negotiate before deciding to take the next steps. Also, marriage then was universally regarded as something more binding and permanent than it is today.

Corry captures some of this in a prayer that she wrote prior to their engagement ('Pierke' and 'Corke' are their terms of endearment for each other in Dutch):

Prayer to prepare for our engagement:

Mother Mary, now Pierke (Corke) and I are so close to our engagement being only weeks away from preparing, we come together full of trust in you.

We come to ask for your help and support, you, who, with St Joseph and Jesus, have formed the most wonderful family of all time.

We really want to remain honest and happy children of God, pure in our courtship.

After all, our engagement is a gateway to marriage, and that is why we are asking you for the blessing of your support and enlightenment in these last weeks, so that we do not take the first big step of our lives unprepared for what will become an eternal commitment to each other.

Give us the strength to always help each other, let us better understand each other, lift us up and may we live a life which follows your example. Strengthen our love, our trust in one another and bring

Part Four: Building Our Life Together ... And Our Family

us speedily to the goal for which you have brought us together.

Together with You, as intercessor with Jesus, everything will be even more beautiful than it has been already. Amen. And so, with enough flower arrangements to open a florist shop, as well as many other gifts, the happy couple celebrated their engagement with a reception for their families and friends, held at the home of Pierre's parents in Helmond.

Three months later, on 11 July 1950, Corry and Pierre were civilly married at Oudenbosch City Hall. This was the normal practice in those times, to have a civil wedding first which would then enable Corry and Pierre to go onto the waiting list for a place to live. Housing for families was then, and remains to this day, very scarce and with an awfully long waiting list.

Corry and Pierre's wedding in the Catholic Church—known as the Sacrament of Marriage—took place in Oudenbosch on Tuesday, 14 August 1951. Their marriage was celebrated in Corry's much-loved Basilica of Sts Agatha and Barbara, the very place where that commando in the green beret stood all those years ago, and where, unknowingly as strangers to each other, Corry and Pierre would both have been praying under the same roof for the first time. Two days after their wedding, Corry and Pierre were in the United Kingdom on their honeymoon, and also took the opportunity to visit some of their wartime friends with whom they had maintained contact. Corry writes:

> We had been married for two whole days and were staying (in London) with Sidney and Muriel. I had met Sid and his friend Frank in 1944, soon after we were liberated by the Americans.
>
> While Pierre was stationed in Eastbourne, after his commando training in Scotland (end 1944), he was billeted with a dear old lady. Everyone called her Mother Christmas. (Christmas was her family name.) Her daughter Alice often came over for a visit, met Pierre there and told him, 'Promise me, if you ever get married, you'll spend your honeymoon with us.'

14ᵗʰ OF AUGUST 1951

The rich tones of Lohengrin's
Bridal March
Echo from the marble columns,
Fill my heart with a surge of happiness
Not experienced before.

At last,
The day we looked forward to with such
Longing
Has arrived.
The long wait finally over,
Wiped away by two simple words.

The laughing eyes of those dear to us
Seem to fade away into the background
Of my youth.

Later today we'll be together
In fulfilment of a once-spoken promise.

You seem so self-assured.
What are your thoughts?

My whole being longs for your touch,
Yet there's a trace of uncertainty
in my heart,
I've never known a man before …

Under this white veil of innocence
I enter a new life,
The Life of a Woman.

We kneel at the altar and
The 'Yes, I do' floats as a breath
of air
Towards the vaulted ceiling.

Corry de Haas

Part Four: Building Our Life Together ... And Our Family

These were the reasons we had chosen England, so Pierre could keep his promise and we both could catch up with very precious friends. We were made very welcome and were spoiled something terrible.

We had timed our trip well. England was in a festive mood celebrating the Festival of Britain, and London was a dream.

We spent three days with Sid and Muriel and were able to see most of the festivities. We walked everywhere until I thought my feet would drop off, but we had to make the most of these few days.

Battersea Park was alive with colour, music and entertainment; we visited some of the exhibitions as well and enjoyed ourselves tremendously. We did all the touristy things. Visited St Paul's and the Tower; walked the length of Pall Mall to Buckingham Palace. There was so much to see. I fell in love with London then. I was absolutely thrilled. To actually see these places I had only read about was beyond anything I'd ever dreamed of.

While walking across Tower Bridge one day, I spotted a London Bobby on patrol on the other side. I nudged Pierre in the ribs, saying, 'Look there, a true London Bobby! Wow! I wish I could have a photo of him. Can you think of anything more English than a Bobby?'

'That's easily fixed,' Pierre said, and much to my embarrassment he waved the chap over, while I stood there open mouthed.

He crossed the road, approached us and asked, 'Yes, sir, how can I help you?'

'Officer, my wife would like me to take a photo of you. Is that all right?'

'But, madam,' he joked, with dry London wit, 'there are so many more beautiful sights to photograph in London than me.'

What could I say? I blushed furiously, and said, 'Well, it will make a great souvenir.'

He complied gracefully. Pierre gestured to me to join him and took the photo, using the Tower Bridge as background, while thoughts of murdering my new husband were foremost in my mind. Still, it remains one of my treasured photographs.

We had a wonderful time and were made very welcome by our friends, both in London and Eastbourne where we spent a week with Alice, and her husband Frank.

As bad as the war years were for us all, they cemented friendships

Engagement and Marriage

that were enduring. Mum and Dad had opened their home to so many lonesome allied soldiers and made them welcome, and they had not forgotten their hospitality, although we could not offer them much more than ersatz tea or coffee and a dry army biscuit. Still, for a few days they had a home, till they had to go back and fight a war, while we could only pray they would come through it unharmed.

Not long after returning home from their honeymoon, Corry and Pierre moved into their first home, a first-floor unit above a corner shop at 31 Veestraat, in the business district of Helmond. This unit was blessed by the parish priest on 15 October 1951, by which time Corry and Pierre were already expecting their first child.

31.   BUSINESS AND BABIES

Corry and Pierre then entered a blur of business and babies which was to demand every moment of their time for the next eight years. There was no time for writing, although initially Corry did painstakingly prepare baby albums to record the first years of each of their oldest children. However, and sadly, as more babies arrived, even this project proved too much for her. Life simply became too busy.

This editor was born in June 1952, followed by:
- Mona: August 1953
- Brigitte: May 1955
- Simone: December 1956
- Veronique: October 1958

The de Haas family remained in Helmond, but when the upstairs unit became too small for their rapidly growing family, Pierre and Corry were allocated a larger terraced house, with a small garden at the rear, at 34 Burgemeester van Houtlaan, Helmond.

Pierre continued to work in his father's business in Helmond until 1955. It seems, however, that, deep down, he remained very restless, unable to settle down within the confines of the post-war Netherlands. Also, the relationship between Pierre and his father remained fraught, and indeed worsened as his father's drinking took an even greater hold.

Like many returned soldiers, Pierre was keen to maintain contact with his comrades. In 1955, he co-organised the first reunion of 3 Company of 8 Battalion, the unit he served in while in the Dutch East Indies. These reunions steadily grew in number, as did similar reunions of his commando unit. Many years later, Pierre returned to the Netherlands to once again be part of this elite group of veterans. Being a commando always remained a high point of Pierre's life, although he never spoke very much about his war experiences.

Business and Babies

On leaving the family business in late 1955, Pierre was keen to emigrate. However, Pierre's mother learned that new shops were being built in Nijmegen. The town's business centre was being rebuilt after the shocking damage it had suffered during WW II when an allied bomber pilot, thinking he had crossed the border into Germany, dropped his entire load on this historic town. Both Pierre's mum and Corry hoped that opening his own business would be the answer to Pierre's deep restlessness and wanderlust.

So, the family moved to Nijmegen, into a first-floor apartment above their shop at 46 Houtstraat. Over time, Pierre built a highly successful home-lighting and bicycle business, but, like most small business owner/operators, found it all-consuming, so that there was little time available for his young family. Taking care of the family was mostly Corry's domain, while Pierre took care of the business. And so their lives steadily grew apart, and the young couple who had fallen madly in love was already a distant memory as a new and much harder reality, the pressures of a young family and a demanding business, set in and kept increasing with each passing year. Something had to give …

First day out at Liedenbos forest

Bikes in Holland were, and still are, the transport of choice

Engagement photo with their parents, and 'al die blommen'...all those flowers

Their civil wedding

On the day of their marriage in the Catholic Church

The bridal party with Ted, Pierre's brother and his wife Mientje

Corry and Pierre

That London Bobby!

The babies, clockwise from the top: Peter, Simone, Veronique, Brigitte, Mona ... and later in Australia, Diana, shown with Pierre

Still time for fun...Corry and Pierre celebrating carnival, February 1955

The de Haas shop in Nijmegen

PART FIVE: EMIGRATION

As their story continues, we will now rely almost exclusively on Corry's unpublished autobiographical story of our family's migration experience. She wrote this many years later, but drew upon her many letters to family, contemporary newspaper articles for a Dutch periodical, and journals, to produce a reliable, and, at times, very detailed account. Where possible, given that I was still a young child during those years, I have added my own recollections of the more significant events.

32.   No Way!

One evening in March 1959, in their flat above the shop, Corry and Pierre were sitting down to enjoy a coffee, shop shut for the day and children all in bed. Little did she know what was coming.

>He dropped the bombshell just when I took the first sip of coffee. Did I hear right?
>
>'What was that?' I asked my husband, hoping I had misunderstood.
>
>'What would you say if I told you I wanted to emigrate?'
>
>Life stopped, as if all the clocks had been put on hold. I felt the blood drain from my face, icy fingers travel down my spine. 'What would I say?' Panic tightened my throat. 'I would say you'd taken leave of your senses, that's what I would say.'
>
>He sighed. 'Please don't start. At least allow me to talk this through. Just think ...'
>
>Really frightened now, I took a gulp of coffee and air at the same time, which made me splutter. 'I do not have to think, I can ... I can tell you here and now, no way. If you want a change, that is fine by me, but I'm not going to emigrate. Just as a matter of curiosity, where would you have us go?'
>
>'Australia,' was his prompt reply.
>
>'To Australia? Good grief, going to the other side of the world? You might as well say Siberia; you wouldn't get back from there either.'
>
>I clattered the cup back on its saucer. 'And another thing, what would you do there? You have always been in business; you are not a tradesman. They are looking for tradesmen there. We have a good income here from the shop. What else do you want? Why is it suddenly so wrong to earn a living this way?'
>
>The bluish-pink burners of the gas heater were going full blast, yet I felt as if I would never be warm again. I looked around the cosy room; everything here had its own story to tell, a story which had

begun at our wedding nine years ago. His voice brought me back to the present.

'I feel we can't go on the way we are. You know things haven't been exactly rosy between us.'

'I know, and whose fault is that?' I shouted, furious now. 'If you were home a bit more, we would all be better for it. We could do things together instead of leading separate lives.'

His face darkened, a deep frown settling on his brow, mouth one straight line. 'Don't let us go into all this now, darling. I am trying to sort it out in my mind. I haven't been happy in the Netherlands, not since I came back from Indonesia.'

'Well, well, that's news. You have only been back eleven years. Now suddenly everything here is wrong?'

'This is not something recent. It started a long time ago. I would like a different life for us. I don't know ... a change of lifestyle maybe? I keep thinking how it would be to live in a country with plenty of sunshine and room to move. Here, I feel fenced in all the time; I've lost all interest in the business.'

'I'll say you've lost interest in the business, but not in your so-called business trips, have you?' God, I sounded like a hag. Was this me talking? He was silent.

I had been knitting, but now threw it down on the table. Eyes streaming, I stomped into the bedroom, slamming the door shut behind me. Here we were again at the exact same point in our marriage where we were four years ago. I had thought, since we opened our own business, all ideas of emigrating had vanished. I was wrong. The unrest and problems with settling down were still there; it had not changed his mind at all, just postponed what I saw as inevitable now.

He followed me into the bedroom, sat down beside me. I turned my head, did not want him to see my tears. He shook my shoulder. 'Corry, please, I want only the best for us all. I don't like it either when things are not right between us. Look,' he said, 'all I ask you is to think about it, nothing else.'

I sat up, steeled myself. 'I can think about this from now until doomsday, but I won't change my mind.' He left me then, quietly closing the door behind him.

Part Five: Emigration

After a restless night, filled with nightmarish dreams, Corry woke to another wet dreary day, a steady soaking drizzle further dampening her spirits as the conversation of the previous evening hit her with renewed force. She knew she had a problem, one that time would not solve and one that would not just fade away.

Nevertheless, the subject of emigration wasn't broached for a few weeks, but that word hung between them, as visible as if it had concrete form. One night, instead of going downstairs to do the books, Pierre told Corry that he had seen a film at the local hall about Australia, and the various migrant centres, also mentioning that he was very surprised at the number of people who were there. Clearly, he was most impressed, and perhaps even more enthusiastic about the sunshine, wide open spaces and beautiful sandy beaches.

Corry's throat felt as if two hands were pressing on her windpipe.

'Too bad you can't live on sunshine.' I tried to swallow; my tears close to the surface once again. 'Tell me, what will we do there? With five little children and no job waiting when we arrive? What will we live on, for Chrissake?' I goaded and saw he was losing patience, and fast.

'The government has made provisions for that. If you can't find a job straight away, they pay you unemployment benefits; from this board and accommodation is deducted, but there will be some money left over for everyday expenses.'

'How much?'

'About one pound six. Not much I know, but there are no further hidden costs.'

'Let me see, that is about ten guilders a week to spend on a family of seven? Throw all this away for one of your whims? No, Pierre, I will never agree to this. If you are sick of the shop, sell it, get a job somewhere. It doesn't matter what. Anything is better than going to the end of the world to live on rosy promises. Who will guarantee you'll get work there?'

'You know I'm not afraid of hard work. I'll find something.' His mouth hardened, lips one grim line.

Lost for words I looked at him, noticed the tightening around his

No Way!

mouth, and knew I was in for a fight I had every chance of losing. My mouth dry, I jumped up, went to the hall, grabbed my raincoat and slammed out the door. My steps sounded hollow on the apartment block's concrete steps; my eyes stinging with unshed tears. A light drizzle filtered down. Oh no, now I had forgotten my umbrella.

I walked, tramped all over town, stopping now and then at the brightly lit windows of the inner-city shops, but I didn't see any of it. My gaze had turned inwards. The cadence of my footsteps tapped out one single word on the pavements, Australia, Australia.

At last, I found myself in the park on the banks of the river Waal. The evening's tranquillity enveloped me, soothed the raw edges of my day, the town's traffic just a low hum in the background. It had stopped raining, and a young moon played hide and seek with the few remaining clouds. I loved this time of day, always had. An early mist crept silently along the river, out of reach, like the answers I sought so desperately. This was all so familiar. There was no peace for me today. Where to turn? Where to go? Who could help me in this? Could anyone?

I realised I alone could answer these questions. Life could not go on as it was. We had not been happy in recent years. Would my husband's wanderlust be the root of all our troubles? Would we be able to start afresh somewhere new? But what to do about the children? Peter and Mona were at school, adored the teachers and had their little friends here. I could not, would not, take them away from the life they knew. Why should I? It was cruel. They were secure here; what would it do to them?

Suddenly I saw a familiar figure approach. I would recognise that stride anywhere, straight, military.

'I knew I would find you here. I began to worry; you were gone so long.'

I did not answer, scanned his face. What went on behind that mask he wore? After nearly ten years of marriage, he was still a stranger in many ways. What winding roads did he travel? What demons did he fight?

'Please, Co, let's talk,' he began. 'I want a better life for us, honest.'

I flared like a blowtorch, the bitterness of past hurts rising to the surface. 'A better life? I don't think you have anything to complain about. Your life has been rather good so far. You have gone your own

Part Five: Emigration

way without any regard for me or the children.'

He had no answer. My heart beat a rhythm totally out of step with the rest of me. 'And you want me to believe that going to the other side of the world will change that? Do you believe this yourself? Be honest with me.'

His face looked dark and yet ... There was something new in his eyes, something hard to define.

'I promise there will be changes, and you know I never go back on a promise.' That much was true; he had proven this in the past.

'Look,' he said, 'you don't have to decide anything yet; just think about a migration now and then and what it would mean for us as a family. Weigh the "for" and "against" in your mind and give yourself a chance to get familiar with the idea. For now, that is all I ask. Why don't you read some of the pamphlets I brought home from the migration office? Find out about the country and don't be afraid—I shan't force you, Co.'

I was silent, sighed and suggested, 'We'd better go back to the children. They're alone.'

He held me back. 'Friends?' I looked into his eyes, a long searching look, and tried to see how much of this he meant. A plea stared back. I hesitated ... took his hand. He embraced me, pressed my head into his shoulder, his lips seeking mine. 'Please, Corry, let's try,' he whispered. 'I want us to get back what we once shared together.'

The rising moon floated like a silver disc behind a wisp of cloud. The river flowed gently, a sheet of polished pewter shimmering in the patchy moonlight. We turned our backs to her and descended the stairs. Whatever the future held for us was waiting in the wings of life's theatre.

33. A POSSIBILITY?

Once again, the word 'emigration' was not mentioned for a few weeks. Business was brisk and there was no time for a serious talk. Nevertheless, the information about Australia grew steadily, as various folders and brochures were strategically placed in their apartment and Corry figured Pierre still attended any information nights in town.

She simply ignored it all.

> I wished secretly for a giant hand with the power to push this Australia further into the surrounding oceans and off the globe. There were subtle changes, however, which I could not ignore. I am no sceptic and could not fail to notice the little extra attention I received. The cold atmosphere of indifference changed to a warmer climate. We often shared a good laugh again and I gradually started to relax, hoping this unrest had been a short hiccup in our life.

Then Pierre came upstairs for his lunch one day and showed Corry a letter from the Immigration Department with an invitation to attend the screening of a film about Queensland.

> He handed me the letter saying, 'This came just now,' and when I finished reading it added, 'Are you coming with me this time? They have some lovely films, and it does not bind you to anything.'
>
> Tempted, despite my misgivings, I agreed, but stipulated at the same time, 'This doesn't mean I've changed my mind, Pierre, it's just an outing.'
>
> 'Okay, okay,' he replied impatiently. 'You will come then?'
>
> I nodded yes.
>
> He wolfed down his lunch—he always ate on the run—then went back down to the shop. For the rest of the day, I felt quite nervous; did not know what to expect. Was this a ploy to sell Australia? Would

Part Five: Emigration

they expect something in return, such as instant applications?

We drove to the hall and on entering I saw it was packed. Were all these people prospective candidates? Future migrants? Impossible. I said as much to Pierre. 'Don't tell me all these people are going to emigrate?'

'A great percentage will,' he replied. 'Don't forget, many young farmers are leaving the country as there's not enough land left to divide between the sons in the family, not enough on which to make a decent living here in the Netherlands. That is why they're venturing out, to New Zealand, Canada and Australia as well.'

I sighed, still couldn't fathom it all, yet in one of her letters Mum had written some of the larger families in Oudenbosch were leaving for New Zealand, and for that very reason, a better future for their children.

The lights dimmed. The murmur of voices abated. Wisps of cigar and cigarette smoke wafted upwards across the screen as the first scenes appeared. I sat back in my chair, thinking that tonight perhaps I would see what this was all about, what people were seeking so far from home. Soon, however, I sat on the edge of my seat, mesmerised by the beautiful scenery. Pure, wide sandy beaches, hazy mountains, a wide sweep of ocean, dancing palm trees on esplanades which seemed to stretch forever. What a pity this was not in colour. It would've been magic. I poked Pierre in the ribs. 'I now know what you meant, when you said it was just like the south of France. It is remarkably similar, but much bigger, wider.'

'I knew you would like it,' he said. 'You still haven't stopped talking about the Riviera since we were there a few years ago. It looks such a lovely country and with plenty of room.'

There were scenes also of the different cities, Sydney, Melbourne and Brisbane, modern cities with lovely old buildings, very similar to the big cities here, and scenes of the countryside which seemed to stretch forever; rock faces and high mountain peaks, and sunset skies stretching to infinity.

All too soon the lights came back on and the lovely aroma of freshly brewed coffee wafted on the air. People helped themselves and moved around the hall, talking to each other while officials of the Australian Immigration Department milled around, having a chat here, a clap on the shoulder for someone else, but I didn't see a single person I knew.

Pierre brought our coffee over, and I sat sipping mine when an immigration officer approached us. We shook hands in turn, then he smiled, and, turning to Pierre, joked, 'You've finally convinced your wife then, Mr de Haas?'

Quick as a flash I butted in, 'No, he hasn't. I would have to find out a lot more before that would happen. Judging by the film you showed, it is a lovely country ... for a holiday. But a migration is not a holiday.'

'I agree, Mrs de Haas, but Australia has so much to offer. In most cases it takes about two years for people to settle down and make a good living there. But'—he checked his watch—'I must get back for the second half of the program, where we show the migrant centres. It was nice meeting you, Mrs de Haas, and please, do not get disheartened when you see clips of these centres. There's a lot of bad publicity about them, but, as you will see, they're not as bad as people make out.'

I looked at Pierre. So this was what he had not told me. They were going to show how new arrivals would be accommodated—the nuts and bolts of a new start—and I was determined to see it all, this flip side of the holiday-like images.

The lights dimmed and once more the screen lit up, and what I saw was a totally different picture. We were shown the migrant centres around Sydney and Melbourne first. Vast tracts of land with rows and rows of barrack-like buildings and Nissan huts, like army camps, and a brassy tropical sun throwing a harsh light on it all. Sparse trees provided little shade. It looked stark and grim. I felt my throat contract watching these endless rows of huts.

So, these were the migrant centres? They expected families, even those with small children, to live there until they found a decent place of their own. A voice droned on and on, but I no longer heard. I had seen enough. How could anyone adjust to such an existence? We were not refugees, for God's sake. I realised it would be only temporary—camping as Pierre put it—but I had switched off.

I was not interested, not even when they showed Wacol later. It certainly looked friendlier, but, as far as I could see, this also lacked essential services and infrastructure.

We lived in the centre of town, in a modern, though small,

apartment with everything at our fingertips: shops, restaurants, theatres, transport, schools, hospitals, etc. etc. Everything a modern society provides. I felt that same iron band tightening around my chest. I could hardly breathe and wanted to go home. How could anyone in his right mind think of leaving here and starting all over again in another country, and in such grim circumstances? No! I would never agree to go to such a place.

The film ran its course and I sat through it, a marble statue, my hands two clumps of ice. Once again, all my objections to such an enormous change rose to the surface, like a huge mountain Pierre wanted me to climb, and I knew I did not have the right equipment to undertake such a challenge. When the lights came on later, I said, 'I want to go home.'

'Don't you want to wait till question time?'

'No, I've had enough.'

One look at my face must have told him more than he wanted to know. He did not argue. When we stepped outside, the rain was bucketing down, overflowing the gutters, the drains swallowing the flood of water with loud gurgling noises. Pierre ran to the car while I waited on the porch until he pulled up. I ran and jumped in, then banged the door shut behind me. We drove home in silence, like two shop manikins. All I wanted was to be home, in familiar surroundings.

On arrival, I asked Pierre, 'Do you want coffee?'

'No, I don't. I have had one. What I want to do is talk.'

'There's nothing to talk about. I've seen enough.'

Fingers splayed, he thumped on the table as if to accentuate each word. 'Corry, Corry, you loved what you saw; I could tell. It is when they showed the migrant centres that you switched off. Will you think for a moment what it would be like for the children? Growing up in a sunny, healthy climate like that, where they can play outside all year round, instead of being cooped up in a small apartment here for eight months of the year? We have to use sunlamps, for God's sake, so they do get a bit of colour. Last year we had eight weeks of constant thick fog, until you felt like a wet towel as soon as you stepped outside. You think that is healthy?'

Deep down I knew he was right. Our doctor had advised us to use a sun lamp for the children during the winter months. It was a long, dark wait for spring and summer each year, and when the calendar told us it should get better, it rarely eventuated. We used to joke summer in the Netherlands falls on a Sunday! Trips to the beach were few and far between.

'Still,' I resumed, 'I don't think this is enough reason to cut ourselves off from all we know and go to the other side of the world, to an unknown country and a dicey future.'

'Australia is screaming for migrants. They need people.'

'Well, they can go and scream for them somewhere else. I am going to bed. If you want to go so badly then go ahead, I won't stop you. When you have found a good job and a decent house for us, I may follow you; and don't think for a minute you can get around me by saying this is for the children. It won't work!'

I slammed the bedroom door behind me, my heart thudding and my mind a maze of mismatched thoughts, yet I was determined not to give in under all this pressure. The problem was, I couldn't go anywhere for advice. Hinting to my parents what was brewing would worry them so much, it could make them sick, and not to speak of Mama. They adored the children. How could we take them away? Pierre followed me into the bedroom, and again I rounded on him. 'Have you thought what it would do to our parents? They would never see their grandchildren again.'

I'd had enough; more than enough for one night. Damn! Damn this whole business. If only I could fetch a glimpse of the future, know what was in store for us, but life does not hand out presents like that.

Sleep was one continuous nightmare yet again. Jumbled pictures of all I had seen. Menacing mountains, grim massive rock faces, jungle vines holding me prisoner; endless beaches stretching to infinity and sand ... all that sand. I tried to walk on a beach, but it took hold of my feet, would not let go. I woke up with a start. My face was wet with perspiration, my nerves jingling with tension. I tried deep breathing to calm down, then quietly stood up, threw on my dressing gown and went to the kitchen to warm up some milk, and later sat in the freezing lounge to think. But the same doubts and angst still hammered in my head.

Finally, cold through and through, I went back to bed and at last fell into a deep sleep, only to be woken by the alarm clock, in what seemed like only a few minutes later. Someone was hurling boulders in my head and it all came back. I still wore my dressing gown. I had

Part Five: Emigration

been too cold to take it off. Sitting up carefully, I pulled the curtain across to see what the weather was like.

Rain again, the sky a dreary dome of lead.

Once again, weeks of uncertainty followed. Corry was torn between the reality of the Netherlands with its familiar way of life, or a dream country somewhere, unknown, untried, and, deep down, unwanted. However, when she picked up one of those colourful brochures Pierre left for her and read its contents, she felt a response, a favourable reaction. There was no denying the photographs showed an ideal environment, the likes of which she and her young family would never experience in the Netherlands.

One day, a newspaper arrived in the mail, its heading proclaiming *Wereld Post (World Post)*. It seemed to be a new Dutch publication and a special newspaper for potential migrants. On leafing through it, Corry found useful information on every aspect of emigration and several letters from migrants telling of their adventures in a new country. It was fascinating reading, especially once she realised others had experienced the same anxieties and doubts plaguing her ever since Pierre first mentioned emigration. Some letters were uplifting, but every letter also told of hardship and difficulties encountered.

It struck me then: I could write about my doubts and misgivings with which I was struggling so intensely and doing so would perhaps help me to see things more clearly. I put the paper aside and carried on with my daily tasks, but during the rest of that week, I often picked it up again and re-read the articles and letters, until I could almost recite them.

Later that same week, there was another intense conversation between them, sparked by a local shopkeeper who had asked Corry if it was true that she was planning to emigrate to Australia! The word, or rumour, had somehow leaked ...

After I had tucked the children in bed that night, I told Pierre of this little episode, asking, 'Do you realise what will happen if this gets out? With our business, I mean. You might as well close the shop now, or have you taken this whole business further than I know?'

'No! I have not! I told you I will not proceed with the plans until I have your okay. This is one thing we have to do together.' He shrugged his shoulders dejectedly and added, 'I just wish you would also look at the positives at times. I've been to several film nights now and you should see how people live over there: free-standing houses, with lovely lawns and beautiful gardens surrounding them. I would dearly love to have something like that, wouldn't you?'

He heaved a tired sigh. 'You know how I enjoyed working in the garden at home. None of the others were interested in gardening, just Dad and me. Have you had a good look around you lately? Have you noticed what is happening here? Enormous apartment blocks are going up everywhere. People live in these concrete boxes, those who are lucky enough to get one allocated to them, and you know as well as I do, couples without children do not stand a chance at all. And this is fourteen years after the war.'

I was quiet; knew he was right. We too had started our married life in one room at his parents'. The flat we had been promised had gone to an emergency case; this after months of haggling, anxiety and negotiations with the different departments. We had waited months before we were finally allowed to move in to our first apartment, and we considered ourselves one of the lucky ones.

'Co, I know what it is like to live in the tropics'—his voice animated now—'and that was in far from ideal circumstances. We were fighting a war in Indonesia, were on patrol every night and yet, despite all that, there were times when I thought, "I could quite easily stay here, never go back …"'

He stood up, took the *Wereld Post* from the magazine rack and spread it out at the letter section. 'Here, look at these stories; people with families larger than we have, off to Canada, New Zealand, Australia, Africa. They're everywhere. They can't all be wrong, can they?'

'I guess not, but Canada would not be an option for me.'

'Nor for me; it's too harsh a climate.'

'I don't know, Pierre.' That same lump in my throat made it hard to talk. 'Maybe it is easier for a man. I can't make decisions like that

Part Five: Emigration

on the spur of the moment.'

'But look at these letters; for most it took two years to settle. Two years out of a lifetime, Corry.'

'What about the children?' It always came down to them in the end.

'They'll be happy as long as we're there for them. Children are so resilient. Peter and Mona will look at it as a great adventure. The younger children are still totally dependent on us. And another thing, do not worry about people gossiping. They will anyway.' He was silent then, his eyes distant, as if he were travelling on a different plain, and perhaps he was. 'I'll tell you what, why don't you go home for a couple of days? It will give you time to think.'

'Oh, I don't know … Then again … Maybe, just for a couple of days. Yes, okay, I think I will.' Maybe a few days on my own could throw some light on this eternal seesaw of decision making.

He took hold of my hands. 'I am serious now, and I promise you, you will never regret it. I know you too well. Trust me.' I was not convinced.

I phoned my mother the following morning, before I could change my mind. Her voice sounded tired. 'Hi, Mum, how are you? And how's Dad?'

'Okay, I guess. Much the same, Corry. There is not much improvement, really.'

'Aw, Mum, I'm sorry.' Maybe it was the right thing to do, going home for a while; it would mean company for Dad and a change for Mum.

'Listen, Mum, could you cope with a visitor for a couple of days? If it is okay with you, I'd like to come over towards the end of this week.

'Oh, that would be lovely,' more enthusiastic now. 'Will you bring any of the children?'

'Not this time, Mum. It might be a bit too noisy for Dad. It is only me this time. I want to catch up on all the news, but I can make some noise if you like?'

She laughed, and, shortly afterwards, the arrangements were all settled.

34. MOVE FORWARD!

The train was packed with commuters. Corry had taken an early one, so she would be with her parents before lunch. Settling into her nook in the rear of the carriage, she watched the scenery glide past as the sun peeped through the heavy clouds, giving her some hope of a few days with fine weather ... at last. Corry relaxed and started to look forward to her visit as the train raced through the lush countryside, the greenest of meadows with Friesian cattle huddled together in little groups.

> The train slowed down, then stopped, and I realised with a start the next stop would be mine. Time had passed and I had not been aware of it. Daydreaming is something I do best, people tell me.
> Now, however, it was time to look out for that beacon, which always welcomed me home: and there it was: the beautiful silver dome of our village church. From kilometres away one could see this magnificent building rise high above the surrounding countryside, the Basilica of Sts Agatha and Barbara. This striking landmark had always meant 'home' to me, and now more than ever.
> The train drew into Oudenbosch station. I took my case down and stepped down onto the almost deserted platform. After the bustling streets of Nijmegen, my hometown seemed smaller each time I visited. I walked to the exit, where the ticket collector stood waiting. A new face, I thought, and wondered whether old Bob had finally retired.
> On the way to the place of my childhood and youth, I entered the basilica and immediately felt at home. I always did this on my visits to Oudenbosch, and, more than anything else, this beautiful, serene place called me back, again and again. I prayed for a while then lit a candle at the statue of Mary and left.
> On reaching my parents' home I walked along the side of the house, where I knew Dad would be sitting in his chair near the window, either reading or dozing. I stopped and knocked on the glass

pane. He looked up, and his eyes lit up when he saw me. He smiled, a little tremor at his lips, then waved and pointed to the back door, where I knew Mum would be waiting. She looked tired.

'Hey, Mum, how are you?' I hugged her and kissed her cheek, still as soft as a young girl's.

'Fine, fine. Had a good trip?'

'Yes, but it was crowded. The train was packed.'

'Come, Dad's been waiting all morning; he'll be pleased to see you.'

On entering the kitchen, delicious smells greeted me, and I knew Mum had cooked my favourite dish, sweet-and-sour red cabbage and rissoles. My mouth watered in anticipation. I often made it myself, but it never tasted quite the same as hers. I put my case on the kitchen table, went through to the lounge and kissed my frail old dad. 'And how are you, Dad?'

'Not too bad, child, no, not too bad. Did you have a good trip? How are Pierre, and the children?'

'They're fine. A friend is looking after them. Pierre is busy in the shop, as usual, but that is a good sign, uh? They send their love.'

Dad was wiping his eyes meanwhile, his tears ducts working overtime, as so often happened nowadays when one of us visited.

After lunch, with Dad asleep in his chair, we did the washing up together, then sat in the kitchen, I in my favourite corner near the cellar door, and Mum opposite me. I asked her how Dad's health was. 'I don't know whether I can tell you anything new, Corry. The doctor comes once a week to check him, but I don't think he can do much. It is just old age, a hardening of the arteries he said last week, and this makes him weak. His system can't cope, it seems.'

While I listened to Mum, I thought what a shame that after a lifetime of hard work, it had come to this. I had never known my parents to ask anything for themselves. They quietly and contentedly cared for us. There had been few luxuries; they had never travelled or wanted to travel.

In these circumstances, how could I possibly raise the subject of emigration? Explain how Pierre saw our future? This would be too hard for them to comprehend, and they would think the whole idea absolute lunacy. I knew exactly what Mum would say: 'Why look for dry bread there, when you eat cake here?' How could I find the words?

Later I asked, 'Would you like to go for a little walk, Dad.'

'Yes, perhaps that would be nice; after I finish my tea then?'

I fetched Dad's overcoat and a woollen scarf and helped him put them on. All his movements were slow, and I wondered briefly where my energetic Dad had gone. The air was still crisp, but everything looked friendlier now. Traces of winter were hanging in the air and I breathed deeply to fill my lungs with its bracing scent. We took it slowly, Dad holding on for support, our roles reversed. I was the carer now.

I remembered how one winter morning the two of us had set out on a hike which would take us all the way to Pagnevaart, a beautiful nature reserve about an hour's walk from Oudenbosch. It had snowed during the night, and, although the main roads were cleared of snow, when we entered the forest, we found a fairy-tale land. The pine trees' branches were heavy with silvery snow, bent almost to the ground. Our boots sank deeply into this soft, snowy carpet. It was eerily quiet. Most of the birds had moved south to a milder climate for winter, but sparrows darted through the trees or sat dozing, heads deeply buried in feather collars.

I remember looking back at our footsteps in the snow, saying, 'Dad, look, we can never lose our way back. All we have to do is follow our footsteps to the road and home again.' We walked in that winter palace for hours that day, then, on arriving home, sat shivering near the wood stove, trying to thaw out our frozen limbs.

It seemed like only yesterday, but this time I was indeed lost. No footsteps in the snow to lead the way. I could only move forward. And it was at that precise moment I knew what I had to do! The clue words: 'Move forward.'

After Dad had retired that night, Mum brought the coffee in, and, as she poured, gave me one of her looks, saying, 'What's on your mind, Corry?' During my entire life I had never been able to conceal anything from my mother. Although I had never told her about any problems I had, Mum somehow knew, and didn't have to be told. Life's wisdom had taught her enough about reading characters and she was always spot-on.

What I was facing now, however, I had to share, for it would also affect my parents. I told her of my dilemma and, as expected, she reacted exactly as I had thought she would. All the arguments she put forward against such a step I had repeated endlessly in my mind

Part Five: Emigration

during the many hours I lay awake at night during the past weeks.

I told her and added, 'What then, Mum? Can you imagine Pierre in a nine-to-five job, or as a sales rep travelling all week? The children would see even less of him than they do now.'

'Pierre wants adventure. That's what he wants,' she replied. 'He will not settle anywhere. Why go to another country to eat dry bread when you have cake here? You have a thriving business he's worked hard to establish, and now he wants to throw it all away?'

To be fair, I answered, 'I don't think it's as simple as that, Mum. I think he's restless because he has seen a different environment. He lived in the tropics for three years, in wide open spaces, taxing his capabilities. He wrote me once he could have stayed there, were it not for his mother. I feel I can't win this one, Mum. He says he will make it work and I know he will. But I have run out of arguments; everything you've said I've told him again and again, but he's waiting for me to say yes, and with his usual determination he'll see it through. It seems all I have to do is pluck up enough courage to take on the challenge, stop fighting it. I don't know honestly whether I can or not …'

I could not go on. My throat was tight with unshed tears, but I didn't want to cry in front of her.

'I can't follow him,' she said at last. 'To have to start all over again, and five young children … I can't find any words for it.'

I was quiet then. I had been voicing the same for weeks and was tired; physically and mentally worn out by the enormity of it. There wasn't a thing I could add, but deep down I knew I had to do something that would restore what Pierre and I once shared, and life had taken away. Five young children and a thriving business had left no time for us.

Maybe a different lifestyle would be the answer?

There was another factor, however, I had not dared touch upon, and I had not admitted even to myself; a tiny thought lingering in the back of my mind ever since Pierre had mentioned migration. A thought I had wiped as soon as it came to mind but was as concrete as if I could see it and a voice that said, 'You always wanted to travel. Here's your chance; maybe your last chance to see the world.'

I had thoroughly enjoyed the few trips we had made in Europe, and I will never forget the rapture of it when for the first time I saw

Move Forward!

the tropical palm trees at the Riviera, the same exotic sights I loved in the photographs Pierre had sent me from Indonesia. Always a nature child, to sit on a sunny terrace blinking in the sunshine seemed as near to heaven as I could get. It was with a sense of loss when, after our holiday, we had to turn the car around and come home. Would a dream of sunny days be enough to sustain me during those first difficult years? Perhaps … Perhaps …

As far as Mum was concerned, I felt the subject was closed and I didn't want to push it any further. In the end she could not make up my mind for me and I did not think my parents would ever understand. Talk drifted to the children and, as usual, it seemed to lighten the atmosphere.

Later, I had just slipped under the covers when Mum came into my bedroom. Without a word she made the sign of the cross on my forehead and tucked me in with a kiss, a nightly ritual when I was a child. 'Are you warm enough, Corry?'

Teary-eyed, I tried to swallow that salty lump in my throat and answered, 'Yes, Mum, thanks. It's nice to sleep in my own bed again,' and knew whatever I decided, the love of my parents would travel with me, even if it meant as far as a strange, unknown Southland. For the first time in weeks, I slept like a baby.

And so, the weekend progressed. We relished each other's company and enjoyed just being together in the home and in the little village which both held so many memories. On Saturday, Mum and I went shopping together and spent some time buying gifts for the children, Mum spoiling them as usual!

On Sunday morning. I woke to the deep bronze voice of the basilica's big bells. The air vibrated with this familiar sound of my childhood. I threw back the covers, opened the curtains and window and looked out. A glorious morning, the soft light of the awakening sun drew patterns of gold across the streets. Clouds scudded across the sky, throwing strange patterns on distant fields.

Sundays had always been special to me, although I had spent most of our free Sundays in church. High Mass in the morning and Benediction in the afternoon put a large hole in my precious 'free' time. For as long as I can remember, I had watched the farmers (from the large properties around Oudenbosch) cycle or walk to church, accompanied by their wives and children. The men, dressed in Sunday

Part Five: Emigration

best, would wear the heavy black serge suits, silk black caps planted firmly on square work-worn faces, rough red hands on the handlebars of their bikes, their wives beside them. The women still wore the traditional dress of the region: full, ankle-length black skirt covered with a grey-and-white checked apron; black woollen stockings and lace-up boots. Richly embroidered bodices showed the strong red arms to advantage (some as thick as young trees). The faces were framed by crisply starched lace caps, adorned with beautifully fashioned gold clips at the side.

Times haven't changed all that much, I thought, watching them. As they greeted acquaintances in passing, their voices carried far over the otherwise quiet morning. Though the younger generation seldom wore traditional dress nowadays, for some the customs—passed down the generations—were still part of the Sunday morning scene.

Later, Mum and I walked arm in arm to church, accompanied by the tolling of the bells, a sound I missed wherever I went. They were part of me, as much a part as the streets I walked, where I knew every house, every shop, little nook or courtyard.

Mass was well attended, and we had trouble finding seats. I sat quietly, listening to the choir singing the beautiful Gregorian Mass. I remembered all the words, could have sung along with the harmonious voices. I was raised on the ancient Latin language, and its voice still echoed in my heart. I knelt on the red upholstered pew, but I can't say I prayed that day. I just let this wonderful music reach my soul, let it engulf me, as I sat, lost in memories. Maybe this too was praying. Now, as I sat in this grand building, the sharp scent of incense drifting on the air, I knew that no matter what happened in the future, this would always be home to me.

Shortly after lunch Pierre and the children arrived, and suddenly the quiet house rang with their voices.

All too soon it was time to go. I went upstairs, quickly packed my bag for Pierre to take down to the car. We gathered children, toys and presents, saw them settled and it was time to say goodbye. Both Mum and Dad came out with us and stood waving until we turned off towards the highway. It saddened me to leave them; they seemed so alone and forlorn.

Later, and once again sitting together enjoying a freshly brewed coffee, Pierre asked, 'Have you told your parents about my plans?'

'Yes, I told Mum, not Dad. I don't think he can handle it at the moment.

'What did Mum say?'

'Exactly what I told you she would. That it was pure lunacy.'

'Did you explain why?'

'Yes, Pierre, I did. I put forward all the arguments I could think of and it didn't help. It's too much for them to comprehend.'

'Can you? That's the big question.'

'I've had time to think while I was home, and I know what you want, but I can't see yet what is best for us as a family.'

'Why can't you trust me in this, Co? I know it's the right thing to do. It will be an enormous challenge, but God, Corry, dare and live a little; dare to step out of this safe, boring existence, the way we will live until we're eighty or so. There's such a wonderful world out there and ...'

'Yes,' I cut in, 'and there are five little children here, who depend on us.'

'I've told you before, as long as we are there for them, they'll be happy.'

Again, we were on the same subject, in the same argument, and there seemed no way out of the dilemma. He shrugged his shoulders in sheer exasperation then suggested, 'Look, why don't you make an appointment to see one of the emigration officers? Have a talk with him, ask all the questions you want; and don't hold back. I'm sure you'll see things differently then. Corry, we are young. We have our whole lives in front of us. We can do what we want, go where we want, and I'll guarantee, when you see the children playing in the sun all day, you'll see it my way.'

'You sound like a damn travel agent,' I said; then we both got the giggles, while tears rolled down my face.

He took me in his arms and whispered, 'No more tears, please. It's time we moved to another stage. If we have each other and the children, what else do we want?'

Yes, whatever else???

35. THE DECISION

On the next Wednesday afternoon, an anxious and nervous Corry found herself in the immigration offices in Nijmegen, staring at the large, colourful posters on the wall. They showed beautiful palm-fringed beaches, magnificent scenes of Sydney Harbour, a jungle scene with a near-impregnable growth of trees, palms and shrubs, much like the small black-and-white photographs Pierre had sent her from Indonesia. To Corry, it all seemed quite exotic, but also intimidating, wild and primitive, and far from civilisation.

A few minutes later, seated in a comfortable chair, Corry commenced the conversation with one of the immigration officers.

I didn't really know where to start and said as much. 'I want to know everything that you think I ought to know if, and when, I decide to proceed with an emigration. I know all there is to know about the sunshine and the beaches, but absolutely nothing about the gritty bits: the migration centres and the conditions there for instance. New arrivals go to these centres first, is that right?'

'Exactly. That is, if they don't have family there, who can arrange other accommodation. Let me tell you the way things are, Mrs de Haas. I won't paint you a nice rosy picture.' He inhaled deeply and blew a cloud of fine grey smoke to the ceiling, then tipped the ash on the edge of the ashtray. His blue eyes gave me a penetrating look as if he was measuring me up, and continued, 'I would be doing you a disservice if I didn't tell you the truth about the type of accommodation you can expect.' He smiled. 'The first two years will be hard; they're hard for everybody. As you can imagine, the changes are enormous.'

'No, I have no idea what to expect,' I answered truthfully. '*Wereld Post* tells some very alarming stories.'

'A lot of the stories you read, Mrs de Haas, are from people who came back after the first two years. They are the ones who didn't make it, and of course all you hear then are negatives. They often have to find excuses because they returned to the Netherlands. and I have heard every one of them, believe me. What I'll do is take you right through the procedures, shall I?'

'Please do. That will be fine.'

'I'll start with your application, which consists of a lot of paperwork about your personal details. You will then be asked to go to The Hague with the family for an interview with the Australian immigration officers. Every member of the family will have to have a thorough medical examination, both by your own doctor and later with an Australian team of doctors. If everything is fine, you may proceed and you will hear, usually within a few weeks, whether you have been accepted as migrants. Only then can you start organising your move. We have at our disposal a list of experts in the removal business and we'll give you all the advice you need.'

'Okay, so far so good. What's next?'

'Then, for most migrants, comes the hard part. You'll have to go through all your possessions and sort out what you want to take.'

'I'll probably want to take the lot.'

'You could of course, but it will cost you. Let me explain. What you can take on board is one suitcase for each family member. The rest of your household goods will have to be crated and shipped to Australia, to be stored until such time you can move into private accommodation. You will have to pay a storage fee for this every month.'

'Good grief, how am I going to manage with five small children?'

'I know it's not much, but remember, Mrs de Haas, one week on board and you'll need only summer clothes as you'll be sailing to a much warmer climate.'

'Yes, of course, I see. So what then?'

It was like playing a quiz game, I thought, as I kept firing questions at him. He was quite pleasant about it; he must have answered the same questions a thousand times before.

'Okay. Now, on arrival in Sydney you will be transferred to your destination in Australia. Where do you and your husband wish to settle?'

'My husband would settle only in Queensland, I think. He wants a better climate than this.'

He frowned. 'Well, that might be a bit of a problem. I believe you must have special permission to go there. Queensland is in the grip of a credit squeeze now. It's worth a try, but I'll have to look into that later.

'Right, then you will probably travel from Sydney overnight by train to Brisbane, where you'll arrive late afternoon. From there, buses will take you to Wacol Migrant Centre, about sixteen kilometres from the inner city.'

'Can you tell me anything about these centres?'

'Well, you're in luck. I've been on an orientation visit recently and I must say it's not too bad. This one sits in an area of parkland, with lots of trees and lovely flowering shrubs. It looks friendly. Still ...'

I jumped right in with my next question. 'What about the accommodation?'

He hesitated, while the ornate clock on the wall behind him ticked away the seconds. 'Are you a strong person, Mrs de Haas?'

'I think so. It all depends how strong I would have to be.'

'Ah, well, the big question. Where to start? Imagine a big camping ground where, instead of tents, there are little wooden buildings and Nissan huts. Wacol was an army camp during the war; migrants have to share housing with other families, depending on the size of the family.'

Just what I thought! Aloud I said, 'Yes, I know. My husband has told me about this. That's the part I don't like!'

He sighed, shrugged his shoulders. 'I agree, it's a tough one. A far from ideal situation, but remember, it's only temporary.'

He riffled through some papers in yet another folder. 'I think I have a photograph somewhere. Yes, here it is. This is taken inside one of the Nissan huts. It doesn't look too bad, does it?'

It was a small black-and-white snap. I studied the little room. It was furnished which what seemed like heavy wooden bunks, a squat table, a narrow hanging cupboard, and a chest of drawers. As far as I could make out, there was some lino on the floor with the walls finished in a light colour. Superimposed on that small photo, I saw my lovely lounge and bedroom suites. My God, could I, would I have to live like that? The so-called furniture looked about ready for the dump.

I sighed, handed back the photograph, and said, 'I don't think sunshine will make this lot look better.'

'I know; it's pretty basic. The authorities can do little about it. With the enormous influx of displaced persons and early migrants, it's the best they can offer now.'

Apprehension shivered down my spine. I seemed to do a lot of sighing this afternoon. 'Ah, well, is there any water in these huts, Mr de Ruyter?'

'No, I'm afraid not. You'll have to get that in the laundries or the kitchen.'

'My God, is there anything positive about this place? Will I have to carry every drop of water we use to the hut? You were talking about laundries a minute ago. What about doing the washing? Is there a central laundry or do we wash everything ourselves?'

'There are two laundries, one on either side of the camp. These are wooden structures, each with three coppers.'

'Coppers?'

'Yes, coppers, to boil the clothes.'

'You mean like my mother used to do when I was a child? Boil the clothes and then scrub them? You are joking, aren't you? Aren't there any washing machines? I have five young children, and you say I'll have to wash everything by hand? Sheets and all?'

'Oh, no; not bed linen, or towels. Clean linen and towels are provided each week.'

'But what about my own washing machine; I can use mine in the camp, can't I?'

'I'm afraid not. It will have to be stored with the rest of your possessions. There are no facilities to store any appliances, Mrs de Haas.'

'I must have my head read, just sitting here. Some holiday camp! Are there any bathing facilities at all, or do we wash with water in the buckets I'll be carting to the hut?' Noticing that I sounded quite aggressive, I apologised. 'I'm sorry, please carry on.' After all, he was doing his job, and I had asked him to tell all, the good and the bad. It was not his fault that there were so few positives to report.

'Again, these are wooden structures, I believe, but I'm not sure about this. I would have to check; but I think there are eight showers and a bathroom in every block. I know it sounds all too much at the moment, Mrs de Haas. However, when you look at the number of people who have left their country and made it there, it can't be all bad, can it? Do you speak English at all?'

'Yes, enough to get by, I think. I read a lot of English magazines now and that goes quite well. I don't think the language will be much of a problem.'

'Well then, half the battle is won. Some people have terrible trouble with the language.'

'I can well imagine. Oh, one more thing. Are there any schools nearby?'

'Yes, as a matter of fact, there is a primary school in the centre and a kindergarten as well. They are absolutely lovely. The classrooms are separate buildings, set between tall eucalypts. The teachers there are specially trained professionals and they're quite capable of coping with migrant children. On arrival, the children are assessed, and once they know enough English to follow the lessons, they will be placed in their corresponding grades.

'By the way, there is also a small surgery, with a fully trained nursing sister always in attendance, and also a lovely little chapel for Sunday services. A Dutch priest celebrates Mass there every Sunday.'

He continued, 'I'm not saying it will be easy; far from it. It is an enormous undertaking and needs a special person to cope with all the changes, but, then again, thousands of migrants can't all be wrong, can they? In the end, what it comes down to is courage, and at least you have a choice. So many didn't.'

'Yes, when you put it that way. But from my point of view, it means many steps back, not forward. As I see it, it will take years to achieve the same standard of living we enjoy here. We'll have to start from scratch. That reminds me, what about cooking and meals?'

'Meals are all served in a canteen adjacent to the kitchen. The men who have jobs are provided with a cut lunch. There are two kitchens and dining rooms in Wacol. You and your family will have your meals there.'

'Have you heard anything about what the food is like?'

'Can I answer that with a question, Mrs de Haas? Are you a good cook?' He smiled, and that question spoke volumes.

'That bad, uh? Yes, a reasonably good one, I think.'

'Then you'll have to grit your teeth a bit more. The so-called chefs are not "Cordon Bleu" graduates! They have to make do with the money available. Do you get the picture?'

'Yes, sharp and clear. As I said, some holiday camp! I have an idea it will be anything but. I have taken up enough of your time. There must be other people waiting.'

Then, before I could stop myself, I asked, 'Do you have any application forms here, so we can study them at home?'

He opened the bottom drawer of his desk, turned around and gave me a second look, then drew out a sheaf of papers, which he sorted into a neat bundle, and handed it to me. 'There you are, Mrs de Haas. I have also given you some extra reading material so you can familiarise yourself with the country.'

I thanked him for his time. We shook hands and, as I left, he said, 'I hope to hear from your husband soon.' He ushered me to the waiting room, where two couples sat waiting, reading a magazine. I stepped outside. Squaring my shoulders, I thought, 'Here you are, girl. The first step is behind you. Now what?'

Only the gods could tell.

So, what now? My resolve weakened. I once again felt hollow and eroded inside through the continuous waves of anxiety and worries about the future.

Once outside, I took a deep breath. What an afternoon. My head reeled with all the input, and I think I realised the enormity of it all for the first time. I didn't feel like going home and decided instead to go for a walk in Kaiser Karel Park. I followed the meandering paths, and after a while found a wooden seat which gave me the best view of the river, and the bridge spanning it. Its enormous spans glistened in the afternoon sun, like a man-made lacework of steel.

It was peaceful here, and I knew decision time had arrived. Despite everything I'd heard just now, a voice deep inside kept repeating the same words, 'How about it, Corry, do you have what it takes, the guts to challenge life? Leave a safe, ordered existence behind and venture out into the world? To see the globe's other half?'

I also heard another voice: Dad's. 'No matter where you go in the world, child, people have to work and make a living everywhere; that will never change.'

A score of seagulls swooped low over the water. For some reason or other they had chosen the fens on the western end of town as their breeding and living quarters. Could it be that in earlier times, the North Sea's beaches were situated here, I wondered? I wished I too had wings, to have a quick look at this mysterious Southland.

Once there, I knew I would have to stand on my own two feet. There would be no family or friends to fall back on. It would be Pierre and I in a strange world of uncertainties.

The river flowed on, an occasional barge breaking the continuous gentle flow of water, and I thought, 'My life will flow on like this, unbroken by upheaval, moves or worries, always onward until it reaches that distant sea.' Reality was centre stage. Sadistic little devils danced around me, encircled me with rings of uncertainties.

Time slipped away and I was not aware of it. I sat in the park for a long, long time until the chill of early twilight reminded me it was time to go home. The tall steeple of St Steven's glowed in the rosy light of the sinking sun, while its bells sounded the full hour. Would there be church bells in Wacol, I wondered?

On coming home, I entered the shop and walked to the rear where Pierre was sorting out the new stock which had arrived that morning. 'And how did it go?' he asked, his eyes searching mine, then pointing to the papers in my hand. 'Did you have a good chat? You were a long time.'

I handed him the papers and shrugged out of my coat. 'Yes, it was very helpful. He explained everything in detail.'

'And?'

'I brought the application forms, so we can check them and fill them in, if you like.'

'Did you? Really? Is it okay, then? Are you sure?'

I nodded yes and promptly burst into tears.

He took me in his arms. 'Shush, shush, it's all right. I promise you, you will never regret this. I'll make it work for us.'

Just then a neighbour walked in and caught us. 'Oh, I beg your pardon. If you're not open for business,' he joked.

I turned around, quickly dried my eyes, while Pierre attended to him, and then faced him and quipped, 'Your timing is way off, Jeff.' I grinned and I thought, *This is life, a smile and a tear.* I knew then I would cope with whatever life would throw at me if there was plenty of laughter as well.

After the children were in bed, we talked for hours, studied the papers I had been given that afternoon, and while we chattered it seemed as if the uncertainties and doubts of the previous months slipped away. I remembered something Pierre had often quoted to me: 'Nothing relieves the mind so much as a decision taken.'

36. Impressions of a Seven-Year-Old

I was seven years old at the time that this major upheaval was brewing in my life. Despite the drama of these months, leading to Corry, our mother, coming to this life-changing decision, none of us children were any the wiser. Did we pick up a 'vibe' that all was not well between our parents during this time? If so, none of us recall this.

I do, however, distinctly remember that we used the sun lamp for short periods while wearing only our underpants and what seemed to be weird little glasses to protect our eyes. We were only exposed for short periods, and I remember how quickly my skin became hot.

From our first-floor apartment above our shop, I was able to wave to my friend, Henk, living across the street inside his family's apartment. It was all very close quarters, living in the Nijmegen CBD.

While we had a small balcony at the rear, facing into an internal parking area or courtyard, I don't have any memories of playing outside, even on our own balcony. Given my mother's account of what seemed to be continual rain, cold and mist, for weeks if not months at a time, this should not be surprising. Nature mostly kept us indoors where we played as children, including with our neighbourhood friends.

My school was a short walk through the CBD, past what is known as Plein 44, a large, open public square surrounded by shops and restaurants. This area was rebuilt after an allied bomber pilot mistook Nijmegen for a target in Germany and dropped the entire load on this part of town.

On a far happier note, we only had half a day of school on Wednesdays and, on my walk home, I was able to obtain (for free) some warm, fried crumbs of batter scooped up from his oil fryer by the nice fish-and-chip man at the market set up that afternoon on Plein 44. I relished these 'treats' and, always enjoying my food, remember this as if it happened yesterday.

Impressions of a Seven-Year-Old

Other clear memories include the Waal River and the Nijmegen bridge, and bombed-out ruins of buildings nearby, probably remnants of Operation Market Garden during World War II.

I had no idea of the changes that were about to come our way.

A letter arrived from the Australian Immigration Department, confirming receipt of our application. It also gave the date for our medicals with their doctors, which meant a trip to The Hague with the children. We decided we would make it a lovely day out for them, with a picnic at the beach afterwards.

I wrote notes to Mona's and Peter's teachers, requesting permission for them to miss school that day, which didn't pose a problem. We knew we would have to tell them about our plans as well, and soon.

So, one night after dinner, the younger children safely tucked into bed, we four sat around the table sipping hot cocoa and nibbling on some biscuits, when Pierre said, 'How would you like to come with us on a long boat trip to another country?'

Peter piped up, 'On a real boat, just the two of us with you?'

'No, all of us will come of course, the whole family.'

'For a holiday, Daddy?' Mona asked.

'No, not just a holiday, but to live there, but we'll have a long holiday on the boat first. All of us, together.'

Peter's face was a study in frowns as he struggled with the idea. 'The teachers won't let us miss school that long, Dad.'

'What it means, Pete, you can go to school in Australia, for we will live there then.'

I added, 'But first we'll be on a lovely big ship for six weeks, and that's two weeks longer than the holidays in August. Doesn't that sound great? We'll be sailing all around the world first. What do you think of that, uh?'

'Where is that Australia, Dad?' Mona asked.

So, Pierre took the world atlas from the bookshelf, opened it at the world map, and, pointing first to the Netherlands, said, 'Look, here's where we live,' and two blond heads bent over the page, 'and this here is Australia. Now, we will travel this way,' pointing out the route for them, 'through this canal here, which is called the Suez Canal, or we

Part Five: Emigration

will go the long way around, via another waterway, called the Panama Canal.'

'Tell me, would you like that?' I asked. There was no answer.

Peter again, 'Can we take our friends, Dad? They would love to be on a big boat like that.'

'I'm afraid not, Peter. Their parents would miss them too much, don't you think?' '

'What about Oma and Opatje (little Opa) Oudenbosch then? Can they come with us?'

'I don't think Opa could make such a long trip, Peter,' I answered. 'You know Opa hasn't been well lately. But, if he gets better, perhaps they can come and visit later. That would be fun, wouldn't it?' I hated myself having to tell lies and fill them with false promises. I knew in my heart Dad would never make it and doubted whether my mother would ever find the courage to travel to the other side of the world.

'Will our teachers let us go, Mum?' Mona wanted to know.

'Oh, sure they will,' Pierre and I spoke as one. 'We couldn't leave you behind now, could we?'

'Do the others know we're going away, Dad?'

'No, they're still a little too young to understand, and we're not absolutely sure yet whether we can go, but we thought to tell you two first.'

We then explained it would take many weeks before everything would be organised, but did not go into too many details, knowing it would only confuse them. 'In a few weeks' time, we will go to The Hague for a check-up with some doctors there, and, if the weather is fine, we'll take a picnic lunch and go to the beach afterwards. How does that sound?'

'Oh, goody, can we have a swim then?' That was Mona, already keen for action.

'It depends,' I answered. 'It might still be a bit too cold for swimming, but you can have a paddle and play on the beach. You can build some sandcastles for Simone and Veronique.'

'Won't Oma cry, Mum, when we go away?' This from my little boy, who had figured out already it would not all be rosy and fun. I couldn't speak, but Mona had another question for us. 'How long are we going to stay in that Australia, Dad? When will we come back?'

'I don't know, sweetheart. Maybe if it is really, really nice there, we

Impressions of a Seven-Year-Old

might stay. Would you like that?'

Two pairs of eyes looked doubtful. 'Our friends would miss us, but.'

'Yes, they might, in the beginning,' I reassured them. 'But just think of all the long letters you'll be able to write them.' My God, this was so difficult to explain. We hardly knew any facts ourselves.

'Now,' Pierre went on, 'can you do one really grown-up thing for us? What we have told you just now, can you keep as a secret between the four of us? You see, it won't be happening for a while yet, or something could even go wrong with our plans. Don't talk about this with your friends yet, uh? Could you do this, for us?'

Two little heads nodded yes.

'That's great and very grown-up, but I think it's time for bed now.'

They kissed their father goodnight, and when I went in later to tuck them in and give them a cuddle, I saw they were still troubled, as both asked the same question. 'You are going with us, eh Mum, you and Dad?'

'Of course we are coming with you,' I assured them. 'I promise we'll all be together, like we are here. Dad and I will be there, always. I'll carry all of you on my back if I have to,' I joked.

Coming back into the lounge, I told Pierre, 'You better go and tuck them in as well. They're feeling a bit apprehensive, I think.' He did and it was a long time before he came back.

'Are they asleep?'

'Near enough. I had to tell them about Australia, and I hope it is all true. I had to give my fantasy free rein there.'

'Will they be okay, you think?'

'I'm sure they will be. They'll be just as excited as their mother once they're on board.'

'Never a truer word said,' I replied. 'Once we're on board.'

I have no recollection of this conversation with my parents!

For Corry and Pierre, these weeks were extremely hectic. There was so much to organise: medical appointments, sorting what would be taken to Australia, and what would be sold or disposed of, including many loads to St Vincent de Paul.

Part Five: Emigration

It was a very emotional time. Although we went about life with a new purpose, every now and then there was a thought of, 'Maybe I'll do this for the last time,' or, 'I wonder if I'll see this again before we leave.' Having said that, deep inside there was a spark of excitement at the thought of changes to come. Maybe my youth played a part in this. I had just turned thirty, and although I had to grow up quickly when we married and the children came along, the young girl inside me still dreamed impossible dreams.

It was a strange time of unreality; it felt like living in a vacuum. Life went on as usual, yet these were the most traumatic months of my life. I could not bring myself yet to tell my parents of our decision but knew full well I would have to do this soon. I had an idea Pierre's parents would not be surprised; they knew he had wanted to go four years ago, and it was only through Mama's intervention and encouragement that we had started out on our own business in Nijmegen.

Summer arrived but the rain was relentless.

At about this time, and since our plans had taken more solid form, I decided to write down my experiences, thoughts, and doubts about this enormous step into the unknown. By doing so, I could then sort it all out in my rather troubled mind and heart. Maybe I would see the real issues clearer, and it would enable me to cope better with all the changes. It was all right to play brave in front of the children, but the reality was quite different.

Another thought stealthily crept into my mind then. What if I also send my thoughts in a letter to *Wereld Post*? Perhaps it would help others who were in the same situation in which I found myself? I knew Pierre didn't have a single doubt that everything would work out fine; he was full of confidence and optimism. And although I was slowly getting used to the idea, I still had to cope with occasional panic attacks.

After careful consideration I decided to do just that. I wrote about the mental struggle I faced, from the moment Pierre had told me of his plans for us, and how I had finally agreed, although against my better judgement. I recorded each event as it occurred, and it did help me. Putting it down on paper was to me as if I could distance myself somehow—as if it were happening to someone else and I could look at it objectively.

Impressions of a Seven-Year-Old

The day of our visit to The Hague and the Australian Health Department dawned with black skies and teeming rain. Our picnic at the beach would be a washout. It came down in buckets. Damn it, the children had looked forward to the day with such expectation. Still, in the hope of it clearing, I fetched fresh bread rolls at the bakery next door, spread them with ham and cheese, filled a big paper bag with fruit, packed a bottle of cordial, little cakes and sweets, and I also took some books and toys. I hoped these would keep them occupied during the trip.

'Well here goes,' Pierre said. 'God, what a day they picked. We could use some of that Australian sun now.'

'We could do with a bit of sun, period,' I said. 'It's been a beastly summer all along. It's one thing that speaks for Australia; at least when planning a day at the beach there, we'll be able to pick any day we like.'

'So, you're sure our application will be approved then?' Pierre joked.

'What could stand in our way? Five healthy children, an old soldier and his pretty wife; especially the pretty wife,' I replied and felt that—despite the ghastly weather—somehow it would be a good day. The old rapport was back, and it was a good feeling. We had lived on opposite sides of the fence for so long, we had hardly dared open the gate which would bring us together again. There would be problems in the future, I knew, but today was okay.

After all the medicals and interviews were successfully concluded, the rest of the day was a complete wash-out: the rain did not let up. We all went to Scheveningen, the seaside resort of The Hague, but had to enjoy the picnic bread rolls and treats while staying in the car as the rain continued to pour, not even able to go for a walk. Nevertheless, I did enjoy eating those ham-and-cheese bread rolls while peering out— through the nearly steamed-up windows of the car—at the deserted, wind- and rain-swept beach of Scheveningen!

37. LIVING ROUGH?

Late in July the school holidays commenced, and, one night shortly afterwards, Pierre came upstairs after finishing in the shop, with some more surprises for Corry. Importantly, this would reveal how deeply Corry was yearning for at least some time in the sun, even though it would only be a short break from the Netherlands' miserable weather. Was this part of Pierre's clever planning, to give her a foretaste of life in sunnier climes—but not nearly as comfortably as Corry might have liked—to prepare her for what would confront her in Australia? But he couldn't have known who they would encounter ... or what would be waiting for them on their return.

Pierre said, 'I've been thinking. Now the children are home from school, why don't we take some time out from all this and take Peter and Mona with us on a holiday to the Riviera?'

'Holidays to France, now? Are you serious?'

'Yes, why not? Show them a bit of Europe, so they'll always remember what it is like, and for us to get a break from the worries of organising everything.'

'But what about the other children? What about the shop?' I should have known he had it all figured out already with trusted friends and shop assistants to take care of the younger children and the business.

Pierre continued, 'It would do us a lot of good not to have to think about an emigration for a while, and the children will never forget the experience.'

It sounded wonderful, although I hated leaving the younger children.

'It wouldn't cost that much,' he went on. 'We can go camping.'

Oh, oh, I knew there was a catch!

'My brother will lend us his tent and camping gear, I'm sure,' he went on with his usual enthusiasm.

'Camping? We have never been camping before'.

'The kids will love it.'

I knew they would, but would their mother? My idea of a perfect holiday at the Riviera was a comfortable hotel room with proper facilities and a lovely big bathroom attached, or at least available, like we had five years ago in Nice. This on top of all the upheaval we were facing. Then I mentally shrugged my shoulders. Why not? If we were going to live like gypsies for the next few years, why not get a taste of it first? 'Okay, let's do it. But then at the end of August, when most holidaymakers have returned home.'

Three weeks later, with two very excited children in the back and our station wagon stacked to the roof, we drove away, seeking adventure.

My introduction to camping was not a success. We had a three-person tent, which was okay, but there were four bodies, and with Mona sleeping at our heads and Peter between us, each time one moved I woke up. In the end I gave up trying to sleep and sat outside, which, as Pierre said later, gave him a terrible fright. He maintained that he saw an Indian squaw sitting in front of the tent, a story he repeatedly told [as did their son!] to anyone who wanted to hear. He, of course, slept very soundly.

The weather was beautiful and quite warm, and the further we travelled south, the warmer it became, and it was not long before I spotted the first palm trees which, for me, symbolise the tropics. They have such grace. Forgetting my lack of sleep, I clasped Pierre's arm, excited as a kitten with its first ball of wool. 'Look, the first palm trees.'

As we neared Cannes, my excitement increased to another level. I was elated to be back where Pierre and I had spent such a lovely week five years ago. How I had missed the sun. Even if only for a little while, we could soak up the sun and enjoy all that the Riviera had to offer, also showing the children a way of life they had not experienced before. We hoped they would remember it always.

We reached our camping site by late afternoon, an enormous area, tents scattered beneath gigantic fir trees like multi-coloured mushrooms. After checking in, we too set up our campsite, having found a lovely spot.

For the next few days, the weather was gorgeous: warm sunny days

Part Five: Emigration

with clear blue skies, and we took the children from beach to beach, and to the different resort towns: St Tropez, Juan les Pins, and of course Frejus, each with their colourful harbours, beach-side restaurants and cafés.

One trip saw us back in Nice, but this time at night. We walked the Promenade Anglais, where luxurious hotels, ablaze with light, lined the esplanade. Coloured lights—strung between the lamp posts—gave a fairy-tale atmosphere, and tall palm trees added to the exotic scene. Its magic still worked, as it had done when Pierre and I were here previously. Now we were here with the children, and to see how they enjoyed this 'life in the sun' doubled our pleasure.

Then the weather turned sour; a dry mistral was coming from the mountains, followed by rain, which made camping far from pleasant. Next day after breakfast we discussed what best to do: wait it out or pack up and look for the sun. We took out the maps and studied the different routes we could take. Go back the same way we'd come, or, as my tour guide suggested, 'What if we go back home via Switzerland and Germany? It would be a different way and much more scenic than northern France.'

So, we packed the car, left Frejus in a haze of drizzle, and just managed to keep ahead of the rain. As we crossed the border into Switzerland, a beautiful blue sky greeted us. The afternoon sun had lost some of its heat, and it was just the right temperature for driving through the magnificent scenery. When we pointed at the eternal snow on the mountain tops, I think the children could not quite grasp how this was possible, driving in the sun and at the same time seeing snow caps.

We had picked a camping site near Interlaken because it lay at the base of the Jungfrau, or so it seemed to us, because wherever we turned this Swiss 'young lady' was looking down on us. It was a marvellous choice, very Swiss, very clean, well-kept and quiet.

We had just put up the tent and organised our beds when another station wagon pulled up beside us, packed tight from top to bottom with clothes, suitcases and children, and an extra roof rack bulging with more luggage. The whole family seemed to be talking at once. They had six children and, as we found out later, were 'doing' Europe. As is usual among campers, Pierre asked where they came from, and the chap said, 'From Australia.'

If this wasn't fate, I don't know what else you would call it; so far from home, and in Switzerland of all places, to meet our first Australians. When Pierre told him we were planning to emigrate there, he answered, 'You could do worse, mate, she's a beaut' country.'

As the sun went down, a chill crept into the air and it became quite cool. I was glad I had packed some woollens as well. We would need blankets tonight, for we sure felt the difference from the warmth of the last few days. A chilly ground mist crept across the camping ground and we made sure to pile up the blankets that night, but I was still cold.

In the morning, disaster: I couldn't move! All my muscles had stiffened with the cold, moist night, and I couldn't turn my head or move my arms. Pierre suggested a hot shower, which relieved the pain a bit, but he still had to help me dress. I felt about eighty.

We had to move on again, so the children helped Pierre get ready for the next leg of our trip. The scenery made it all worthwhile. Everywhere we looked we saw the high peaks of the mountains, with a sprinkling of snow on top and along the slopes, the air pure and crisp, while the sun made the snow glisten and sparkle like crystal. My tears were welling up as I realised how beautiful Europe is, and how little we had seen of it. I was so glad we had taken this opportunity.

I remarked on this to Pierre at one stage, and he answered, 'I knew this would do the trick. This was a good transition period. Once we are home it will be very busy again, but no one can take this away from us, and the children won't stop talking about it. Let's hope the others will get a chance to see all this later.'

Sadly, we packed the car for the last time, and I silently said goodbye to the palms, the lakes and the rivers. Perhaps I would find my palm trees again in a few months' time, in that faraway part of the world ... Now, it was a hopeful thought.

What a welcome we received when we arrived home, so many hugs and kisses, and it seemed everything was fine. A festive afternoon tea had been prepared for our home coming. It was party time, with everyone talking at once.

Later, with the children in bed, our babies happily asleep with the few presents we'd bought them, Pierre brought up the business correspondence and went through the letters one by one.

Then he picked up a large manila envelope, and, as he did this, it

Part Five: Emigration

seemed as if all movement stilled. Without a word he handed me the letter. His face did not give anything away. It was an official letter from the Immigration Department informing us that our application to emigrate had been approved. Our date of departure was stipulated as December 11 on SS *Waterman*. The details of our accommodation on board would be forwarded as soon as they had been finalised.

I started to shiver as if someone had just doused me with icy water. Reality had caught up with us. Now, there would be no turning back …

38. STEPPING OUT … IN FAITH

This wonderful but brief holiday in France rapidly became a distant memory. Now the greatest stress for Corry and Pierre was in selling their business. While the necessary advertisements had been placed in various national and provincial papers, reactions were slow in coming. So, with each passing day, with the gap to the day of departure inexorably narrowing, the level of anxiety and stress continually increased. It was a nerve-wracking time.

A deep underlying Catholic faith was interwoven through the lives of my parents. This faith was not so much spoken about by them as it was lived. Many years later when my mother was ravaged by dementia, she could still easily remember, and say, her prayers, and she understood what Communion meant to her.

What happens now mirrors my own experiences of what can occur when one steps out in faith, trusting in God's grace and love, but holding nothing back in what we ourselves are able to do. Sometimes, there might even be miracles!

> One night, after closing, Pierre came in and said, 'I've been thinking …'
> As soon as I hear this I think, 'Oh, oh, here comes another scheme.' I was totally taken aback by this one, however.
> 'I'm a bit worried,' he continued. 'Time marches on and we haven't had any luck selling the shop, so I thought I'd go on pilgrimage to Grave.'
> We were both raised in the Catholic faith, and had a great devotion to Mary, the mother of Christ. Near Pierre's hometown, Helmond, is a small township called Binderen, where a little chapel had been erected and devoted to Mary. Many people went there to pray, to ask for help in sickness or hardship.

When we were engaged, we used to visit this little chapel often, to say a few Hail Marys and light a candle. It was a lovely custom, adhered to by many. It was part of daily life, and May and October are months of special devotion to Mary. Scattered across the Netherlands are many such places, including in Grave about 30 km from Nijmegen. People walked or cycled to these places as pilgrimages.

'You never know,' Pierre continued. 'Maybe if I walk that distance next Sunday and say a few prayers there, we might sell. I'll take the train back of course.'

'You're sure you want to walk that distance?' I asked incredulously.

'Yes, why not? It may help. I can do it.'

I looked at his face. Determination looked back. I knew then, whatever I said would not make any difference. I had to admire him; he was so sure of this. 'Okay, if you think it will help.'

'I'm sure it will. I'll light a few candles, pray for a while, have a rest and something to eat and take the train back home. It all depends on the weather; if it rains, I'll go another day.'

So, on Sunday, a glorious September day, we waved him off, while I wondered whether he would really last the distance. The day dragged on. I stood at the window perhaps a thousand times, although I knew he could not possibly be home before dark. I had just finished dinner with the children when we heard the key in the front door and their dad walked in. A very tired Pierre who, when questioned, did not want any dinner; he was too tired to eat. 'Just give me lots of cold water,' he sighed.

I poured him a big tumbler of water straight from the fridge, left the jug on the table, and asked, 'And? How was it?'

'It was okay. The last few kilometres were the worst, of course. I'm out of practice, after all, and it's different when you're walking on your own. Still, I enjoyed it. Let's hope something good will come of it. Mary will have to come to the party now.'

Nothing happened, however. There were a few enquiries, but still no sale. Maybe it is hard to understand that this was such a difficult and mentally exhausting time for us. We had mentally prepared for this move and were now held captive in uncertainty. I wished sometimes it would all go away, and we could wind back the clock. It was hard to be positive and believe everything would fall into place.

Stepping Out ... In Faith

When, after a couple of weeks of fruitless negotiations, we still had not found a successful candidate for the shop, Pierre suddenly said one day, 'It's not been far enough.'

'What're you on about?' I asked, not catching on straight away.

'My walk; it hasn't been far enough. I should have gone to Binderen. I'm sure if I walk that distance, Our Lady of Binderen will help us. She's helped us before, remember, when we needed a house.'

'Pierre, that's 60 km you're talking about. You'll kill yourself.'

'No, I won't. I feel sure about this: if I walk to Binderen, we'll sell!'

'Pierre, you can't! Not sixty kilometres.'

'Yes, I can, and I will.'

I knew him well enough to not take it any further. Obviously, his mind was made up.

'I'll go next Sunday, the first Sunday in October. Maybe that will be our lucky day.'

'I sincerely hope so because I've wondered whether we will get everything done by 11 December!'

On the following Saturday, 3 October, we were plumb in the middle of our autumn sale, and people in the Netherlands—aware of the long winter nights ahead—had started thinking of buying new ceiling and wall lights, and various electrical appliances, like heaters and electric blankets. All this to make the bitter winter nights easier to bear, and their homes more welcoming. It was our busiest time of the year. There were five of us serving in the shop that day: Pierre and I, two shop assistants and one of Pierre's teammates from the volleyball club, who generally took care of deliveries or helped in the shop where needed.

One of our clients was a well-dressed gentleman, who walked around the shop, inspecting the merchandise as if he were looking for something special. He went outside to look at the window display, came back in, to then start the same routine all over again. When Pierre was free at last to attend to him, he approached this customer and asked, 'Can I help you with anything, sir?'

'No, thank you, I'm all right for the moment. I'm just having a look around.' We didn't give it much thought; people often came in for a browse, so we continued serving the customers and, sure enough, he left sometime later.

About an hour later he was back again, waiting patiently at the

Part Five: Emigration

door, until Pierre asked him again, 'Can I be of assistance, perhaps?'

The chap replied, 'I believe this business is for sale?'

Quite taken aback, Pierre replied, 'Yes, sir, that's right.'

This mysterious gentleman then floored Pierre with, 'It's sold.'

Pierre was absolutely stunned. They shook hands and he introduced himself as a Mr Maurits, an engineer, who had travelled from Leiden that morning to look at the shop.

Of course, I, occupied with serving customers, was unaware of what was happening. I did notice that Pierre ushered him into the office, offering him a chair, then came back and asked me to make some coffee, only then adding in a whispered aside, 'I think we sold.'

'WE WHAT?'

He nodded, silently putting a finger to his lips.

I couldn't take it in; this was not happening, not like this, surely. There would be hassles. My legs turned to water and, nerves jingling, I ran up the stairs to make the coffee, and when I brought the tray downstairs, I found them deep in conversation.

Pierre and Mr Maurits talked in the office for several hours, poring over books and figures. The rest of us carried on as if nothing out of the ordinary was taking place, but my mind was not on the job at all! Near closing time, he finally left. He shook my hand, thanked me for the coffee and said, 'Nice meeting you Mrs de Haas. I'll see you next week,' and to Pierre, 'I'll phone you Tuesday or Wednesday at the latest, Mr de Haas, and I will definitely see you on Sunday then.'

'And?' I asked, as I followed Pierre into the office.

He gave me a big hug, kissed me soundly and began to stash away books and paperwork. 'He has a meeting with his bank manager Monday and we'll probably hear something definite then.'

'How did he sound? Was he truly interested?'

'Very; enthusiastic even, the way he stood there observing everything. We're going to sell, I feel it, and to celebrate I'm going to take you out to the "Lakenhal" tonight. I've already organised someone to look after the children.'

'What about Binderen tomorrow? Are you still going?'

'Of course; a promise is a promise. Early tomorrow morning I'll put on my walking boots and you can wave me off. Tonight, we celebrate!'

'Don't you think it's a bit premature? Wouldn't you rather wait until it is all confirmed? You're tempting fate here.'

'Nonsense. Go on,' when I hesitated. 'I'll ring and book.'

I ran upstairs, excitement galloping wildly inside. The Lakenhal was our favourite restaurant, situated in the centre of town. It stood on the edge of Nijmegen's old town with its narrow streets and alleys, where it was not hard to imagine yourself in the Middle Ages.

Early next morning Pierre left for his pilgrimage to Binderen, a sixty-kilometre march, and I knew he would need every ounce of determination for this one. Once again, we waved him off with a promise that we would meet him at the station, once we knew what time to expect him.

It was a long day.

We had just sat down to dinner when the phone rang. I picked up and a very tired husband told me, 'I've arrived at the Molenstraat just now. Mum is fixing me something to eat.'

'How are you? Did it go all right?'

'Very sore and very tired. No one here wanted to believe me when I told them I had walked all the way. They kept asking where the car was with you and the children. Only when I asked Mum for a basin of water for my sore feet did she realise I wasn't making it up! But I did what I promised.' He sounded absolutely spent.

'Give Mama a kiss for me.'

'Will do, and Co, I have a surprise for you. I think you'll love it.'

He then told me what time he would be home, but I suggested, 'Why don't you stay the night and come home tomorrow morning?'

'No, I'll be all right. I'll see you at the station.'

'Okay then, and, Pierre, congratulations. You did it! We'll be there with bells on.'

His home crew was at the station in plenty of time, Veronique in the stroller with Peter pushing her, the others beside me, all ready to welcome the 'conquering hero'.

There were no laurels at the station's flower stall, but we bought two big bunches of flowers so the children could present them to Pierre. As he walked towards us later, I knew what a mammoth effort it had been. His face drawn with fatigue, he walked towards us slowly, then handed me a carefully wrapped parcel. 'Regards from Our Lady. Don't drop it. It cost me a year of my life to get this.'

The children had hidden the flowers behind their backs and

handed them to Pierre. 'Look, Daddy, these are for you for walking so far.' He nodded and smiled, but I could see he was too tired to talk. All he wanted was a hot shower, a drink. Once refreshed, he then tumbled into bed, relieved to at last get the weight off his feet.

When I unwrapped the parcel later, I found a beautiful ceramic wall plaque, a sculpture of Mary and child with a little lamb at Her feet, and I knew this would travel with us to that wide and sunny Southern Land.

On Tuesday the following week, we received a phone call from Mr Maurits informing us finances had been approved by his bank, and he would be in Nijmegen next Sunday to finalise the sale. He requested our accountant be present so we could sign the contract. The business had finally been sold and, at last, we could confidently organise for our departure ...

39. LETTING GO

Now Corry and Pierre entered the final stages of preparation, which were by no means any less stressful or less draining emotionally. Step by step, the ties to our lives in the Netherlands were being cut, each one with its own unique sense of loss and pain. Corry's account doesn't mince words.

> The hardest thing I have ever had to do in my life was to go home with Pierre and tell Mum and Dad we were going ahead with our plans and the business was sold. Of course, they couldn't understand why, and it was beyond us to explain how we could exchange a secure existence for an unknown and dicey future in the antipodes. I didn't understand it myself. And the promises of keeping in touch and future holidays home did not bandage their wounded hearts at the thought of never seeing their grandchildren again. It was a very quiet drive home.
> The handover date for the business was set for a fortnight before our departure, which also meant the flat above had to be empty by that date so the new owners could move in. We thought it best to try and find places in Helmond for the four older children, seeing as we would be departing from there. Family and friends were fantastic. We asked Mama whether she would look after Peter for us, to which she readily agreed, and friends of ours, who lived opposite, offered to have Simone. This was ideal as they had two little girls Simone's age, and Oma and big brother were nearby to keep an eye on her. Needless to say, we accepted gratefully.
> Pierre's eldest brother and his wife told us they would take Mona, who had holidayed with them before, and Pierre's auntie was happy to have Brigitte. Auntie Dora and her husband doted on our little miss, and Brigitte loved being there and had spent time with them before. At least there she didn't have to vie for attention with her siblings!

Part Five: Emigration

Our baby could 'board' with friends in Nijmegen, which I thought best, as she was still so small and would need me most. Our wonderful neighbours, who lived in the flat above us had offered accommodation to Pierre and me, which was ideal since Pierre had to be close to the shop to help the new owners settle in. It all seemed to fall into place neatly. Now my only hope was that the children would not fret. We had prepared them, told them it was only for a little while, but, as I said before, how do you explain time to a child? I think Peter and Mona understood. I was most uneasy about the younger children, however.

Then, a few days later, the flat above the shop stood empty, except for two suitcases, Pierre's and mine. I was miserable; everything ached. A mixed feeling of apprehension and nausea settled in my stomach. I walked the silent rooms. There were no bright children's voices; no toys strewn haphazardly on the floor. In the girl's bedroom a little doll lay deserted in the corner. One of its arms had come off, obviously not fit to emigrate; had not passed its medical. Little finger marks on the wall where Veronique's cot stood; at least I would see my baby often. I shivered; the flat had died around me, a home no longer. Only the memories remained …

I walked back into the lounge and stood at the window. Across the road Chris and Geoff sat down at dinner. Soft light from the wall fixtures created a cosy atmosphere. She caught me standing there and waved, as we always did first thing in the morning. It was a sign all was well. I waved back, thinking, 'I'll never be able to do this again.'

Two strange weeks followed, with Pierre working in the shop, while I spent most of my time getting some last-minute shopping done and finishing some sewing. I had started in my other 'life'. I visited my baby girl often, but each time I left, Veronique started to cry, which upset me terribly. I held her close and, looking at her beautiful dark eyes, I kissed her silky hair and promised her silently she would never have to cry for me again. I would never leave her, no matter what the future would bring.

In all this hyper-busyness, the otherwise exciting period leading up to St Nicolas Day on the sixth of December now seemed to be a non-event. Instead of weeks planning and shopping for each other and the children, it was a strange and quiet time for us. We had decided not to give each other presents, as it meant more luggage; but how I

Letting Go

missed the children, especially taking them into town to see the decorated windows, their eyes full of wonder at the magic of it. Instead of weeks of excitement in preparation, I could buy only a small gift now, which would fit into their suitcases.

On the afternoon of the 4 December, Pierre's mum rang. 'Corry, I've bought presents for the children and I wonder will you and Pierre come home on the sixth? I've arranged for all the grandchildren to be here in the morning, and I'll have a table ready for them as usual.'

My eyes filled to overflowing, and with a voice thick with tears I said, 'Oh, Mama, that's lovely. Thank you, Mam, thanks so much for thinking of them. They'll love it, especially with all their cousins present as well!'

As usual she waived all thanks with, 'Seeing it's the last …' then swiftly broke the connection.

Mama certainly excelled herself. On the morning of the sixth we took an early train to Helmond and were met at the door by four excited children and their cousins, who had waited impatiently to see what St Nicolas had brought them. Peter was first to unwrap a big parcel and was beside himself when he found a genuine cable car, a first in remote-control toys, and of course had to try it out at once. Peter, his face a study in concentration at the controls, made the car creep along a fine cable across the lounge, his little face aglow with happiness. It was the girls' turn next. St Nicolas had not forgotten them after all!

One by one the other de Haas families arrived and there was much excitement for their children as well. It was a fantastic day. Mama had twenty-one for lunch that day, and I don't know how she managed it all. It was the last time we would all be together like this. Around seven, we called it a day, as we still had to get back to Nijmegen. Mr Maurits would be waiting for Pierre in the morning.

It had been a wonderful family day; one we would always remember and one we realised would never be repeated. We would be far away, in another country with other traditions and folklore. I had left a present for her and Dad in their bedroom, which they would find later. We thanked her with a big hug and kiss, and Pierre said, 'We'll see you on the tenth, Mam.'

We had planned it so that our entire family would be in Helmond on that date. Two of Pierre's brothers, Ted and Jan, had offered to

Part Five: Emigration

drive us to Rotterdam, where we would embark, and Mama had asked the neighbours whether we could stay the night there, to which they readily agreed.

Our last week in the Netherlands sped by with finalising details at the bank regarding the sale of the business. There were papers to be signed amidst assurances our interests in the Netherlands would be taken care of.

Then the hardest task of all: we had to say goodbye to all our friends and neighbours in the flats around us, who had been so kind during our last weeks in Nijmegen. We had to close so many doors behind us, and it was quite devastating. Several representatives of our business associates travelled all the way from Amsterdam to say farewell, which touched us deeply. We were drawing a line, a dividing line between past and future.

For the first time, I deeply knew the meaning of that adage, 'burning bridges behind you'. I felt hollow.

But at least we left with very many happy memories.

40. FAREWELL!

Corry continues:

Before we left Nijmegen, we phoned my parents, but I still cannot write about this. A few weeks before, we had taken the children home, to Oudenbosch, and had spent a happy day with them. I didn't tell my parents then we would not bring them back again to say goodbye. They had a happy memory now and I thought it too cruel to formally say farewell.

Pierre and I had also made the time to spend a few days with them. They still couldn't understand what we were seeking in that faraway land, and we could not explain it either. It was so hard to put into words; however, there were no harsh words spoken and, as they had done so wisely throughout, kept their misgivings to themselves. I can only bless them for their understanding. The promise I would come and visit as soon as we were settled made parting perhaps a little easier for them. Not for me though. I knew I would not see my gentle dad again …

Then the day of our departure dawned; a cold, dreary December day, with heavy fog hanging low across the roofs. Gutters dripped and a biting wind shrieked around the house. We had been made very welcome, but, although I had piled on the blankets, I could not get warm that night and had hardly slept at all. Too many pictures tumbled through my mind, like a jumbled kaleidoscope. Pierre lay beside me, softly snoring, and I envied him the peace of mind to be able to sleep so soundly after all the upheaval of the last four months.

I was glad he had set the alarm for 5.30 am—there were still so many last-minute things to take care of before we could leave. I wanted to be gone; and the day stored away deep inside. We had received notice we could board from eleven o'clock onwards, with the approximate time of departure set at 2 pm. We wanted to leave

Part Five: Emigration

ourselves plenty of time, this with the workday traffic in mind. We also didn't know how long it would take to clear customs and for checking of papers etc.

Breakfast with Mama was a very quiet affair, our son doing most of the talking. Our little boy was so excited to be finally leaving on this great adventure. I managed a cup of tea and a piece of toast, my otherwise healthy appetite lost somewhere in that griping feeling where my stomach used to be. Mama had made us two big bags of lovely fresh bread rolls, 'just in case lunch is later today,' she said, 'with so many people boarding and all.'

Our other children arrived soon after.

Then, it was time to check the suitcases, and lock them. Pierre put them in the hall, together with two travelling bags and my handbag, when suddenly Peter appeared, carrying his treasure, the cable car in its big carton box. Oh no, I thought; we had forgotten about it. This won't fit in the suitcases anymore. They're packed tight, full to bursting. We tried every one, but it was no use. There just wasn't any room. There was nothing for it: we had to leave it behind.

How to tell my little boy this? I couldn't. Simply could not. Not after all we had to let go and leave behind. I tried, but the words wouldn't come. So, in the end, it was Pierre who said, 'Peter, I'm sorry, son, but we can't take this with us now. I'm afraid you'll have to leave it here with Oma, so she can look after it for you.' I can still see his little face, thick tears rolling down as he handed his cable car over, saying, 'But when I come back, I want it back!'

Yes, I do remember this very well, and, twenty-five years later, as an adult, I met my cousin in the Netherlands who had inherited my cable car. He didn't give it back to me!! Mum never forgot this moment … It released all the emotions she had been feeling into a flood of tears.

That was it for me. I ran upstairs and howled. Of all we had to leave behind today, this was the last straw. I cried and cried until I had no tears left, then washed my face, applied new make-up and took a deep breath. I went down, took Peter aside and promised him, 'If I can get a cable car in Australia, I'll buy one for you there, okay? I promise,' but he was inconsolable, and I hugged him as if that would

Farewell!

make it all go away. It was one of the worst moments of my life.

It was just as well that when the time came to say goodbye, there were no tears left. Dry eyed I kissed Mama goodbye, thanked her for everything she had done for us, after which I left some space for Pierre and his mother. His dad was still in bed, hadn't come to say goodbye, so I knocked on the bedroom door, opened it a chink and said goodbye that way. He mumbled something, I don't know what, so I quickly closed the door on it. Pierre didn't bother. That was so sad ...

It was time. The men took the suitcases down and put them in the cars, a last hug and kiss for the children, then, before we turned the corner, a last wave from Mama, and from the neighbours, who had gathered outside to see us off. 'Good luck,' and 'Goodbye!'

I don't remember too much about this drive, except that it was raining and miserable. In the car, no one spoke very much, and, in that silence, I sensed some of the gravity and finality of what, as a family, we were embarking on.

Two hours later we arrived in Rotterdam. On reaching the harbour we had to drive at a snail's pace to snake our way through the crowds gathered there. Each family embarking on SS *Waterman* was accompanied by some family members of course. It seemed to be like a scene from a motion picture with hundreds of walk-on extras.

An icy wind blew in from the North Sea, and the early fog had turned into an annoying drizzle. I was glad I dressed the children warmly. Jan and Ted accompanied us to the customs building, where a sign read, 'Passengers only.' It was time to say goodbye once again. Jan seemed to be okay, but poor Ted dissolved in tears as he embraced us all. People were queuing behind us, so we made it brief and maybe this was just as well.

'We'll wait until the boat leaves,' Jan said. 'I'll wave with my umbrella,' and I wondered how we would find them in this mass of people. Customs was a mini-nightmare, with Pierre inching forward seven big suitcases, and me checking on the children every few minutes, meanwhile shifting the baby from one arm to the other, until I thought they'd both drop off. It took ages and I wondered how they could possibly process everyone by departure time.

I scanned the faces of my fellow passengers and knew their expressions mirrored mine: apprehension, fear, sadness and doubts about a decision we had taken and would only know years from now whether it had been the right one. At last, it was our turn. We handed over the different forms, all properly filled out, passports were duly stamped and then relief at last. A steward appeared with a lovely big trolley to take our suitcases to the gangplank, where others were waiting to carry them on board.

Pierre took Veronique from me, and, bags slung around my shoulder, I took Simone and Brigitte by the hand while Mona and Peter followed close behind Pierre to close ranks. Once on board a cabin boy showed us our cabin. He unlocked the door, switched on the lights, and explained the layout and facilities in perfect Dutch. He assured us our luggage would follow soon. Our cabin was not big, but because of our big family we had it all to ourselves, possibly because we'd had to pay part of our voyage ourselves.

Our cabin had three bunk beds and there was a little cot for Veronique, which was great. The cabin lay aft near the deck and had two portholes which would provide a nice cross breeze through the cabin when we reached the tropics. Everything was spotless: lovely clean linen, hand basin and mirror shining. It also had a small wardrobe to hang up some clothes, which was ideal. I knew we would be living out of suitcases for the duration, but the hanging space would make it a bit easier.

After our suitcases arrived, I quickly sorted out what we first wanted, shoved them out of sight under the beds, and we seemed settled. Veronique, thumb in her mouth, sat in her cot, quite contentedly watching all the activity, while the others were trying out the 'bounce' of their beds, and arguing who should sleep on top. Things were back to normal.

With our boarding passes we had received a deck plan of the SS *Waterman*, and Pierre was studying the layout. We planned to take Mona and Peter on deck when the ship left the harbour, so we had to locate the nursery and playroom. We wanted to take the younger children there for a half hour or so, while we said goodbye to the Netherlands.

With two o'clock approaching, we took them down, and, after we introduced ourselves to the young woman in charge, she said, 'I've been expecting you, Mr and Mrs de Haas.'

'Expecting us?'

'Yes, Mrs de Haas, your cousin Netty asked me to give you this,' and handed me a beautifully wrapped parcel. 'Netty is a close friend of mine,' she explained. 'When she found out you were sailing on the *Waterman*, she wanted to surprise you.'

Pierre and I looked at each other, lost for words. Trust Netty to think of this. As children and teenagers, we had spent every free minute together. We were the same age, were always in the same class, true bosom-buddies, and remained this through our teenage years. 'But how did you meet Netty?' I asked.

'Through school. I'm also a pre-school teacher and her two eldest boys were in my class.'

This was an amazing coincidence. After we were married, we kept in touch, and it was nice to know someone who provided a link to my youth. 'Now I know the children will be well looked after when they have to spend some time here,' I joked. 'You are going to Australia with us, aren't you?'

She smiled. 'Yes, all the way. This is my third trip and I love it. It is a tremendous change from a classroom, and it is fantastic to see a bit of the world.'

'We'll pick the younger children up again after the departure then, Miss ... Sorry, what's your name?'

'Oh, of course, I'm sorry; must be all the excitement of meeting you. My name is Mary.'

A few minutes later, all rugged up against the biting cold outside, we climbed the outer stairs which led to the top deck, where frantic last-minute activity greeted us. There were people everywhere. Peter and Mona leant on the railing and watched in fascination as big wooden crates were hauled up and deposited into the gaping mouth of the cargo holds beneath us, while I prayed silently the massive cranes would have a good grip on our crate.

The quay was a sea of waving arms. Last minute messages were shouted, but with all the noise and the distance they were impossible to understand. We searched through the masses, trying to pick out Pierre's brothers amongst the crowd, but it was too much to hope for. We waved anyway, hoping they could see us!

Part Five: Emigration

Two o'clock, ten past two, quarter past; we watched the gangplank rise, the mooring ropes thrown clear, and with an ear-splitting rattle the anchor was raised. A rumble of heavy engines, a tremor shuddered through the *Waterman*, the thump, thump grew louder; an acrid smell of diesel oil rose in the air, and a roar went up from the throng on the quay.

These moments, as the engine started with a cloud of smoke and diesel fumes, the mooring ropes thrown clear and the ship slowly drawing away from the quay, are indelibly imprinted in my memories. Even as a young boy, I could sense the import of what was happening. This was real and there would be no going back, but I was also quite excited. I stayed on deck as our ship slowly navigated through the channels of Rotterdam harbour and enjoyed seeing all the large cranes and other huge ships at anchor or berthed along the wharves.

Slowly the gap between ship and shore widened. In the distance, one red hanky tied to an umbrella: arms waving, waving. I took my children's hands in mine for reassurance while Pierre's arm rested around my shoulder, but at that moment I stood totally alone. We slowly steamed towards the open sea, past the many ships at anchor; faces became a blur, the quay disappeared into the misty distance; then there was just the sea, a cold, grey sea.

41.   LIFE AT SEA

On leaving the safety of Rotterdam harbour, the SS *Waterman* steamed straight into a North Sea storm, and the emotional roller coaster of the past months was now replaced by a challenging physical one as the ship heaved and bucked in the wildly dancing waves driven by a howling gale. For Corry, it must have seemed like some sort of sick joke, or a living nightmare, especially when we all started to succumb to seasickness, Pierre being the first!

> Those first days on board SS *Waterman* were certainly different from all I had known so far. The weather was not helping. Wild seas fought her for every mile. Our little cabin could not replace the comfortable home we had known. I was like a bird that had landed in a strange nest and didn't know how to get out.
> What I remember most vividly was that I was terribly cold all the time.
> I ran around getting everyone drinks, then to the toilets—which I had to find first—with sick bags. I was so busy those first days, I didn't get time to notice whether I was seasick or not and surprised myself. (Every time I fell pregnant, I was sick for five months. If they had given out Oscars for throwing up, I would have won them all.)
> When I felt a bit queasy, I went outside and marched up and down the gangways, fighting the fierce wind and the heaving deck, and filling my lungs with huge gasps of fresh air which kept me going. On one occasion, I found myself on the prow and watched the ship in her fight to conquer the massive waves; watched as they crashed across the bow and felt as if I was part of this battle, for one was raging deep inside me as well. I held on to whatever was near, felt each shudder, each creak and sigh of her, while I fought down the nausea that swept through me, refusing to give in. If I went down, there would be no one to look after the children, so I decided against getting seasick. I wasn't, not a single day.

Part Five: Emigration

Those first days dragged on. The children sat up in bed, pale little faces peering at me from their bunks while the hours crept by slowly, ever so slowly. When the dinner gong sounded, I went down alone. Again, the dining room was nearly deserted, but the soft light of the wall lights created a warm atmosphere, far nicer than the cold grey light of day. I had promised the children I would order something for them, but there was not much choice in the circumstances. Anything decent was out of the question for it would make them feel sick again, so I asked for dry biscuits and weak tea, which were delivered to our 'hotel room' later and just as well! I didn't have any spare hands; I needed both to stay upright.

I decided to forego bathing the children, just washed their faces and hands, and popped them back into bed, promising they would feel a lot better come morning. I was immensely grateful we had the cabin to ourselves. If we'd had to share, it would have been extremely difficult.

As one day slowly merged with another, with no sign of the sea abating, Corry found some space and time for herself in the evening after we (including Pierre) were all asleep. She found a place on deck which was sheltered from the wind and wrapped herself in a blanket.

> It was lovely and quiet here, away from the wind, no sound other than the steady growl of the engines and the wash of waves against the ship. I tucked the blanket close around me and leaned back, enjoying the elements. I felt one with the wind and the sea; en route to an unknown future, already far removed from all that was familiar.
>
> This transition period would be good for us. After all the hassles of the last few months we were free now to enjoy ourselves on what, especially for Pierre and me, would be the last adventure of such magnitude. Listening to the wind proved to be a calming influence and it felt good to be alone for a while. Breathing deeply, I let the salty air clear my mind of all anxiety. Here I was at peace. The worst was over, for now.
>
> A young sailor, coming off duty, stepped outside to light a cigarette and spotted me. 'I beg your pardon, madam, I didn't see you there. You must be the only one on board still up.'

Life at Sea

'Well, I had a very busy day, and now I'm enjoying a few moments alone.'

'I hope I'm not disturbing you?'

'Oh, no, not at all.'

'Last cigarette, you see, before I turn in.' He stood at the railing, smoking, finished his cigarette and, with a 'Goodnight', left me alone with my thoughts. Shortly afterwards I retired as well but doubted whether my sleep would be as sound and undisturbed as his.

I didn't sleep much. I had not been trained for sleeping on a roller coaster, and many times I expected to find myself on the floor as the ship shuddered through the night. I was pleased to see dawn creeping through the portholes at last.

Four days later, on nearing the Azores, the weather improved, and the sea became much calmer. Together with most of the other passengers, we all quickly recovered from *mal de mer* and were finally able to explore our 'home' for the next five weeks. From this time on, until our crossing of the Tasman, life on board became a holiday, not dissimilar to what is now so relished on modern cruise ships.

We all stood at the railing that afternoon when Pierre called out, 'Look, kids, there!' He pointed down. 'There's a school of porpoises following the boat. Can you see them?' He was right. As we watched, they approached our ship, and, like some sort of official escort, swam with us, jumping out of the water to then dive again, putting on a wonderful display of agility and grace. The children were thrilled as they watched the glistening bodies jump up like frolicking children. They swam with us for some time, then, tiring of the game, they disappeared.

With the bad weather behind us, life on board was exciting, especially for me. At times I felt like a movie star, sitting on deck winking at the sun, not a worry in the world; no cooking to do or serving of meals. It was all done for us. Talk about a holiday! Morning and afternoon tea served when we wanted it ... 'I can take this for a few months,' I said to Pierre.

We soon established a wonderful routine. All the children had their meals at a special sitting before the parents had theirs. There was a waiter at every table and I only had to look after Veronique. The Indonesian waiters seemed to love children, for they could not do enough for them, which was lovely to see. We felt as if we were staying in a five-star hotel. At all meals, the waiters were always close by and attentive, and when Pierre started to converse with them in Malay, they could not do enough for us.

On board we met some genuinely nice people, couples with young children about the same age as ours, and we soon sought each other's company and later spent a lot of time together.

From time to time, the entertainment officer organised games for the children in which they could win little prizes. Peter and Mona eagerly took part and loved it. There was a library on board if you wanted a quiet read, or to write a letter. We also had classes in English, which Pierre and I decided were a must, since we would be living in an English-speaking country.

I loved this special time on the ship. I often sat and watched the V of white foam the *Waterman* left in her wake, dreaming a little, the horizon somewhat undefined, like our lives now: sailing between two worlds, the old and the new. I enjoyed every day.

42. Christmas at Panama

As Christmas Eve dawned, the SS *Waterman* was approaching the Panama Canal, a milestone on our journey which would leave an indelible memory with me, with images as fresh today as they were sixty years ago. However, first things first.

December 24 is also my sister, Simone's, birthday. So, while she was still asleep, we all decorated her bunk and the rest of the cabin with colourful streamers, and then, as she awoke, we greeted her by singing: '*Lang zal ze leven*' (roughly translated as: 'long shall she live'). Then she unwrapped her presents; an exciting and happy morning for all of us. As we entered the canal itself, we spotted a big sign on one of the buildings which read 'Merry Christmas and a Happy New Year', which further heightened our festive mood.

Like many other passengers, I spent much of the day on deck completely engrossed with our ship being manoeuvred through what seemed to be the tiniest locks by little locomotives, up to four at a time. I was fascinated, not only by these little engines but also by the operation of the locks themselves, with their massive gates, and how the ship rose or fell as it passed through them. As a seven-year-old, I was amazed by this engineering marvel—I had never seen anything remotely like it.

As that day was also Christmas Eve there was a growing excitement in our family, as this was always such a special time which Corry and Pierre always held very, very dear.

> The Christmas atmosphere took a firm hold on us. I sent up a quick prayer of thanks for being able to experience all of this. I knew whatever happened in the future, no one could take these impressions away from me.

Later that night, Midnight Mass was a most uplifting start to the

Part Five: Emigration

Christmas celebrations on board. When we arrived, the cinema was already packed, but we were in luck; there were still a few seats at the front. Peter and Mona had made their first communions and went to church with us every Sunday, so they knew the liturgy, and followed everything with great interest. They sang the beautiful traditional carols with us, and I was so happy to have this special time together.

It was a very moving occasion. When the first tones of 'Silent Night' sounded, I knew there wouldn't be a dry eye anywhere. We remembered previous Christmases and thought of those we left behind.

After Mass, the captain told us coffee and fresh bread rolls would be served in the dining room, so that we would have a chance to wish each other the best of the season. Petty differences seemed forgotten; passengers celebrated with a true feeling of good will; after all, we were all in the same boat!

We took Peter and Mona to the cabin and, when they had settled down, we met with our friends on deck. The padre joined us there later, and we talked and talked as if there were no tomorrow. We didn't want this night to end. The sky was dusted with diamonds, and the moon threw ribbons of silver on the waves. We talked the night away ... then said goodnight and sought our cabin.

We passed the crew's quarters and noticed they too were still up, enjoying a few drinks and a smoke, seeing the night out. They were celebrating Christmas as well and invited us to stay a while, which we happily did. Later, much later, we tumbled into our bunks, when I remarked, 'Well, I know we will never have such an unusual and happy Christmas Eve again. I never thought it could be like this.'

It was 4.30 am, and dawn's early light crept along the portholes. Christmas Day 1959.

That day was unforgettable. From the children's breakfast sitting onwards it was one big celebration. It was hard to imagine we were on a migrant ship, and the efforts of the captain and crew went far beyond any expectations that anyone could have held. They could not have done more for us.

When Christmas dinner was announced, we found the children had special menus, printed on lovely, decorated cards; all the dishes had names of fairy-tale characters; and the tables were tastefully decorated with green and red ribbons, and strewn with confetti. When our children walked into the room, their eyes were as big as saucers. I could well imagine the amount of work it had taken to make this so special, and I decided I would send a thank-you note to the captain and ask him to also convey our thanks to the crew.

The adults' Christmas dinner was an eight-course affair, presided over by the captain, accompanied by some of the officers who were off duty. Talk was animated and cheerful; tonight was a night of celebration and our good old ship felt like home for a while. It was a night with a golden edge, and I remembered thinking, 'If our parents could see us now, it would lift their spirits and dispel some of their worries.'

Then Boxing Day was totally geared to preparing for the Christmas ball that night, and, I dare say, we ladies sparkled! Hair wavy and shining, we had dressed in lovely summer frocks and sandals, with the men wearing suits and ties. Jackets were soon discarded, however, when the music started.

We had a wonderful time dancing all night, until at 10.30 pm the captain finally declared the bar closed. Although we protested loudly, he would not budge. Then one of the officers began to sing a well-known popular folk song, a favourite from the Dutch province, Limburg, where the captain was born. Suddenly the entire crowd erupted in song as we all joined in, until he relented and said, 'Oh, all right, you lot, one more drink for everyone.' It earned him an enormous round of applause.

43.   ON TO AUSTRALIA

The usual routine of life on board resumed after we had left the Panama Canal in our wake. The equator was crossed on 29 December, and 'celebrated' by King Neptune in the presence of many of the crew and passengers. The ceremony was held on the largest deck with everyone gathered around an impromptu stage, some standing and some sitting. I sat close to the front, all the time not knowing that those poor unfortunates, who were subjected to this King's trident and other depredations, were all volunteers. They had put their names down in advance! So, I was terrified that, just like these folks who seemed to me to be randomly selected, I too would soon be hauled out of my seat and subjected to the horrible spectacle I had been witnessing and had never in my young life seen the likes of.

One by one the victims were led to King Neptune, who ordered them 'soaped'. This was a terrible mix of pink porridge, soot and flour, which was rubbed on their arms, legs, hair and clothes. Next, they were locked in the stocks, where they were fed a raw herring, followed by a big glass of gin which they had to scull, to then be dumped into an enormous tub of water. Each time they tried to climb out, Neptune, with his trident, pushed them under again.

Apparently, it was considered very funny by all the adults watching, but I only remember how gross and scary it all was. Afterwards, like all the passengers crossing the equator for the first time, Corry and Pierre received a citation with their names and date of crossing duly displayed. They were lucky to have earned theirs in such a leisurely manner!

Two days later it was New Year's Eve …

New Year's Eve was a wonderful night of fun and dancing, but despite the outward appearance of celebration, I was sure each of us nurtured a big question mark inside, wondering what 1960 would bring. When we were counting down the last minutes of this very eventful 1959, I hoped the new one would not be too grim. I knew we were right to enjoy every moment of this wonderful cruise, for as soon as we set foot in our new country, it would be full-on once again. I prayed I would find it in me to meet this enormous challenge head on … and see it through.

Pierre and I sat aft on the deck for a long time on that first morning of the New Year. We didn't talk, but let the tropical night soothe away our uncertainties. We watched the ship's wake trail behind, the dull hum of the engines now the only sound. It was strangely calming, this vast expanse of ocean, the sky and sea as company. I wished this could go on forever, this pure existence with the moon throwing glitter on the waves; we two part of the greater unknown, part of this great mystery of life.

It was during our next stop, in Tahiti, when Corry experienced an entirely new insight, full of gratitude, into the adventure that she and Pierre, and we children, were embarked upon. Perhaps it was the tropical air and the palm trees, or was it the exotic nature of this beautiful paradise with its 'buzz'? Whatever the reason, it reveals a remarkable transformation for someone who first reacted so strongly to any thought of emigration only a few months beforehand!

> We took the children ashore to explore the town, which looked just as quaint as Willemstad [the capital of Curaçao, a Dutch Caribbean island, where the ship had stopped briefly], only more exotic—if that was possible—lush and green; almost voluptuous in growth, like the sarong-clad girls. Pierre bought us all gigantic ice creams, which we thoroughly enjoyed while sitting on a little terrace, soaking in the local atmosphere.
>
> After dinner that night, Pierre and I went ashore again to see whether we could capture 'some of the action', a performance or a dance somewhere. We landed outside the 'Tahitian Hut', where some 'performances' were happening already, but not the kind we sought.
>
> We watched 'on the sidelines' for a while, but soon tired of this

Part Five: Emigration

and looked for a spot on the patio, where we could still hear the music and enjoy a cool drink. The music was hot and energising, the Polynesian rhythm and the girls' grass skirts moved in tandem, twirled and swayed around the smooth young bellies, and you couldn't help but be swept along on the electric atmosphere.

We thoroughly enjoyed this view of a totally different world and took our time over our drinks; watched as the gyrating bodies turned into glistening young goddesses. The unattached young passengers were part of this scene, and I'm sure their very married brethren watched with envy, and could only wish … and wish …

It was a beautiful night, the air soft as silk, and the moon's friendly face floodlit the white caps of the breakers as they rolled to the shore. A night made for romance. We walked along the beach, arms around each other. I think we both realised this transition between the life we knew and what was to come had been of enormous value. I would have hated to emigrate by stepping on a plane and landing in Australia only a few days later. I now understood what Pierre meant when he wrote, 'I like being underway, travelling between two worlds.'

Maybe my ancestors had endowed me with some adventurous blood. I enjoyed this so much, seeing part of a wide world I would not have seen otherwise. Admittedly, we travelled with five young children, but somehow, they seemed to enhance our pleasure. They seemed so interested in everything new. I was sure the older children would never forget this and hoped one day they would thank us for it.

I realised also how incredibly beautiful our world is and what a mess people make of it at times, through greed and selfishness and petty little grievances. This voyage had opened my eyes, and I would be eternally grateful for it.

In that one moment I felt what true happiness means. We had no house, an uncertain future, no idea where we would settle, and I fervently wished Mum and Dad could have seen this, especially Dad. 'Yes, Papa,' I thought, 'people everywhere must work for a living, but, by God, look how they can enjoy their leisure time, so close to nature. You would have loved this.' More and more I began to realise how Pierre must have felt when he came home after living in the tropics for three years; the unrest that troubled him constantly. How small the Netherlands must have felt after Indonesia!

Next morning, with much grinding and rattling, the anchor was hauled up once again and we followed the pilot boat out towards the open sea. I felt sad and doubted whether I would ever see this little paradise again. Perhaps some places are just too beautiful to see more than once in a lifetime. I, like many of us, wanted the dream to last.

After leaving Tahiti, and with each passing day, Corry's anxiety steadily increased as Australia, and what it would entail, came closer to the horizon with each turn of the propellor. She didn't want this comparatively care-free voyage to end.

Having completed a short overnight stop in Wellington, New Zealand, once again the SS *Waterman* found itself battling very heavy seas as it crept across the Tasman. True to form, Pierre was again seasick and in bed. To Corry it seemed that the voyage finishing as it had begun—being tossed around by the waves—was a 'wake-up call' and a final preparation for what was to come.

With the bad weather, the atmosphere on board changed as well. I was sure each one of us was apprehensive of the days to come, and the carefree weeks on our ship were already just a memory.

We were due to arrive in Sydney on the 16 January; so, on leaving New Zealand, we started to prepare for our arrival as best we could despite the best efforts of the heaving waves. I sorted clothes we needed, repacked suitcases and bags, and went walking gangways once again. The children had lost much of their appetite during the bad weather, but, luckily, they weren't sick. Pierre was not so lucky.

Then, at last, we caught our first glimpse of the Australian coast as the weather changed for the better. Not long afterwards, under an extremely hot, tropical sun, we were sailing into Sydney harbour. We all stood on deck to take in this magnificent sight, the first glimpse of our future country. As we sailed underneath the Sydney Harbour Bridge, the children pointed excitedly at the little island we passed. Boats lay at anchor at luxurious houses, and a ferry was taking its passengers for a ride to the other side.

I remained on deck the whole time from when we steamed through

Part Five: Emigration

the Heads of this stunning harbour. However, as one who tends to worry, I became quite convinced, as we steadily approached the bridge, that it was far too low for the ship to pass underneath. The SS *Waterman* was obviously going to lose its masts and the funnels. I was wrong!

It was so beautiful, and it gave me hope for the future.

But ... beauty disappeared immediately when we berthed at a run-down, deserted quay, where long snakes of corrugated-iron sheds lay waiting, serpents which would swallow us whole. Now that we lay still, the heat felt like a steaming wall around us, and a strange pungent smell hung in the air. Dejection settled inside me like a lump of lead. Dreams were a thing of the past, and reality had taken their place.

Lunch was a very quiet affair. Even the children were subdued as if my mood had superimposed itself on our offspring, and my healthy appetite took a holiday. It was sad to say goodbye to the dining room personnel; they had taken such good care of us

Shortly afterwards it was time to clear customs, have our luggage checked and readied for transfer to the interstate railway station. We descended the gangplank, Pierre struggling once again with our seven suitcases, while I kept an eye on the children. Progress was slow, and we waited and waited until at last it was our turn.

Several long trestle tables were set up in the hall where the customs officers were waiting. We approached the one nearest to us and he addressed Pierre with, 'Please, sir, put your suitcases on the bench here and open them, so we can have a look at the contents.' Pierre heaved them onto the tables one by one, when the chap exclaimed, 'Seven?'

'Yes,' said my husband, 'there are seven in our family. Do I have to open all of them?'

'No,' he answered, 'I don't think that's necessary. I'll check the first two and, if you buy me a beer, I'll take your word for the rest.' He went through the cases, checked the forms, and said, 'These seem to be in order.'

Crossing the cases with a piece of chalk, he moved them to the far side of the bench, where some wharfies were waiting to put them on trolleys. Meanwhile Pierre reached into his pocket, took out a couple of two-shilling pieces, handed them to the officer, and said, 'Will this do?'

'Yeah, yeah, that's fine.' He pocketed them and called out, 'Next, please.'

First hurdle overcome. Passport checks were next, and these were found to be in order as well. Much relieved, we went back to our cabin with a long wait ahead of us and at a total loss what to do in the meantime. Luckily, we heard afternoon tea would be served as usual, which was a small distraction. We lingered there a while, then went for a walk on the quay, but there was very little to see, apart from deserted sheds and warehouses; it was a dismal sight.

It was a strange, long and sad afternoon, and I felt totally out of tune with this environment. The sun was still shining, but it was as if its rays had lost their brilliance somehow, and it seemed that a sense of apprehension had settled in to stay. It was a relief when the crew did their rounds, asking us to assemble on the quay so we could board the buses which would take us to the station. A last look at our cabin, our home for almost six weeks, a last look out of the porthole, a check under the bunks and in the one cupboard.

We closed the door behind us, leaving the old, ready for the new. A few crew members, arms on the railings, waved us off, while we made our way to the gangplank for the last time. It was, without a doubt, the longest walk I ever took.

44. OVERNIGHT TRAIN TO BRISBANE

A new expression, which has only recently entered everyday use, is 'living in a bubble'. While this may once have had negative connotations, suggesting someone cut off from reality, in 2020 it took on an entirely different meaning: understood as being in a safe, protective space, in a comparatively small group, cut off from the risk of infection from a dreadful pandemic. Back in 1960, the five weeks in transit on the SS *Waterman* would have been a 'living in a bubble' experience for Corry and Pierre, and less so for my siblings and me. Yes, the seas were sometimes very rough, but on board, Dutch was spoken, familiar meals were prepared, and the Christmas festivities would have had that Dutch 'touch' about them.

The experience of suddenly leaving this pampered and safe cocoon, and entering what was indeed a new world, can only be fully appreciated by those who have made a similar plunge into the unknown, where everything is completely new: the heat, the sights, the smells, the culture. Yes, it is exciting and stimulating, but can also be overwhelming, and extremely draining.

All things considered, we all did rather well in those first hours and days.

> Sydney seemed like a town deserted, vastly different to what I had envisaged. Being a Saturday afternoon, all the shops were closed, and there was little traffic apart from buses and trams. Maybe its people, eager to catch a breeze, had sought relief from this extreme heat at the beach.
>
> On arrival at the station, we were escorted to a platform where the train stood waiting and were allotted a compartment, which we had to ourselves—once again, an advantage in having a big family. Pierre and I slung our hand luggage onto the racks while the children tried

to figure out where everyone should be sitting, which of course brought the usual squabbles. Father soon fixed this by telling them, 'That's enough, settle down now.'

We tried to get comfortable in the scorching heat. Although late afternoon, it was stifling, and the humidity was almost unbearable. Within minutes my dress was glued to my back.

Finally, the train pulled out of the station and gave us our first look at an Australian city. Like all railway lines, these too ran mostly through industrial sections, with dull grey warehouses and factories, until we left the built-up area behind and entered open country, sprinkled here and there with small rural towns.

Darkness was sudden, and a long, drawn-out night began. It was still hot and humid, though, and we had to leave the windows open. The soot from the steam engine billowed freely into the carriage, until everything was covered in layers of grime, including the clothes we wore.

On boarding the train, we had received a luncheon packet, and as soon as the children were settled, Pierre went to the canteen to buy some drinks for our first Australian picnic, a picnic on wheels. It was a long time since lunch and it went down very well, except for the babies. I think Simone and Veronique were too tired to eat. I didn't worry too much, just made sure they had a good drink. I then bedded them down on the seats.

Brigitte, still a bit off-colour through a slight throat infection, and Peter and Mona found it hard to get comfortable. They fidgeted and wriggled until a lady in the next compartment came to the rescue. She'd had the foresight to have a couple of blankets with her and she kindly offered us the use of one.

'I've put the children on a blanket on the floor,' she said. 'At least they can stretch out then.' I thanked her and, while Pierre put it down, I rolled up their coats for a pillow, and they too were asleep within minutes. Not so their mum and dad.

Pierre, an old soldier, was dozing in one corner. I'm sure the military can sleep standing up, but mothers don't have that training. In normal circumstances we mothers sleep with one ear tuned to the needs of our children, and now even more so. Try as I might I could not doze. It seemed as if I was counting every minute of every hour of that endless night.

Part Five: Emigration

Conversation was sporadic. 'Just settle down,' Pierre said. 'Try and at least get some rest.' I tried, but my jumbled thoughts danced a jig in my head. In the end I gave up. The screeching sound of steel on steel, the groan of wooden carriages, and the swing and sway of a long train was not conducive to sleep. Well, I'd had sleepless nights before and I was sure there would be others.

Later that night we had a visitor, namely an officer from the Immigration Department in Brisbane, who apparently accompanied new arrivals to see us safely to our destination. We made room for him on the seat opposite us and were extremely pleased with the diversion and for the opportunity to ask the many questions that had been on our minds for so long: about Wacol Migrant Centre; procedures on arrival there; and about work opportunities. He answered them all patiently and was very friendly and helpful. Perhaps he was glad also to break the monotony of this long night. Finally, towards morning, he took his leave after assuring us if, at any time, we needed help we could always contact him at the Immigration Office in Brisbane.

The sky started to lighten, and a new day announced its arrival with the most beautiful sunrise I had ever seen. The sky was painted with an artist's palette of colours in varied hues of pink, orange and lilac, like one gigantic canvas. It lifted my mood and instilled me with hope for the future. A country enriched with beauty of such grandeur would be worth the challenge of an emigration. At that same moment, I suddenly realised what a big wide country Australia was. As far as the eye could see, sunburnt brown grasses; tufts along the railway lines—bleached by a relentless sun—waved in a strange ritual dance.

I sat up a bit straighter, glad about the new light of day, then stood up and stretched my aching back. One by one the children woke up and, as usual, were full of beans and enthusiasm for the day ahead. They looked like miniature chimney sweeps and no wonder: soot lay on every surface of the compartment. I brushed them down, then washed hands and faces at the small drinking fountain in the aisle, shook out the borrowed blanket and handed it back to the lady next door, thanking her for its use.

She asked, 'Have you heard anything about the time we'll be in Brisbane?' What a country, eh? Did you have any idea of its size?'

'I'm afraid not. Yes, we talked to an immigration officer last night

Overnight Train to Brisbane

and he thought around four or five this afternoon. Apparently, it will be another nine or ten hours. Can you believe it? If we covered this distance from the Netherlands, we'd be in Moscow by now.'

'Still, at least it won't be cold where we're going,' she joked.

'No, it will be just the opposite. Thanks again. I'll see you later then.'

It was with a deep sigh of relief when we finally arrived at Casino, where—as we were told the night before—breakfast would be served. At last, a chance to stretch our legs, walk around and get the stiffness out of our muscles! They were expecting us. When the train pulled into the station, we noticed long trestle tables, set up on the platform, the tables laid with plates, mugs and cutlery, and, alongside, long benches where we all found a seat.

As soon as everyone was seated breakfast was served; a lovely hot breakfast with scrambled eggs, tomato and bacon, mashed potatoes, and as many slices of bread and butter as we wanted. There was milk for the children and tea for the adults, which was poured from enormous tea kettles by the railway staff. It was very good indeed, a lovely start to the day, certainly lifting both my energy and spirits.

After breakfast we strolled along the platform for a while, so the children could let off some steam, then sought our carriage again for the next leg of our long journey. I was starting to appreciate firsthand the term: 'Timeless Land'. Can one really measure time in such a big country? Measure it in hours and days?

Slow hours passed as the sunburnt landscape crept by with each turn of the wheels, the utter vastness and isolation occasionally relieved by small townships with quaint little station buildings, mostly in need of a fresh coat of paint. As soon as the sun climbed higher it became uncomfortably hot again, which added to the exhaustion of a night without sleep.

Just as we thought this trip would never end, Pierre—who had followed the route on a map—said, 'We're getting closer, I think,' and just as well. The children were getting restless, and we had exhausted all the games we usually played to entertain them. Still, they'd been very good considering all the upheaval we had been through over the past months.

Finally, by late afternoon, we reached the outskirts of Brisbane. Standing at the window, as did our fellow passengers, my first thought

Part Five: Emigration

was how strange it all looked. Pierre and I were both amazed to see so many wooden houses; queer-looking structures sitting on long poles like so many stilt walkers, the rusty-red roofs like old hats worn on top.

'Aren't the windows small?' I said to Pierre. 'And that in such a hot climate.'

'I wonder what those strange little outbuildings are. They seem like little afterthoughts,' he said. 'You see, there on the side, with those corrugated iron roofs.'

'Yes, I see what you mean. It seems as if they're glued onto the wall.'

The houses were all free-standing, surrounded by lovely lawns and well-tended gardens with beautiful flowering trees and shrubs. Gracious palm trees called out a welcome to us. It looked very friendly and colourful. Oh, to have a house with a few palm trees one day. Would we be so lucky?

The train crawled into town. Meanwhile I suffered renewed pangs of anxiety at what we would find at the end of our journey. Fear of an unknown future—which I had pushed far to the background while on the *Waterman*—now flared up again. Pierre and I took the hand luggage down, once again checking carefully that we had everything ready for arrival at South Brisbane Station. 'I'll look after the bags and coats,' Pierre said, 'if you take Veronique, then I can help the children down first,' then warned the children, 'stay close to Mum and Dad, now.' I knew they would, like limpet mines!

I looked at our five little imps and wondered briefly what was going on in their minds. Little faces pinched with fatigue, they took all this in their stride as if it were the most natural thing in the world, and I marvelled at their resilient little souls. It strengthened me in my resolve to make a go of this adventure and to try and look at it in the right frame of mind, positively. They deserved this much.

Finally, the train drew to a stop. Luggage handlers and immigration officers stood waiting on the platform and, after a last check of papers and passports, escorted us to the waiting buses in front of the station.

On boarding the bus, our driver gave us an instant weather report. 'Welcome to Brisbane, folks. We're in a right old heat wave now. It's still ninety degrees out.' Perspiration dripped down the necks and faces of his passengers, and my dress clung to my back like a wet second skin.

What do they say? 'A kingdom for a cold shower!' We left the station and I sat praying silently, 'Please, let us have a little house. Don't let us land in one of those Nissan huts,' while my stomach did somersaults, and my throat was tight with nervous tension.

Again, we were on our way. Sydney yesterday and now Brisbane; it seemed strangely deserted with very little traffic apart from the trams. Where was everybody? We had been told Brisbane was a big town. Where were its people? We soon reached the outskirts and travelled through what seemed a large industrial area. Here, too, big corrugated-iron buildings stood deserted along the roads, red roofs reflecting their own heat, an uncomfortable oppressive heat. Then the scenery changed. Our route took us down a tree-lined road, with cute wooden houses, surrounded by lawns and colourful gardens. It looked very friendly.

Opposite stood a sprawl of military buildings; long wooden barracks and offices, the one road leading towards them closed by a barrier where a sentry stood guard. A sign read 'Wacol' ... and some army number. A sad-looking Australian flag hung limply from a flagpole. I nudged Pierre in the ribs. 'There, look, it says Wacol. We must be getting close.' Minutes later, the bus turned off the highway where another sign read, 'Commonwealth of Australia. Department of Immigration. Wacol Migrant Centre.'

Some of the surviving *Wereld Post* articles that Corry wrote; in English: 'Actually, emigrating is a serious business …and we haven't even left the country'; 'we did a good job there…after only one week at school, our children are settling in very well'; 'it was a good year our first year in Australia'; 'don't take too much baggage with you when you emigrate' (and here Corry wasn't referring to suitcases!)

Camping in Frejus

Last photo in our Nijmegen apartment

Just before departure on the SS Waterman

Peter and Mona on deck during departure from Holland

Going through the Panama Canal ... a very clear memory!

Family picnic ashore at Tahiti with the SS Waterman in the background

Simone's birthday on board

Corry sailing under the Sydney Harbour Bridge…only a few minutes before docking

Our first steps in our new country

PART 6: WACOL MIGRANT HOSTEL

45. First Days

Corry's account continues to record our arrival, and the 'culture shock' of the first two days in Wacol:

> We turned into a lane edged with flowering bushes and shrubs. Then we came to an open area surrounded by several wooden houses and Nissan huts, and the bus came to a stop. 'Okay, folks,' the driver said, 'Wacol Migrant Centre. Please step down and wait outside.'
>
> Trees towered above us, yet gave little shade, and I had a first good look at the place which would be home to us; for how long? Everything looked deserted and dry, and my heart plunged into my shoes.
>
> We stood waiting in the hot sun, when suddenly a young woman approached us, handed me a bottle and said, in Dutch, 'You must be so hot. I've brought you some ice water.' I gratefully accepted the proffered drink, thanked her, and let the children have a good drink first. They were parched, as were Pierre and me. We quickly emptied the bottle and I handed it back to her, thanking her again, while she said, 'That's quite okay. I know what that train trip is like.' It was a lovely gesture, lifting my mood somewhat.
>
> Meanwhile a small group of people had gathered, our welcoming committee, I suppose, when one smartly dressed gentleman stepped forward and introduced himself.
>
> 'My name is Mr Home. I'd like to welcome you to Wacol Migrant

Centre. This gentleman to my left is Mr Macnamara. Mr Macnamara and I are the administrators of the centre. This gentleman'—pointing to a dark-haired chap, with what I thought were decidedly Italian features—'is your block supervisor, Mr Barbieri, who lives in the centre.' (I was right.) 'He will handle any queries during your stay with us. We hope it will be a happy one. I know the circumstances and housing are far from ideal. We are quite aware of this, but here at least you will be safe and well looked after until such time you are ready to move into other accommodation. If there are any problems, don't hesitate to come and see either Mr Macnamara or myself. I hope you will come to love your new country, and I know he joins me in wishing you well.'

He then added, 'Mr Barbieri will show you to your temporary home. I hope you will be patient a little longer until he can attend to you. Your suitcases will arrive soon and will be delivered to your rooms.' We waited our turn until Mr Barbieri, carrying a sheaf of papers, approached us and escorted us to our rooms.

I had to smile at the thought that here we were, Dutch nationals, on the other side of the planet, talking English to an Italian! He asked us about the trip and where we lived in the Netherlands, all in very accented English. I thought we didn't do too badly ourselves, for he remarked, 'You won't have much trouble settling in, Mr and Mrs de Haas. Speaking the language is half the battle, believe me. Some people have terrible trouble because they don't even know a few words of English. We have English classes here. I hope you'll join in. They're held at the school and will resume after the holidays.'

'We certainly will,' we promised him. 'That is very important to us.'

'Then I wish you well. If I can be of any help, don't hesitate to come and see me.' He then took us to our accommodation, a Nissan hut after all! We had been allocated three rooms, two adjoining and one around the other side, which I found quite disturbing. There was no connecting door to the other rooms. This was not a very good arrangement with small children.

We entered our temporary domain, I with heart in my throat, but I must admit the first impression was not that bad. At least it looked clean, though very basic. Green linoleum on the floors, the walls seemed freshly painted in a greenish-lemon colour and wooden furniture. Rough tables and chairs decorated with scratches, names

First Days

carved into them, all painted in a regulation army colour of brown creosote. So too the bunk beds, the three dressers and hanging cupboards, which, at a pinch, had room for only two uniforms. We also had a cot for the baby, a baby bath and potty, but I decided to give these a good scrub before we used them for Veronique. There was one hitch, though: there were only four beds for five children, and there were no curtains nor screens at the windows.

Soon Mr Barbieri returned with an official Department of Immigration form for us to sign, a contract detailing the charges for board and lodging as guests of the Commonwealth. We noticed then that Brigitte was not listed on the form. When Pierre pointed this out to him, he said, 'I'm sorry, Mr de Haas, we'll see to this first thing in the morning. We'll get you another bed. Can you manage for tonight?'

'Yes, yes, we'll double up our youngest. They're so tired from the trip they'll be asleep within minutes,' I assured him. 'I am concerned, though, that one of our rooms has no connecting door with the other two, which means the children will be alone at night. I don't like that.'

'Don't worry, Mrs de Haas, they'll be quite safe here. We've had so many people here and not in all the years have we had any cause for concern. By the way, dinner will be served in the dining room at 6.30 pm. Just bring your tray and you'll be served at the counter.'

On one of the dressers stood our 'china' and cutlery, this all displayed on aluminium trays, together with a note which read, 'This is the property of the Commonwealth of Australia, any losses will have to be replaced and paid for.' It also stated mealtimes and a note: 'All meals must be taken in the dining room, adjacent to the kitchen. Under no circumstances should food be taken to the huts for reasons of hygiene and the prevention of disease.'

In a corner of the room stood two buckets, a mop, broom, dustpan and brush and a mosquito spray. After Mr Barbieri left, I checked the beds. These were neatly made up with clean sheets, although 'clean' would be a generous assessment. They seemed freshly laundered, but some still had large areas of stains and dirty marks which had not come out in the wash. Still, they would have to do for now.

Reaction set in. I needed all my willpower to overcome this sinking feeling of desolation and dismay. I heard voices of children at play, noises of families going about the business of living, yet I felt completely shut away in a strange unreal world, far removed from all that was familiar and known.

The heat was beating down on the corrugated iron roof. It seemed to sap the last trace of resolve from me, and I was quite prepared to finally let go and have a darn good cry. The children's voices saved me, however. Peter and Mona burst into the room, saying, 'We've seen the school, Mum, and there's a cinema and a shop and a church.'

'And, Mum, a big playground with swings, and a kindergarten too, and the school looks really nice, Mum,' Mona added.

Pierre followed them in and said, 'The camp is bigger than I thought. It's quite a large area and there are a lot of people here. At a guess, I'd say it's nearly fully occupied.'

'You reckon? Where are all those people, then? I can't see any around here.'

'They're keeping indoors because of the heat, I'm sure. We might go for a walk, eh, after dinner. It will be cooler then.'

What was left of the afternoon dragged on, as if time moved at a slower pace. We had a rest, but there was no escape from the sweltering heat, nor escape from my dismal thoughts. Around six o'clock we gathered children, trays, plates and cutlery and walked to the canteen. It was a big wooden building, with kitchen and dining in one, the two divided by a full-length bar, its interior painted the same colour as our 'house'.

It looked clean and fresh. Cooking smells teased our taste buds and I wondered what our first meal here would be. We selected a large table which would seat us all and, as if we had arranged this beforehand, today's new arrivals found places nearby, so that we formed one big family of newcomers. We scanned the blackboard's menu: soup, sausage and salad vegetables.

'Forget the soup,' I said to Pierre, who with Peter would collect our dinners at the counter, like we saw others do. 'It's too hot for soup, but salad will be fine. See if there's something different for Veronique, though. She's too young for salads.'

Within minutes they were back. I looked at the offerings, a slice of cold sausage each, half a cucumber, a big chunk of carrot, some tomatoes cut in quarters, lettuce leaves, mashed potato and pumpkin for the baby, two slices of bread each with butter. There was tea for the adults and milk for the children.

Now, how to feed my family? The knives were too blunt to cut carrots or tomatoes and I didn't have any salad dressing to make it more appetising. Still, I sliced the tomatoes as well as I could, cut up the lettuce leaves and made sandwiches with the sausage slices. The children must have been hungry, for they tucked in with their usual enthusiasm and, to my surprise, Veronique finished her vegetables as well. There was an orange each for dessert. Pierre gave me a look across the table. 'Okay?' Well, I had not expected a gourmet dinner, and salad was healthy so I nodded. What could I say?

The noise in the room was something else. With so many in the one small area and lots of children, our usually quiet meals seemed something of a distant past. Youngsters ran around the room, shouting and yelling, while ours looked on in amazement and forgot to eat until I urged them, 'Come on, eat your dinner.'

One chap, a big burly fellow, who with wife and children had travelled with us to Brisbane, looked at his plate of raw vegetables, shoved it aside in disgust and hollered, 'What do they think we are, cattle?' We roared at his disenchantment, but, to be frank, it was a come down. I'm sure we all felt the same. After six weeks on the *Waterman* this was nothing like the Dutch wholesome meals which, beautifully presented, had enhanced our appetite. And even then, there had been people who had dared to complain.

To me, the bare Formica tabletops—more than anything else—proclaimed that reality had arrived. I tried to look at the positive side, telling myself at least it's healthy. It's too hot for anything else. Then made a mental note to buy some salad dressing first thing in the morning. I had an idea we'd be eating lots of salads. On finishing, I gathered plates and cutlery and went to a wooden annex, where women who knew the drill were doing the washing up in big concrete laundry tubs. Luckily, there was steaming hot water, but no detergent, so I rinsed everything then put it on the trays to dry. I didn't have a tea towel either, (two more items for my shopping list) so the hot air would have to do the job for me this time.

After dinner we all went for a walk, located shower and laundry blocks, which were fancy names for those old, dilapidated wooden structures. They were situated about a hundred meters from the hut. I expected I would have to do a lot of fetching and carrying come wash day. There were no taps in the hut, so every drop of water we used had to be carted in. It would certainly keep me slim.

And so we came to our new, temporary 'home', just bedrooms and a sitting area, with no water, no toilets, no kitchen, no fans or air-conditioning, no phone, no car. But on that very first evening at Wacol, I was jumping up and down on the beds with some of my sisters in sheer delight that we had finally arrived! They would also be the first beds that would be our own indefinitely, and they didn't move! Meanwhile, Dad was madly pumping and fumigating everything indoors with the DDT mosquito sprayer, not that it helped much …

Our suitcases arrived later. I took out the essentials—soap, face cloths and pyjamas—bathed the babies while Peter and Mona showered in the next stall. They enjoyed playing under the cool water, until I called time. I popped them into bed, with Simone and Brigitte doubling up, which, for once, didn't cause any arguments. I think they were just too exhausted and were asleep within minutes. Pierre meanwhile pushed the suitcases under the beds to be unpacked later.

After we tidied up, we sat on the steps for a while, his arm around my shoulders, and watched the day go to sleep. A small breath of breeze touched my face with feather fingers, the night sky sparkling with stars; the only lights, pinpointing the different huts around us, and the few streetlamps in the camp.

'Tell me,' Pierre said, 'what do you think? Will you manage?'

'Gee, I don't know. It's too soon to tell. I must say I expected worse. At least we have a roof over our heads and beds, just essentials. We'll have to take the rest as it presents itself. The hut seems clean and I can certainly keep it that way, and hopefully the family on the other side will do the same. Otherwise we're in trouble.'

Our Australian adventure had begun, and I could only accept whatever came with it.

'I would love a cup of coffee,' I said later, sitting down on the porch. 'First thing tomorrow morning I'll write down a few things we. We can get some hot water from the taps at the dining room, until we get a kettle or something to boil water. Everything is so strange. I haven't got a clue what we'll need to function.'

'No, but we can find out by asking around,' Pierre replied. 'People who have been here longer will surely be able to help. But I'll make certain you'll have a cup of coffee tomorrow. I'm sure the little shop here will stock most things like that.'

'We better get ready for bed now, or I'll fall asleep on the steps here.' I yawned. 'We didn't get much sleep last night, nor the night before, and the children will be awake at first light.'

We gathered towels and soap and walked to the shower block arm in arm. I needed his arm, for the night was of such an intense blackness it was like walking through black curtains, the only light coming from a single streetlamp and, in the distance, the two pale yellow bulbs of the shower block. Pierre was used to tropical nights, but I was not. Nevertheless, looking up at that jewelled sky nearly took my breath away!

The shower/toilet block was a wooden contraption. The walls of the stalls didn't quite reach to the roof, nor did they reach the ground. We separated. I stepped into the toilet and got the shock of my life! On the seat sat a big ugly toad. It frightened me half to death and I quickly jumped back ... quickly deciding to have a shower first. I kept a nervous eye on my surroundings, however; there could be other 'Queenslanders' here, eager to welcome me.

I think that night I was asleep as soon as my head was on my pillow!

Next morning, I woke up and in that first instant did not know where I was. The unfamiliar room seemed totally foreign to me. I felt out of place in a strange alien world. Voices from the past came to me like faint whispers on the wind, a cuckoo's call and the twitter of sparrows on the roof ... I listened for familiar sounds: the swift swoosh of cars in the street below, the shrilling of bicycle bells and high voices of children going to school. Then a kookaburra laughed ...

Our second day in Wacol started with brilliant sunshine, and by eight o'clock it was hot once again. The children, as expected, had woken early, which was just as well. I wanted them showered and dressed before breakfast. Pierre fetched warm water for Veronique's bath and, after scrubbing it thoroughly, I bathed and dressed her, while Pierre helped the other children.

I didn't have a clue how or where to start and get organised but realised it would take time (and work) to establish a smoothly running daily routine. Everything was difficult; nothing was simple. The lack of water in the hut was terrible. During those first days in Wacol, I turned around a thousand times to turn on the tap to wet a washer, to wipe the children's hands, or give them a drink of water. We didn't have any jugs, only the two buckets in which to cart the water we needed into the hut, so I had to make sure to keep one scrupulously clean for drinking water.

We breakfasted in the dining hall and found the food was quite good. There was a choice of porridge or cornflakes, followed by scrambled eggs with tomato; two slices of bread and butter each; tea for the adults, and lovely cold milk for the children. We all enjoyed this.

There was a sign up which said there would be fresh milk for the children at 10 am and 2 pm, to be collected at the hall. Now, where could I get a big enough container in which to carry it? I saw some women who carried a small aluminium can with a lid. I pointed this out to Pierre, saying, 'Now that seems to be a good idea. When you go to the shop later, see if they have something like that.'

After breakfast, Pierre went shopping and soon came home triumphantly carrying his purchases. 'Found everything,' he said. 'Nescafé for Mum, sweets for the children, a tea towel, salad dressing and this,' holding up an aluminium can. 'Do you know what this is called?' he asked. 'This is a billy can. A real Australian billy can. The lady in the shop said this is what people use for making tea in the bush.'

'Oh, go on,' I countered. 'They'd take a thermos, wouldn't they?'

'I wouldn't know. I only go by what she said. I brought some biscuits too.'

Life certainly looked better already. Pierre went to get some hot water, and minutes later we made ourselves comfortable on the steps of our villa, sipping the lovely hot brew, while the children sat on the grassy plot in front. Quite content, they nibbled a biscuit and drank their milk, and again I marvelled how they seemed to take everything in their stride and how easily they adapted to different circumstances. Here we were, thousands of miles away from all they had known, and not a peep out of them. Young as they were, they had travelled much further than their mother in her thirty-two years. They truly taught me a lesson in acceptance. Looking at them, I sent up a quick prayer that this would be the case for as long as they needed us and that we had made the right choice.

Slowly, hour by hot hour, we organised ourselves, tidied up, swept and mopped the hut, until it started to look like a home. I found a place for everything in the end. At ten o'clock I sent Peter to the canteen for milk, which he proudly carried home in our very own billy can, and I poured us all a lovely cold drink. After another salad lunch, we all had a much-needed rest as the heat was stifling, and energy sapping.

That evening, our second at Wacol, we walked to the far side of the centre, which was quite a distance, taking our time to explore the school, the chapel, the surgery, and the kindergarten opposite. This looked lovely. It was painted in bright colours, had swings and seesaws, a little playhouse and sandpit, plenty of things to amuse small children. It seemed that we would have most of the facilities we needed. It was enough for now.

We spent that first week in Wacol getting our bearings, exploring the camp, finding out about school, office hours and the general run of things, and acclimatising and socialising with our fellow immigrants. Pierre spent a lot of time with employment officers, who travelled to the centre from Brisbane to interview the men.

At night, when the cooling breezes gathered and the children were in bed, we adults tended to meet in front of one of the huts to talk. Mosquitoes swarmed in the light of the open doors and our words were punctuated by frequent slaps on any exposed skin. At times, the men gathered some dry leaves and twigs and built a small campfire. We then placed slices of bread on thin sticks, held them above the flames until they were toasted, spread them with butter and had a picnic. Rations were small, and we adults seemed to be hungry all the time. These 'picnics' staved off the worst hunger pangs; there was always enough bread and butter.

In a lot of ways those first days and weeks were quite hilarious. That is, if one had a sense of humour. Everything was different, and to be placed in such an environment was a daunting experience. We had to learn about the most basic things, and for some of us it was just impossible to communicate. Therefore, there were all kinds of misunderstandings and problems. Doing the washing for instance: used to a lovely modern washing machine and dryer, doing the washing in Wacol proved to be a completely new experience. Our 'laundry' was an old wooden building, an open shed with four coppers. Wood to stoke the coppers was provided by the groundsmen. We needed newspapers; yes, we had those, but no matches.

Pierre was off to the shop for matches, while I sorted clothes, meanwhile standing watch near the copper, in case someone else decided to do her washing first. (I had learnt quickly.) I filled it, put the whites in for boiling, the paper and kindling ready. When Pierre rolled up with the matches, I lit it. Furtive flames licked lamely at the newspaper, then died out. Then it was Pierre's turn; no fiery flames.

After several attempts, we enlisted the help of 'Sunny Boy', one of the cleaners and groundsmen, who we had met earlier; a chap with a sunny disposition, which, I am sure, had given him this name. Sunny Boy always wore the same uniform: black singlet, blue shorts, high rubber boots and a broad smile. Whenever I met him going about his duties, his usual greeting was, 'Hello, Missus, lovely sunny Australia, eh?' I had a slight suspicion these were the only English words he knew, but he was an absolute gem.

He gestured to wait, came back minutes later with a can of kerosine. He sprinkled some on the wood and whoosh! We had lift-off! I thanked him profusely, but he waved it aside, saying, 'Isse all right, Missus.' With the copper finally doing what it was told, I made suds for the rest of the load and, with a newly bought scrubbing brush, started scrubbing, while longing for my smart little washing machine. I would never kick it again; not even when it boiled over as it sometimes had in the past. (I could boil the clothes in it as well, you see.)

Standing there, my thoughts went to Mum, who never owned a washing machine, washed everything by hand, heavy work clothes from the men as well. It was a sobering thought. The strange part was, you don't realise this as a child, and I doubted my children would give it a thought later in life.

46. First Separation

Foremost in their minds during those first weeks was the job situation. As forewarned by the emigration officials in the Netherlands, Queensland was indeed in the grip of a credit squeeze (as it was called then) and jobs were scarce. While tradesmen were still in demand, Pierre quickly discovered that, even though he had years of experience in selling and fitting electrical goods in the Netherlands, he lacked the piece of paper (or ticket) to certify that he was a qualified tradesman. Nevertheless, he went by train to the immigration employment service in Brisbane every second day. Then he found a job, but hardly one that he could have imagined, let alone anticipated, but it came with a big drawback ... If Corry had hoped that migration would mean more time together with Pierre, that hope would have to be deferred ...

> One day, after yet another trip into town, he came home, waving a bit of paper and said, 'I've got a job! You remember the immigration officer we met on the train? Well, he knows about a tobacco farmer who needs help with the harvest. It's just for a few weeks, but at least it is a job.' I was thrilled, but then came the crunch. 'The only thing is, it is all the way in Yelarbon, near the New South Wales border. It means I won't be able to come home nights, Corry, but I'll try and make it once a fortnight. What do you think? Will I give it a go?'
>
> My heart sank. Newly arrived, only a few weeks in Wacol and me alone with the children? This was not something I could sing and dance about. I knew at one stage we had talked of opportunities on the land, but so soon?
>
> Pierre liked working outdoors, was the only one in a family of five brothers who, with his father, looked after the gardens at home. Would this give us an insight into what life in the bush would be like? Still, I felt extremely uncomfortable about the distance. It was so far away. I kept my reservations to myself, however.

He went on with his usual enthusiasm for all things new. 'My fares will be paid by the Commonwealth. I will be earning seven shillings an hour and I can work there as long as I want.' And, as an afterthought, 'Will you be okay?' What could I say? I hated the thought of being on my own so soon, but at least if something happened, I could call on people here to help me. 'I can start on Monday.'

I sighed, my stomach already in tight knots. 'If that's what you want. We said we would try different avenues. At least we'll know then what opportunities there are on the land. It's so far away though.'

He was dying to go, I could see. I read it in his eyes … I gave in.

On Sunday night, I packed his suitcase and we waved him goodbye early on Monday morning so he could catch his connecting train in Brisbane. I felt terrible; utterly alone in this wide big land, where everything was new and daunting. I felt sick with apprehension and was glad I still had the children for company. I drew new strength from them and knew I would never be totally alone if they were with me. I was close to tears, but heaved a few deep sighs, stood up and started the chores.

Now I could establish an everyday routine, so the children had a stable home life once again. For weeks everything had been topsy-turvy. Now it was time to try and create a normal life. Although they had adjusted well to all the changes, they had had a lot to contend with over the past months. They had taught me a lesson in acceptance and never questioned the changes. And so it should be. Youth happens only once in life, and they had every right to be young and carefree.

The previous week we had received information about the new school year which started the day after Australia Day. So, on the Tuesday morning we all walked to the school and were met by a Mr Milton, the headmaster. He seemed a very gentle man, with kind, intelligent eyes behind dark-rimmed glasses. He was dressed in crisply ironed slacks and a light-blue short-sleeved shirt. I liked him on sight.

I introduced myself, and Peter and Mona. He took them by the hand and showed them the classrooms, which were free standing buildings, then asked me, 'What were their grades in the Netherlands, Mrs de Haas?'

'Peter was in grade three and Mona in second grade.'

First Separation

'What I'll do, then, we'll put them in a lower grade for the time being and once they've settled in and can manage the language, we will re-evaluate the situation and they will be moved to their proper grades. Is that okay with you?'

'Yes, thank you, that will be fine. Have you any idea how long this will take?'

'Oh, not long; give them six weeks, Mrs de Haas, and they'll speak English with the best of them.'

'Only six weeks?'

'That's our experience with these children. The playground is the best teacher, we found.' I could not believe this, but he would know best, of course.

We took Mona and Peter to their respective classrooms, introduced them to the teachers, and then it was time for me to say goodbye. They looked a bit apprehensive and I really felt sorry for my two eldest. They were certainly thrown in at the deep end, poor moppets.

The headmaster must have read my thoughts, for he asked me, 'Would you like to see the children at work, Mrs de Haas?'

'Oh, yes, I'd love that. I've often wondered how children with such diverse nationalities cope with lessons.'

He steered me to one of the rooms, where a charming young teacher, a lovely blond with a slim figure, smartly dressed in a colourful summer frock, was explaining something on the blackboard. Mr Milton pointed to three children who sat in the front row. 'They arrived shortly before the Christmas holidays, so only a little bit earlier than your Peter and Mona.' They sat playing a noughts and crosses game. I was amazed and asked the reason why, and he replied, 'We don't pressure the children, you see. While they're playing, they develop a "feel" for the language and pick up a word or two, and before you know it, they are fluent. It just comes naturally to them.'

I was not fully convinced, but I could see the sense in this. I thanked him most sincerely and knew the children would be in good hands.

We had also made enquiries about enrolment in the kindergarten for Brigitte and Simone, but just then those two little imps went down with measles and would be with me a little while longer. They were disappointed; had looked forward to 'going to school'. But school would start soon enough.

When Peter and Mona arrived home from school, they were full of chatter about their first day. 'Gee,' Mona said, 'they talk so strange, Mum. I can't understand them, but I have a friend, another girl who just came to live here, like us. We sit next to each other. She comes from Germany, and she knows a few words already, so she can teach me. We haven't done much work yet, but we're allowed to play a few games. I tried to follow what the teacher wrote on the blackboard, Mum, but it was too hard.'

'Tommy and Rob from the boat are at school too, and we played together,' Peter added. 'It's a nice school, Mum. I like it already.'

Tom and Rob Boogers were great friends with me through our time in Wacol, and afterwards in Inala. We were in the Cub Scouts together in Inala. Rob and I are still in contact all these years later.

'Oh, that's okay then. You have your friends back, and before you know it, you'll be able to talk to the other children.' And hoped I was right, and they'd soon learn to adjust to the different circumstances.

Brigitte and Simone went to kindergarten in the mornings and loved it. The teachers I met seemed lovely and fond of all the little newcomers. This just left Veronique at home, and she saved me from a desert of loneliness and brightened my days. She chatted all day, a baby language only I understood, and so kept my spirits up. Together we took the children to school and kindy, and later had another little walk to collect the milk.

Then a scorching heat wave descended upon Wacol, with temperatures hovering around one hundred degrees Fahrenheit. There was not a breath of air, and the heat bore down with a ferocity I had not experienced before; it was too hot to do anything, and cold showers were the only way to get any relief. The grass around the huts crackled under our feet and, when the children came home from school, I let them play under the showers for a while. I also gave Veronique frequent baths to keep her cool.

My babies helped me through those first days alone—chirping and chattering like birds—for if anything got to me it was the absolute quiet. The centre was far removed from mainstream Australian society, and during the day there was hardly a sound apart from the cicadas, the early morning laughter of the kookaburras, and the hourly train from Brisbane to Ipswich, which was the only sign there was life outside.

There was another factor which helped me to fill in the lonely hours, namely the articles I wrote for *Wereld Post*. I tried to write about subjects that would be of interest to future migrants and gave some information we had found lacking. I did not embroider too much on the circumstances in which we lived, nor did I go overboard writing about negative experiences. I wrote down what I saw and experienced, what life was like in this rather sober environment, and how to adjust to this.

Despite the drawbacks, I felt a migrant centre was the best solution for new arrivals. We had a roof over our heads (although a hot one) and food on the table, which at times left a lot to be desired; the children had schooling and, while playing, learned the language of their new country. Of course, the first word they took to heart was a firm 'Shudup!' I couldn't believe my ears when that little three-turf-high baby of mine called out one day, 'Shudup!' This in the right context as well. I laughed till I cried, and it was golden moments like this that kept me sane. Luckily, my sense of humour often came to the rescue, plus the fact there was this brilliant blue sky every day, something we rarely knew in the Netherlands.

When I was scrubbing clothes at those ugly concrete tubs, I caught myself at times humming a tune. I don't know what it was, but this country spoke to me in a very special way, even then. Only eight weeks separated us from an icy European winter, but this feeling was much more than time. More even than distance. I had crossed a timeless barrier into this timeless land. Nevertheless, I was dreadfully lonely. I missed my family, missed the luxury of a big city; but as I sat on the steps of my hut at night and looked up at the sky, with countless stars glittering like diamonds, I knew it would be okay, that we would be okay.

Most mornings, we ladies managed to have a cup of coffee together; it was a welcome break in the monotony of life. Housework was finished quickly, and we took turns to play hostess, although we didn't have any fancy china, or fancy cakes. Still, we looked forward to these simple pleasures, while the children played happily together.

I was amazed how content I was. My children were so happy in their new surroundings. They relished playing outside after school and quickly made new friends. What amazed me most was they rarely talked of their friends back home and accepted these enormous changes as a matter of fact. I tried to do the same, and to look at things in a positive manner. How could anyone be sad with this beautiful sunshine every day? Sure, it was hot, but we would get used to it. Everything looked and felt so much better in the sun.

Peter and his friends often wandered through the surrounding bush, playing cowboys and Indians, and came home dusty and dirty, but with exciting tales to tell. For children who had spent the greater part of the year indoors, this was heaven.

Mona took Brigitte and Simone on long walks to explore our surroundings. Sometimes they had a picnic out in the bush. Apparently, they had found a nice grassy plot, they told me. 'We've called it our playground, Mummy. It's so nice there.' I often made them sandwiches, filled a bottle with cordial, gave them a couple of oranges to share, and they would set out quite happily for their next adventure. They had never known such freedom and absolutely thrived on it.

I too walked everywhere. If I needed something from the shops, I walked the two miles to Darra, following a rough, narrow path that ran along the railway line. There were just a few essential shops: chemist, newsagency, butcher, haberdashery, and grocery. Still, it was an outing of sorts and very relaxing. The sun warm on my face, everything around me at peace, no sound other than the crickets and, now and then, the call of a kookaburra. I felt happy then. Life could wait, and these few months between two worlds proved to be a good transition time. One can't hurry life along. It walks its own pace, always.

Later that first week of Pierre's absence, I received two letters: one was from Mum and one from Pierre. On coming home, I opened Mum's letter first in which she told me Dad's health had deteriorated and he had to go into hospital. This worried me greatly. I had hoped he would recoup again after we left, although, perhaps, this had been too much to hope for. He looked so frail and weak when I kissed him goodbye. Yet this news came as a shock. Being so far away the feeling of helplessness was the worst. All I could do was pray.

I opened Pierre's letter next. He wrote:

My dear Corry,

I'm staying with a Dutch family, who are share farmers together with two Italian tobacco growers. I work fifty hours per week, Corry, and it is very hard work and hot between those tall plants. We pick the leaves that are ripe for picking, bundle them up, and leave them at the end of each row, where they're picked up later to be hung in the drying shed. Everyone seems to help, even the children when they come home from school.

It seems like a very isolated existence. The nearest town is thirty miles from here. There is no water, other than rainwater, nor electricity. The mailman calls twice a week, so does the butcher and baker. After a solid day's work, my back is speaking to me—painfully! Luckily, there is a river nearby and I can have a swim twice a day. The fridge runs on kerosene. Distances are enormous. You have no idea. The plantations are crop-dusted by PLANE they tell me. Can you imagine that? All meals are provided here, and Mrs M is a good cook; better than the 'chef' in the centre.

I'll write again soon. Kiss the children for me and oh, all right, I can spare one for you as well. I miss you,

Pierre.

I could not imagine life on the land, or in the bush as they say here, but I knew one thing: it would not be for me. So far from civilisation and no home comforts was too much to ask of someone who liked to live, not necessarily in a city, but at least near enough to go shopping now and then! Although I had grown up in a small village, the concept of a 'country town' had a different meaning in the Netherlands.

Later I told the children, 'I received a letter from Oma this morning, and Opatje Oudenbosch is very sick, so you children will have to say a special prayer for him tonight.'

'Oh, if Opa is sick I'll get a plane, Mum, and I'll fly to the Netherlands.'

'That's a good idea, Peter. I might go with you.'

'Can I come too then?' This was Brigitte, who drifted somewhere between the eldest and younger children, but was always keen to join in with the others.

'Of course,' I joked. 'I'll take all of you,' thinking meanwhile, *I wish* …

The days ran into each other. I tried to fill them as best I could, but time lay heavy on my spirits. The nights were long and lonely. It seemed as if all sound faded away and there were just the crickets to keep me company. I often sat on the steps, thinking back on recent months. So much had happened since the time Pierre had first mentioned the word 'migration'.

How opposed I had been to his plans; how I had fought him on this issue. After only a few weeks here, however, I began to understand what he had missed in the Netherlands. Pierre is an outdoor man, had enjoyed Indonesia's climate, despite the fact there was a war on and that he had faced danger every day. He had volunteered for service there and arrived back in the Netherlands after three years in a tropical climate. How, with such an experience behind him, could he then revert to living in the Netherlands' bleak climate with its dark winter days?

One night, after I had put the children to bed, there was a knock on the door. I wondered who it could be. Usually, people knocked and walked straight in. Doors and windows were always open to catch the tiniest breeze. I went to the door, to see who this late visitor was, and there stood my husband, a big grin on his face. What a surprise! We hugged and kissed, and I was so pleased to see him, I could've cried.

Questions tumbled out. 'What are you doing home? How did you get here? Have you lost your job?' meanwhile trying to make him a cup of coffee. 'How did you get here?' I asked again.

'I hitched a ride,' he said. 'I thought I'd save the fare.'

'Hitched a ride? How come you're home so soon? I thought you could only come home once a fortnight?' I handed him his coffee, then poured myself one.

He stirred his slowly, saying, 'We finished the harvest and were put on one day on, one day off, so whatever I earned one day, I lost the

First Separation

next. I decided to come home. I didn't come to Australia to twiddle my thumbs all day. I'll try for somewhere else, but, Corry, I earned twenty-six pounds. Not bad, eh, for ten days work?'

'It's great,' I said. 'What was it like?'

'Quite an experience. You have to laugh. Just as well I was trained to sleep rough in the army. That first night, when it was time to go to bed, I asked my Italian boss where I could sleep. I was so tired with the work being so unusual and all.

'My boss said, "No problem, come." So, I followed him, and he leads me to this small storage room in the drying shed, no bed in sight. "I get bed," he added. Minutes later he's back with an old wooden door, puts it down, shoves four bricks underneath the corners, gets a couple of black horse-blankets from somewhere and says, "You okay, eh?" I was speechless. Oh, he also gave me a little kerosene lamp, so I would have a light. Luckily, I was so tired I could have slept standing up, I think. I used one of the blankets as a pillow and was asleep within minutes.'

'At least you had a bed there,' I joked. 'That's more than you have here. They came and took your bed away, the day after you left for Yelarbon. I was so upset.' I told him what had happened and finished with, 'It looks as if we have to double up some of the children again.'

'We mightn't even have to do that.' He gave me a cheeky wink. 'I missed my wife, you know.' Then, more serious, 'We'll see what happens. It seems most tobacco farmers are harvesting now. There might be some work somewhere else. I'll go into town this week and see what's available.'

I didn't even want to think about another stretch on my own, and said as much, but he countered with, 'For the moment this is all part of the learning process. Finding out where the work is and how best to earn a living. I've said it in the past: I'm open to anything, although life on the land as I saw it there is very basic. There are no comforts whatsoever; life seems very hard. Come harvest time the whole family is involved, including the children.'

We talked deep into the night, and much later he held me close in those familiar strong arms and all was well in my little world. When the children woke up, they were so surprised and delighted to find Daddy home again, and even more so when after breakfast he took them to the shop for ice creams and some sweets and cakes. I let them stay home from school that day. We needed to be together as a family. Luckily, the heat wave had given up its battering of poor new migrants and we could sit outside enjoying all these lovely treats.

A few days later, coming home from one of his trips to the Commonwealth Employment Office in Brisbane, Pierre arrived home with a big box under his arm and said, 'I've bought you a present from my first wages.' He helped me unpack this and there, out of reams of paper, appeared a lovely new radio.

My eyes filled with tears. 'Oh this is lovely. How did you know I missed my music?'

'I just knew. It might help a bit; in case I must go away again. There are just no jobs in Brisbane. I must go back the day after tomorrow; maybe they will have something then. Do you like it?'

My arms were around his neck as I embraced and kissed him. 'I love it.' It was a streamlined little number and just the right thing to cheer up lonely days. We plugged it in and soon 'Running Bear' was charging through the room.

He had bought a bottle of sherry as well. He opened this and poured a small tot into our special Wacol sherry glasses—the grey plastic mugs—and, sitting down on the steps, we drank a toast to the future.

47. Second Separation and Crisis

If Corry had thought that the separation from Pierre while he was tobacco picking was difficult and lonely for a young mother in a strange new country, what happens next would challenge and test her to the very limits of her strength and resilience. Pierre, being an adventurer, and used to doing what he felt was necessary to support his young family, had the easier part by far, and this is not to say that he didn't work hard or 'put himself out there'.

But I am getting ahead of their story … and, as you read on, please remember that most of the things we now take for granted simply weren't available or did not exist, useful things like mobile phones! What was available, and so generously provided to help cope with an unexpected crisis, was the support of other 'New Australians' and those seeking to help them settle into their new country.

> On 24 February, I was informed at the centre's administration of a job vacancy at Mount Isa Mines for Pierre. I had no idea where Mount Isa was, but was still very excited about some good news at last. Apparently, this was a permanent position; a nice change from all the starts and stops of recent weeks. It seemed that free accommodation went with the job. Wages would be twelve pounds per week, and there would be free milk for the children.
>
> I could not sit still and was restless all morning, eager to tell Pierre the good news. Shortly after lunch he arrived back, very disheartened. The trip to a prospective employer in Brisbane had been a waste of time.
>
> Eagerly I blurted out, 'I received a call from the office this morning. They have a permanent job for you at Mount Isa Mines. They want you to go to the employment office in town to discuss this. Sounds good, eh?'
>
> His face lit up. 'Really? That's wonderful. It's too late now, but we

can go first thing in the morning. That is, if you want to come.'

'Of course I'll come.' This, I felt, we should do together. We talked of nothing else for the rest of that day: wondering what sort of job it would be; hoping it would be one on which we could build a future.

Early next morning, full of excited anticipation, we arrived at the Commonwealth Employment Office in Brisbane. What we heard soon turned my excitement into dismay: we learnt that Mount Isa is 2000 miles from Brisbane. There would be no accommodation for the family. Pierre would start as a labourer, his wages sixteen pounds per week. He would also receive an eight-pound bonus. Board and accommodation would cost five pound per week, and his accommodation would be provided by Mount Isa Mines with a room in their barracks. Apparently, they employed a lot of single men.

The crunch came at the end: there would be no leave for the first six months, and I felt sick. To be on my own with five young children for six months? The officer went on, 'After the first six months, there could be some assistance in finding a home for your family, or some help in financing a home. If you decide to accept the position, Mr de Haas, you also will have to have a medical first.'

'Oh, that's fine,' Pierre answered, 'but I would like to discuss this with my wife if I may. Can I let you know later?'

'Could you phone me first thing in the morning then? You understand we have a lot of people on our files.'

'Yes, of course. I'll ring you tomorrow.'

We thanked him for his time, left the office with me totally thrown out of kilter. Not again, not so soon after the other weeks on my own. I had five little children to care for. What if anything happened to me or if one of the children got sick? We walked out into the hot sun, but I shivered with apprehension and fear.

Over a coffee we talked. Pierre was all for it, as I knew he would be. His restless, adventurous nature was ready for this new challenge. I was not. I could not face being alone again in this vast country, where everything was strange and unfamiliar, and carry by myself the daily routine of caring for the children; long days and nights in which I would only have myself to fall back on. Yet another frightening thought entered my mind. Was this the pattern our life would follow here?

My head reeled as I pondered all this.

Second Separation and Crisis

However, I had to admire Pierre: not a moment of doubt about what he would find at the end of this journey. The train trip would take three days! It was something I could not comprehend. It made me realise, however, the enormous distance which would separate us. I was afraid, simple as that. Also, my decision to finally agree to an emigration was on the premise there would be more time for family.

Pierre must have seen the expression on my face and said, 'You won't be totally alone, Co. There will be people around you. You're safe there. I promise I will look for a house as soon as I get there.' Yet he could not convince me this was the right thing to do. I had no family here; I was surrounded by strangers, who we'd just met. We talked on the train going home; talked till late into the night. In the end, still not fully convinced, I finally agreed, yet again, against my better judgement. The thought we might be able to find accommodation there, however, was the deciding factor.

The following week was a jumble of strange emotions, with Pierre spending most days in Brisbane. His medical was fine, so there was nothing to prevent his leaving. 'I'll be working at the Mica-Creek Powerhouse there,' he told me, 'but before I go, I want to try and get a temporary ticket. I have plenty of experience and all the certificates to show for it.'

Apparently, most migrant tradesmen had to sit for an exam before they could work in their field. Maybe it was a safeguard for lack of knowledge in terms of the specific trade, or lack of mastery of the language. With his usual determination and 'gift of the gab', he received his temporary ticket, which also meant an immediate increase in wages of four pounds per week.

In the final days prior to his departure Pierre suggested, 'Why don't you have a day in town before I leave? Ask Margareth to come with you. Do some shopping and have a good look around. Once I'm gone there will not be many opportunities, and I can look after the children now.' Yes, of course we could do this. Great! It would be fun. Within five minutes it was all arranged. We girls would have a day out.

'It's quite easy to find your way around,' Pierre said later. 'All the streets with names of the English queens run one way, the ones with names of the kings cross these.' He handed me a small map. 'Look, here's City Hall. If you keep your eyes on that, you can't get lost.'

'Okay, great.'

Part Six: Wacol Migrant Hostel

Two days later we set out on this great adventure. We each had a few pound notes in our purses so that we could learn to handle the foreign currency. We made an early start and walked to Wacol station, a grand name for a building which was barely the size of my rooms in the hut. Like two ditzy teenagers we were already giggly when we tried to buy our tickets. Getting used to the Australian idiom was quite an experience.

This was fun. For one whole day, we could forget about the circumstances in which we lived. We would be amongst people who didn't have an inkling we were so new, and so we were filled with excited anticipation.

By late morning, all our exploring had made us thirsty, and the search was on for a small café. We finally found one in Albert Street, the 'Cabana'.

'You do the talking,' Margareth decided. 'I wouldn't know where to start.'

'How about you practise your English?'

'Oh, come on now, don't be mean.'

'Okay then.' Full of confidence I approached the counter, where a starlet was serving customers. We scanned the list of drinks available and decided on an ananas (Dutch for pineapple) drink. 'Two ananas drinks, please.' That was me.

'I beg your pardon?' from our beauty.

I repeated, 'Two ananas drinks please.'

A blank stare. Suddenly it dawned on me. 'Oh, oh, sorry, I meant two pineapple drinks.' Once again, we dissolved in laughter. The young lady was not amused! Within minutes we were enjoying a delicious fresh drink.

We then went shopping in earnest.

Oh, we were drunk that day, drunk not on alcohol but on all the new impressions, the sunshine and the freedom. We decided to have a last treat before going home and went to Coles' department store. A snack bar near the front entrance had an enormous counter served by a conveyer belt. The orders were shouted to the kitchen below and soon would magically appear to start their journey towards the hungry. This saved the waitresses traipsing endlessly along the full length of the counter.

In no time at all we saw our Peach Melbas approaching. They rode

Second Separation and Crisis

the bar like thoroughbreds, and while the girls swept orders from the conveyer belt left, right and centre, our delicacies were still travelling. We could see it happen. Any moment now and the Peach Melbas would topple over the side. As in one voice we cried, 'Ho! Ho maar!' in pure Dutch, (Stop! Stop!) then broke up as the waitress grabbed our ice creams and placed them in front of us. Weak with laughter, tears running into our peaches and cream, we managed a couple of mouthfuls.

The waitress, a very curious expression on her face, could stand it no longer and asked, 'What's so funny? Haven't you ever seen this before?' Oh, Lord, no we hadn't. The poor girl went back to her job, while Margareth tried to pick up the artificial flowers she'd bought, hiccupping with laughter, and two new Australians were gasping for breath.

We could face life again, hard as it was.

A few days later, the day of Pierre's departure dawned, arriving far too quickly. It was a quiet breakfast, and we did not talk very much. Even the usual children's quarrels were absent. I felt dreadful; it was so hard to say goodbye. This was the first time since we were married that we would spend months apart, and it seemed such a long, lonely stretch ahead. Although Pierre promised he would write as often as he could, it did not help much.

I was glad about having the children's company that day. Nevertheless, while their voices chased away the void I felt, I couldn't settle down to anything. I felt totally out of tune. Forlornly I walked from room to room, picked up something only to put it down minutes later. I tried to read but couldn't concentrate; the day dragged on. Finally, when I put my little girl down for her nap, I broke down and cried. It helped, but only a little. I knew I could not look back, only ahead to the future.

But worse was to follow. Less than a week later I was rushed into hospital for an emergency operation.

Several times in the past few months I had felt rather sick and nauseous, with bad pains in the lower right of my abdomen. This had happened also while onboard the *Waterman*, but at the time I put it down to something I had eaten or a stomach bug.

Shortly after our arrival in Wacol, I saw the doctor, who told me it could be my appendix playing up. This time however the pain was severe, so I decided to go and see the sister at the centre's clinic. When I explained the symptoms, it was enough to convince her I needed help, and soon.

'I'm going to phone for an ambulance, Mrs de Haas.'

'An ambulance? It's not that serious, surely? Is it?'

'Yes, I think you ought to go home, pack a few things you need, in case they keep you in hospital for a few days. Have you got a friend who can take care of the children for you, just in case?'

'I don't know. Oh my God, I only know the few people who arrived with us ... I can ask ...'

'You do that, Mrs de Haas. I think that's wise. If you can't get anyone to look after the children, we sometimes place them in a children's home in Brisbane for the duration the mother is in hospital.' To me this was not an option. No way. Not after all the changes they'd experienced in recent weeks.

What now? How could I ask the only two families I knew reasonably well? What would it mean to them, living in cramped quarters as we were, to suddenly see their families double in size? Still there was no other way out. I went to see them, explained the situation and asked for their help; told them I could be back home that same day, but was not sure about this. They were marvellous and came to my rescue without a moment's hesitation. I could not thank them enough, but they waved it all away with, 'You would do the same for us. Don't worry, the children will be fine.' I looked at them both, lost for words.

'I'll take the three younger ones, Brigitte, Simone and Veronique,' Margareth said.

'Could you look after Peter and Mona then, Ria?'

'Sure. Ours play together anyway, so it's just meal- and bedtimes that will be a bit hectic.' It was all arranged within minutes.

I gathered some toiletries, nighties etc and, amid assurances of these wonderful friends I was not to worry, the ambulance arrived, and I was taken to hospital. My heart was heavy, my spirit at the lowest ebb it had ever been.

After several examinations by different surgeons, they decided to operate that same night at 11.30 pm, which gave me an indication how urgent this was. I'd had no idea at all. Apparently, I had a big cyst on one of my ovaries and it could have turned quite nasty. Sister had been right; there had been no time to waste.

It's hard to describe what I went through. I was in hospital for five days and can't remember ever being so miserable. Far away from my family, in a strange country, my husband 2000 miles away, the children with people we'd only met six weeks ago ... I could have crawled back to the Netherlands on my knees.

After the operation, a reaction set in. I cried and cried and could not stop. In those first days I had only one visitor, our padre, who walked in one afternoon, carrying a big bunch of grapes. He brought some consolation, and I blessed his kind heart. He promised to bring Peter and Mona next time. I was so pleased to see him.

He told me, 'Now, you don't have to worry about the children, Mrs de Haas. They are well looked after; everything is going smoothly. Peter and Mona help as well.' This eased the anxiety somewhat.

I wrote Pierre a letter while in hospital, told him what had happened, that he was not to rush home, because I was over the worst. It would take a week before he could get home anyway, and by that time I could be back in Wacol.

Father Tiedink was as good as his word and brought Peter and Mona on his next visit. I was so pleased to see them; they looked fine and were full of stories of their 'holiday' with our friends. Suddenly Peter piped up, 'Maybe you'll get another baby, Mummy, now you're so sick.'

'Well, son, you never know,' I answered, and wished I could laugh, but my stitches prevented me. It cheered me up. I missed the children terribly and couldn't help fretting about them, but my son had found the right words to bring some light into my days.

I truly believe the lady in the bed next to me and her kind husband kept me sane that week. Whenever he visited, he drew me into the conversation, which helped to pass the long, lonely hours. Towards the end of my stay in hospital there was one comical episode, however. One morning a young nurse entered the room, a dark-haired girl. She had a beautiful tan and deep-brown eyes and was a very friendly lass. As was routine, she picked up my chart, checked it and asked me, 'Have you moved your bowels today, Mrs de Haas?' (Six weeks in Australia—did I know what she was talking about? I was far too green to know the correct terms for bodily functions.)

Part Six: Wacol Migrant Hostel

'I beg your pardon?'

She tried a bit louder, 'HAVE YOU MOVED YOUR BOWELS TODAY?' I was still no wiser. The same question was repeated three times, each time a little louder, as if I were not only ignorant but deaf as well. 'HAVE YOU MOVED YOUR BOWELS TODAY?' My fellow patient came to the rescue. 'She wants to know whether you have been to the toilet,' she said slowly.

I looked the nurse straight in the eye and confessed, 'No.' Blushing furiously, the nurse made a note on the chart and left the room. Another lesson learned.

On the day I was discharged, the padre came and took me home. When we neared the hut, I saw the children waiting at the door. Each had a little posy of wildflowers in their hands. Their faces lit up when they saw me. I struggled to my feet and walked towards them, then broke down in a flood of tears, clasped them in my arms to never let go. I was home, poor as it was.

Recovery was slow, however. I had no strength or energy. Although the stitches were later removed, and I could—more or less—walk upright, I was not my usual cheerful self. Some action was needed here. I sent Peter to the local butcher shop near Wacol station for some veal and made myself some nourishing broth, for the food in the centre was far from nutritious. I was sure this would do the trick.

Peter and Mona were wonderful during those weeks. Small as they were, they helped me where they could. Pierre wrote every day and looked forward to my letters. He was constantly looking for accommodation for us, but apparently there was little housing available. 'I was so worried,' he wrote. 'Are you sure you are all right?'

Of course, deep down I wasn't, but what use was it to tell him this? It would unsettle him as well. However, in the end I wrote to him, 'Look, if it takes longer than three months to find something, I want you to come home and look for work in Brisbane. I do not want to be alone any longer.'

His letters were cheerful and positive. 'I'm earning terrific wages. I made thirty-seven pounds last week! I share a room with another fellow. We have three hot meals a day and the food is very good. It is extremely hot here. Just as well I spent three years in Indonesia, eh, Corry?

Second Separation and Crisis

'Guess what! I met a chap who did his commando training in Scotland with me. He has lived here for several years. A small world, eh? He's married and has two children and has invited me over. I'll certainly take him up on that! There's not much entertainment here, other than the pictures. We can buy land here for about a hundred pounds, which is crown land, but it will have to be approved by the state.'

So, what were we to do? How could we work something out, being so far apart? Mount Isa seemed like the end of the earth to me.

One day, Peter and Mona came home with big grins on their little snouts, and, feeling very proud of themselves, asked me, 'Mum, guess what?'

'What?'

'We're back in our own grades! Mr Milton said we know enough English now to go to a higher grade.'

'Well, that's good news. You better write a letter to Dad and tell him all about it. He'll be so proud of you.' Two little heads nodded yes, and I marvelled how soon the children had integrated into the school system. I was so pleased for them.

The climate also did its best to be kind to us now. The nights were a bit cooler, and the days lovely and sunny, ideal days for the children to play outside.

One day I was sitting on the steps of the hut, sipping a cup of coffee, when suddenly I thought, 'I never want to leave here,' and completely surprised myself. The air was fragrant with eucalyptus, and in the distance a choir of crickets sang a midday song. There was no sound other than the few children's voices in the background. It was all so peaceful.

Despite this moment of truth, my body thought otherwise, however. That night, shortly after dinner, I nearly collapsed with a searing pain in my stomach. It was so fierce it took my breath away and I was gasping for air. Perspiration dripped down my face and I knew I should go for help, but I couldn't walk. For a second my breathing stopped completely, which frightened me senseless. I knew I had to reach someone. I struggled to my feet and, doubled over, arms supporting my stomach, went to Margareth's hut. She needed only one look and ran to the clinic, where, luckily, the sister was still in attendance. She immediately phoned the doctor in Darra, who arrived four hours later. He examined me, gave me a penicillin injection, which didn't help very much. I still could not speak.

After a few days of resting up I felt a bit better, but the pain persisted. I knew then it was time for Pierre to come home. I tried, but simply could not cope any longer on my own. I had two more attacks, but luckily the pain was not so severe and did not last as long. To make matters worse, in his last letter he'd written, 'There is no chance of getting a house in Mount Isa. To buy one is very, very expensive as all the materials have to come from such a distance.'

I saw no point therefore to try and wait things out. We might as well start all over again, but in Brisbane and together. I sent him a telegram, asking him to come home for Easter, so we could discuss this. He immediately sent one back, saying he would fly home on Easter Sunday. This made me feel a lot better. It was such a relief. It felt as if a huge weight had fallen off my shoulders. When I told the children, they were so excited. They had made special Easter bunnies at school, little cardboard bunnies with cotton wool tails—one bunny for each of us—and of course they would have to make one more now.

48. TOGETHER AGAIN

Corry's story continues:

Margareth and I planned a party for Easter Sunday (17 April 1960). We had prepared a nice meal including cake and lemonade for the children, the cake saved from our rations. Margareth's husband, John, and two young Dutchmen, who recently had arrived from the Netherlands, had gathered wood to build a campfire. The children were very busy meanwhile, decorating the tables with all the Easter bunnies.

Our two young guests had brought their guitars and played the so familiar Dutch songs and, just when the light was beginning to fade, John lit the fire. Soon the flames danced high in the balmy night air, and we joined hands with the children and danced around the fire, while our guests accompanied us on their guitars. It was most enjoyable, especially for the children. They thought it was magic. We sang all their favourite songs they had learned at school in the Netherlands.

For a while even adults could forget about the challenging circumstances in which we lived and just be young with the children. Then, amid all these festivities, Pierre appeared and gave us all a surprise. We had not expected him so early, seeing the distance he had to travel. It was a wonderful reunion and timed perfectly. The children were so excited. They crowded around him, each one eager to tell him the latest. So was their mother. There was so much to talk about after such a long absence. But I could wait. He looked extremely well, had put on weight, quite in contrast to his wife.

Later, with all the children asleep, Pierre and I sat down at last to talk. His deep voice seemed to chase all worries and misgivings from my mind. I wanted to know all about Mount Isa. His letters took a full week to reach me and I didn't know the latest about the housing situation.

'What's the town like?' I asked.

'Well, it's a real country town. The centre is quite small actually, nothing like Brisbane. It's very dry and very, very hot, but it is a different heat than here. As I explained in my letter, there are a lot of single men working at the mine, and there's not much going on after work other than go to the pub and have a few beers, or the other alternative, the open-air cinema.

'But boredom creates some heavy drinkers, I noticed. I had figured that out quite soon. What I really liked is Lake Moondarra. It is an artificial lake, where people go for picnics or a swim. Zena and John—you know, the friends I met there—took me one Sunday. It was wonderful and so many people there.'

In one of his letters Pierre had written about this surprise meeting with John who was employed at Mount Isa mines as a painter. It was one of those eerie coincidences. One morning, when Pierre went to work, John had approached him and said, 'Don't I know you from somewhere?'

Pierre had a second look, 'Well, if you take off your hat, I might recognise you.' John took off his hat, and recognition was immediate.

What a reunion that was. John had also joined the resistance during the German occupation of the Netherlands and, like Pierre, had made his way to England and Scotland for commando training. They both received the green beret and were with Number II Dutch Troop. This unexpected meeting led to many visits and outings with Zena, John's wife, and their two children.

When I asked him about the housing situation, he sighed and shrugged his shoulders saying, 'I really don't know. I tried everything and talked to so many people, but housing seems to be THE problem there. It's simple for single men; they have a room in the barracks and don't need much else.

'It all depends on what I hear when I go back to Mount Isa's offices after the weekend. I hope they will reinstate me, but that's by no means a sure thing. Apparently, they are quite ruthless.'

'They can make an exception, surely? After all, it was an emergency. It might not look like that now, but believe me, it was then! What I went through that week …'

'I would've come home, you know, but you wrote not to.'

'No, I didn't see the point, not then anyway. But when I had those attacks, that scared me. I'm awfully glad you're home now.' I put my arms around him. 'Let's not worry about Mount Isa for a few days. We're on holidays and we have to make the most of it for the children. We'll have to cheer them on tomorrow.'

'Do you know, Corry, John has built his own house in Mount Isa?'

'Did he? Really? On his own?'

'Yes, and that one is his third. He built two in Brisbane as well, when they first arrived here. I wouldn't mind doing something like that.'

'How long did it take him?'

'A couple of years,' he said.

'Goodness. Where did they live meanwhile then?'

'In a caravan. They own one. It's parked in the backyard.'

'My God, when did the poor man sleep?'

'I don't know. It's quite a mammoth undertaking, eh? Talking about sleep, where do I sleep, or is that a silly question,' he said cheekily.

When I lay in his arms that night, it was the first time in many weeks I felt secure and safe. I didn't have to carry the load alone for a while. To have him home with us was a good feeling. Also, for the first time in weeks I slept right through.

Early on the following Wednesday, Pierre went to Brisbane, to the Electricity Board to find out about procedures in getting a permanent ticket. He also went to the Immigration Office to enquire about jobs in Brisbane, just in case. While he sat waiting there, he spotted a *Wereld Post* on a low table, together with other magazines. On leafing through it, he found an article I had written, an early one about Wacol Migrant Centre. On coming home, he proudly showed me the paper.

I was thrilled. It was nice to know my work was appreciated even though I had not painted a rosy picture. I just wrote about the facts of living in a migrant hostel. It was wonderful to see it in print. I felt I had achieved something and helped future Dutch migrants.

Pierre brought me back to reality when he told me, 'I also went to the office of Mount Isa Mines, but they had not yet made up their minds about my re-employment. I wonder whether they will now. It doesn't sound very encouraging, does it?'

'Never mind, we'll wait and see.' I did not add anything further, but, to be quite honest, I hoped they wouldn't. I'd had enough of being on my own and coping with the primitive circumstances in which we lived.

The following week Pierre went back for his second interview with Mount Isa Mines. He arrived home late in the afternoon, and one look at his face was enough: seven days of bad weather. On my question, 'How did it go?' he answered curtly, 'They didn't re-instate me.'

'But … But … Why?'

'Why?' All the frustration of recent months rose to the surface. 'Because I left before the six months were up,' he thundered. 'Now see what you've done!'

I was speechless. As a matter of fact, I was speechless for a week. What had I done? Clipped his wings?

Soon, however, we were sailing calmer waters again and, thankfully, Pierre found work with an electrical firm, wiring new houses. His new boss asked him whether he could work weekends as well. Of course, he could; it meant extra money. I hoped this would mean permanent work, finally.

He was to start on the following Monday, but instead of going to work, he had to go to Princess Alexandra hospital with a shocking cheekbone infection, which required a daily injection at the hospital. This was yet another setback. Would the job still be open after this cleared up? Not good for the nervous system, all this upheaval. When Pierre went in to explain it all to his future boss, he assured him the job was still his, if he still wanted it, which brought big sighs of relief for us both.

Meanwhile I had been busy as well. I had interviewed several people in the centre, asking their opinion about conditions. This with the view of recording it all for my next article for *Wereld Post*. Most of the women I spoke with complained about the food and I could relate to this, as we were far from happy about this ourselves. Portions were very small, and what food we had was badly prepared. I wrote it all down, then went to the office and asked to speak with someone in charge.

It happened that both the manager and chef were there, and we talked while I put my case. They must have known; all they had to do was look at the overflowing rubbish bins at the kitchens every day, where most of the offerings ended up.

Just when I was ready to go and thanking them for their time, a

Together Again

journalist arrived who worked for the *Daily Telegraph*. I was called back. 'Oh, Mrs de Haas? Have you got a minute?'

'Yes, of course.'

'Do you know of anyone here who has an unusual profession? This reporter wants to write an article for his paper and make a few photos.'

'I don't know off hand. We have not been here long enough to learn what people do for a living.' I then added spontaneously, 'Unless he's interested in my story. I write articles also.' I still do not know where this came from or how I had the nerve to say this.

'Do you really?'

'Mrs de Haas writes articles for a Dutch migration paper,' the manager explained. 'We had one translated recently.' Well, the journalist became extremely interested, while the manager promised me, 'I'll ring the newspaper, Mrs de Haas,' which I thought was wonderful.

I thanked him and left and walked home on clouds, although somewhere in the back of my mind was this little devil saying, 'Don't get your hopes up too much. It might not lead to anything.' I was wrong.

Two days later a big Commonwealth car stopped in front of the hut. There was a knock on the door and there stood the centre manager. He had come to take me to the office where a journalist and photographer were waiting for me. The interview went very well. They wanted to know the reasons for our emigration, why we had chosen Queensland, and about my first impressions here, and we later went to the hut for a photo session.

Two days later, the front page of the *Telegraph* carried a big photo of my little girls and me, together with an article with a headline that read, 'SHE LIKES OUR STATE.'

That same week, I received a letter in the mail which was sent from Murwillumbah in northern New South Wales, signed by a Mrs Alison A Luxford, which read as follows,

Dear Mrs de Haas,

I loved your photo in the *Daily Telegraph* of May 24th and those lovely little children. I think Mona, the closest to you, is you over again. I keep saying to my family, 'Oh, isn't this a lovely mother and family.'

I hope and pray that God will bless you and your husband and those little children in this, your new country.

These are the sincere wishes of an old grandma.

All the best,
Mrs A Luxford.

I was truly touched by this heartfelt letter, and if I had ever doubted how we new Australians would 'fit' into an Australian society, on receiving such a kind letter I knew we would not have any problems at all. If we could reach out and accept a hand in friendship, if we could accept a new way of life and adjust to it fully, then we would cross the barriers and come out more than okay on the other side. I was fully convinced of this and, much later in life, I came to realise that I had subconsciously kept to these guidelines for years.

A few days later, when I went to collect the mail, I received a lovely surprise. There, among some letters from home, I found one from the *Daily Telegraph* with two copies of our photo. I was thrilled. This was a great souvenir of a very exciting event, and I decided one would be on its way to my parents by the next mail.

49. HOUSE AND LAND DEALS?

Looking for a block of land in 1960 was a vastly different experience to what it is today, more like a family adventure rather than the clinical business transaction it has become! Before Pierre departed to work in Mount Isa, he was keen to buy his first piece of Australia so that he 'would have something to work for'. In areas surrounding Brisbane, there were several major new developments opening, each promoted with substantial advertisements in the newspapers. Corry describes our adventure in finding our 'block', clearly from a very different time, when perhaps the pace of life was more gentle and less driven, even for real estate agents!

>All we had to do was dial a phone number and ask for a sales agent to come out and take us to the different estates. (All this was free.) As Alfred Grant was a big real estate company at the time, we decided to try this firm first and booked for Sunday, the week before Pierre's departure.
>
>It was a glorious day, sunny, not too hot, a perfect day for a trip and a first outing for us as a family. I'm sure the poor chap received the shock of his life when he saw who was waiting for him at the gate. Take a family of seven to look at land? But we had promised the children a day out, and that's what they would have. It might be a long time before we could do something like this again, and it would be fun.
>
>By late afternoon, we arrived at Redcliffe where a new development had recently been released. The land had been sub-divided and included a grove of beautiful tall pine trees. I immediately liked the look of this; for one, the heady scent of pines reminded me of home. Pierre also seemed impressed and, as a bonus, it was close to the seaside town and the beach, ideal for children. The roads were sealed and kerbed, and the agent assured us water and electricity would be connected by the time we were ready to build.

Part Six: Wacol Migrant Hostel

We decided there and then and selected a big corner block. The price: three hundred pounds, and we paid a deposit that same afternoon. This would be the foundation for a new future. 'If you can come into town to sign the papers next week, Mr de Haas, I'll have them all ready for you.' It was as easy as this, and I was building already!

The children had been so good I decided they should have a little treat, so I asked our 'tour guide', 'Could you drive back along the beach perhaps? Maybe I can buy the children an ice cream there?' He obliged, and we stopped at a small wooden building on the beach front, which was painted a hideous green, where large colourful posters advertised, 'Cool and refreshing Lifesavers, Lipton tea, fishing bait and tackle.' Luckily, they sold ice creams as well, and within minutes the children were happily enjoying their treat. So were we adults, including the salesman.

We were all very excited about our new 'property', and on coming home talked at length about the future. It was still early days, of course, but making plans helped to alleviate negative thoughts and doubts. It was fun to see the older children full of enthusiasm, making plans with us. They had everything figured out already: 'We can go to the beach after school, eh Mum, when we live there, and we can have our friends over in the holidays, eh Mum?' Of course, they could, but when?

After Pierre had returned from Mount Isa, there was another real estate expedition with a different Alfred Grant agent as our 'tour guide', just as surprised with the number of 'prospective buyers' that trooped into his car, which was only just big enough to cope.

After visiting new developments in Kenmore, he took us to Chermside. As soon as we arrived there, Pierre and I looked at each other and read the same message. It was stunning. High up in the hills, the blocks set out on sloping land, the same as in Kenmore, but smaller in size. 'There's a school nearby, only a seven-minute walk, and so are the shops,' the salesman explained. 'It will be ready for building in three months' time. Would that suit you, Mr and Mrs de Haas?'

Would it ever! 'Yes, definitely,' answered Pierre. 'We're thinking of paying cash for this, so there shouldn't be any delay.'

'Well, as soon as the registration is completed, I can't see any difficulties ahead.'

We selected a block in a quiet cul-de-sac, with a beautiful view over the surrounding countryside and part of Brisbane. The roads were already finished, which was a bonus. I was thrilled. It looked magnificent. The children must have sensed my excitement because the questions started coming fast. 'Are you going to buy this, Dad? And can we have our own room? Can I have Tom and Rob over then? Can we have a look at the school?'

'Just imagine, kids, we could be in our own house by Christmas,' I said, and my heart was doing somersaults. Oh, imagine, living in a house again.

'Would you like to look at some houses now, Mrs de Haas? We have a couple on display in other estates.'

'Could we?' I looked at my watch: eleven. 'Are they near here? We have to be back in Wacol by lunchtime.'

'Yes, it's not too far. It will give you an idea what is available now.'

To see a house, the interior complete, was a new experience for us. However, the first one we saw did not really impress me. It had few interesting features and squatted squarely on the land like a tired duck. The second, however, I loved on sight. It was built in an L-shape, with large picture windows at the front, the panels underneath painted in pastel colours, and a good-size garage on the side. I promptly got a stomach-ache, a sure sign of excitement. The salesman opened the door, we stepped inside, and I was sold. It was ideal.

I looked at Pierre and saw he was impressed as well. Before getting back in the car I looked back. Yes, I could live in this house. During the drive home, Pierre made an appointment for the following week to go into town and draw up the papers to finalise the sale of the land. It was as easy as that; unbelievable. 'I'll send someone out to the land next week, Mr de Haas, to see what sort of house would suit the block. We usually do this in a hilly area. It is to do with the drainage of rainwater etc. Okay?'

After our experiences in waiting for housing in the Netherlands, I could not fathom it could be this easy. We had just bought a piece of our future, and I was as excited as a kitten with its first ball of wool.

Part Six: Wacol Migrant Hostel

It was a great feeling, different than when we bought at Redcliffe. I wondered then as I did now whether we would ever build there. I preferred to be closer to town, and this meant building in suburban Brisbane, with the town's centre within easy reach of public transport.

Later, when I had tucked our youngest in bed for a nap, and the others were playing outside, Pierre and I could finally talk. I was so excited I could hardly sit still. 'Now, Corry,' Pierre admonished, 'don't put your hopes up too much. We still have to wait and see what they tell us next week, and they have to find out which house will suit the block.'

'I know, I know, but I can dream, can't I?'

'I just don't want you to get all excited in case something happens that puts a damper on the whole thing.' He stood up, poured us a glass of sherry, and said, 'Anyway, let's at least drink to it. You never know, Lady Luck might be with us this time.'

But it wasn't! After a week and a half of excitement and high hopes, spending hours poring over different plans for houses that might suit their chosen block, Pierre arrived home with bad news that put an end to these plans and dreams.

Pierre had called in at the Alfred Grant office in town to hear how the second inspection went when he was told, due to the enormous boom in land sales, there was a back log of eighteen months before the land could be registered.

I knew something was wrong as soon as Pierre walked through the door that night. When he told me this, I sat down and had a good cry. That door certainly slammed shut in our faces. We would have to start planning all over again.

Finally, I dried my eyes and made a cup of coffee, while Pierre poured a glass of sherry, saying, 'Here, Corry, drink this first. I know it comes as a blow, but we'll find something else, I'm sure. This was only a first try and we'll try again. I'm sure something will turn up.'

'There goes that lovely stainless-steel sink.' I hiccupped then laughed at that ridiculous thought, while hot tears ran down my face.

After this setback, Pierre and Corry nevertheless bought the block of land in Chermside, knowing that there would be a long delay for its registration. They continued to explore brochures for different housing designs, but nothing emerged on which they could confidently make any decisions. Then, as sometimes happens in a stalemate situation, a completely different pathway to owning their own home became apparent. Was this destiny?

> On one of my trips to the shop, I met a woman who lived opposite us. She told me, 'We're moving out on the weekend. My husband has built our new home in Wacol, and it's ready for occupation. We can finish the rest while we're living there.'
> I was amazed and asked her, 'How long did that take?'
> 'About two and a half years,' she answered. 'But at least it won't be so hectic now, while we live there.'
> 'That is a big job,' I said. 'I admire your husband. He must have worked day and night.'
> 'We certainly didn't see a lot of each other, but it was worth it.'
> 'Yes, I can imagine. I'll come and say goodbye before you leave, and best of luck with the move.'
> 'Thanks. Look, why don't you and your husband walk over one Sunday and come and see the house.'
> 'Yes, I'd like that. You are the second couple I have heard of who built their own home. I'm sure Pierre would be extremely interested.'

A few weeks later, Corry and Pierre visited this couple on a quiet Sunday afternoon. They proudly showed off their new home and freely chatted about the many hurdles they had overcome through the various stages of building. Pierre was incredibly impressed with what they had achieved ... and, indeed, that one visit changed everything. Any previous plans for buying a house were immediately forgotten in favour of an entirely different idea!

> On walking home later, Pierre said suddenly, 'Now THAT is something I would love to do; build our own house. When you see what that chap has achieved in a few years, amazing. I feel as if I haven't achieved anything since we came here.'

'Hey, hang on, you! Give it time, for goodness' sake. We have only been here for a few months. They came here at least four years before us, considering that it took them three years to build their house.'

I thought that would be the last of it, but I was so wrong. After work one night we were having a cup of tea when he said, 'On walking home from Darra station, I saw that house for sale. You know the one I mean, where that family lives in a tent? There is just the concrete slab and a few walls. It doesn't look as if they will ever finish the job. He hasn't done a thing on it in months.'

I knew the one he meant. People had told us there were seven children and the family had lived in that tent for six years. Apparently, the husband drank, and, whenever we passed the house on our way to the shops, we had not noticed any activity.

'What would you think if we were to buy it off him? I could finish it off. I believe it is a double block, so plenty of room for the children and a garden.'

I was lost for words. What in heaven's name was he planning now? Talk about surprises! 'Build it yourself, you mean? How? You've never done any carpentry or bricklaying.'

'Well, it's never too late to learn, is it? John's done the same, and the chap in Wacol. I think it is marvellous what they have accomplished.'

An icy hand squeezed my heart, which started beating so hard I could feel it. I could hardly breathe. 'What about the land in Chermside? We've just bought that, I thought with the idea of building a house there.'

'That's still a good investment and will only improve in value. If we buy this block, we can finance it ourselves; there would be no mortgage or bank involved. The money we have from the sale of the business will be enough to build it. The only thing against it, we would be living here longer than intended. Could you cope with that?'

My nerves twitched like they were electrified. My God, now what to say? I was dying to get out of this place and into decent surroundings again, in a place I could call home. 'I don't know, Pierre. Another two years in this hut? I don't think I could stand it.' I was sick at the thought. It was all right for him. He was here only to sleep. I had to cope with all the negatives day in, day out, on the outer edge of a normal life in Australian society.

I saw he was dead keen, and I didn't know how to handle this. I knew he would do this, without ever questioning his ability to do the job. 'Do you know how much he wants for the land?'

'I don't know, but I can find out. He won't be able to charge for those walls. They look as if one good push could bring them down.'

'I don't know. This is something I will have to give a lot of thought to. It's our future, and not what I think best for the family.'

'If we do this, we'll be ahead financially for the rest of our lives. We won't have to pay off a mortgage while the children are growing up. It is close to the shops, schools and transport into town.'

'Okay, as far as that is concerned, you're right. But I don't like the place itself. It's rather rough.'

'I know, I know, but it is only a start, don't you see?'

I breathed deeply, trying to overcome the sick feeling in my stomach, looked at him and knew he was determined to give it a try. 'I won't say yes, Pierre. Not now, maybe not ever. I don't think I could stand it. You will have to find out a lot more. How much he wants for the land etc.'

'Oh, I won't jump in with my eyes closed, don't worry. I'll see what I can find out tomorrow. I pass there every day anyway.'

Once again, I was facing a dilemma. Was this ever going to end? What to do for the best? Was it feasible? Again, I had another sleepless night. I knew Pierre. Once he put his mind to it, he would be able to do this, but was I able to put up with this life for an indefinite time? I would prefer to have a nice house built in Chermside and be done with it. I wanted a normal existence; not living like gypsies any longer was an attractive option. Still, if it helped us financially ... I gave up. The land could be sold anyway by now.

It wasn't. When Pierre came home from work the next day, he told me, 'I saw that chap in Darra just now. He wants a sale as soon as possible. Apparently, the family is moving to Townsville. He's been in Australia for nine years, and for seven of it they've been living in that tent. He's asking seven hundred pounds for the land. He seems to be in debt as well; hasn't paid his rates for eighteen months. What d'you think?'

'Not a good proposition. What does the lot look like close up?'

'Like a dump. He told me he hadn't worked at the house for months. He reeked of drink, so I can't see him ever finishing it. I offered him six hundred, but he wanted seven. Maybe we should let him stew over it for a while.'

'Listen, why don't you stop running around for a few weeks. All you've done since we arrived here is going from one office to the next, finding out things, planning, looking at land, at houses. Give it a rest, and then we'll see. This doesn't sound good. We might buy a lot of trouble there.'

Pierre replied, 'There are certain agreements in place between our governments to assist migrants with building a house. It comes with a lot of red tape. To help with a loan, we must pay fifty pounds to find out whether we are eligible, plus fifteen pounds for different costs, plus a mortgage insurance, which is fifteen pounds a year. It's all a bit much. Anyway, we'll see what happens.'

In the days that followed, Pierre and I had many discussions on what to do with the land in Darra. It was hard to decide what was best for the family. I knew Pierre was dead keen to do this, but could I face spending another two years in the camp? We had looked at other options, did some sums, checked our finances and found that building ourselves still seemed to have the most benefits in the long run.

Pierre had also spoken to a builder to seek some advice. 'If that's what you want to do,' he said, 'go for it. I know of a good draughtsman, who can help you draw up the plans.' Of course, by then Pierre was building already. The chap had built his own home as well, so perhaps it was not so unusual here.

He confessed to me one day, he could not sleep nights because he was so excited about the idea, so how could I not agree? After much serious soul-searching we finally decided to go ahead and build in Darra. Within a few days everything was properly signed, witnessed by a solicitor, and, by the end of that week, the previous owner had left for Townsville.

And then the fun started!

As soon as we knew they'd left we walked to the land for our first close-up inspection, only to find that the previous owner had planted a very unusual crop. The high grass was littered with beer bottles, cans, carton packets in all sorts and sizes, remnants from a tent and, last but not least, an old sewing machine. We looked at this lot, then at each other, while Pierre—seeing the look on my face— said, 'Don't worry, I'll have it tidied up in no time.' I very much doubted this. He

House and Land Deals?

would need a bulldozer to do the job properly.

It was indeed a corner block and double the size of a normal building block, with plenty of room for a nice garden later. Much later, I thought. A strong smell of wood smoke still hung over the land; they had probably used a woodstove to cook. Well, my man would have his hands full for the next few years, yet he did not seem at all daunted by the prospect.

On coming home from work at night, he quickly ate his dinner, then paper and pencils came out and he started drawing different plans, which changed quite a few times during those first weeks. Still, it gradually took shape, and I quite liked what I saw. A patio at front and back, three good-sized bedrooms, bathroom with shower stall, bath and basin, a lovely big lounge-kitchen and a laundry. Of course, these were only rough sketches, and a proper plan would have to be drawn by a professional draughtsman later.

Towards the neighbour's fence on one side stood a sort of lean-to which could serve as a shed for Pierre to keep his tools. It had no door, so his first job was making one, after which the big clean-up started. He gathered all the beer bottles, stacked them, ready for the scouts to collect, and made a big bonfire with all the rubbish. Then the big building adventure could begin.

But just at this time, Pierre was being asked to work many hours of overtime once again. He was very keen to start on the house, but it would just have to wait. He did ask me, however, to go and see the chef and ask whether he had a big empty tin in which he could mix cement! We were in luck. The cook found an enormous tin which would do the job until there was time to do some serious shopping, although Pierre had bought some small trowels—a small start for such a gigantic project indeed. However, he now had the essentials so that he could start whenever some spare time became available.

His first chance to work on the house came in late October. With plans properly drawn up and approved by the council, the first bricks were laid. However, it was already extremely hot, with temperatures already soaring above 90 degrees Fahrenheit. Nevertheless, to mark this special occasion, the children and I walked over with a picnic afternoon tea and had a little celebration.

On Wednesday of the following week, Peter asked Mr Milton whether he could have the afternoon off. When the headmaster asked why, he answered, 'I have to help Dad build our house.' Of course, Mr Milton laughingly agreed, and our dapper little man went with his Dad quite happily to do his bit for the family. He was so keen, and we adults had a good laugh about it.

While our house was being built, I spent many hours helping Dad and, in the process, by observation and limited practice, learnt a great deal about some of the practical arts involved in the building trades. An early achievement was learning how to mix 'mud' (cement for the brickwork), and to carry and place all the large—and quite heavy, for an eight-year-old—concrete Besser blocks nearby so Dad could easily place them on the row he was working on. I guess this qualified me as a 'bricky's labourer'! Another big job, which came later, was mixing all the concrete (in a concrete mixer) for the floors of some of the rooms, and then helping Dad do the levelling and finishing.

One morning, when Pierre left for work, he asked me to go to the sawmill and brick factory in Darra to order materials. These factories were situated on the Brisbane side of Darra, and it meant an hour's walk there and back. There was no transport, of course, so I put Veronique in the stroller, and we set off. It was steaming hot on the track, the sun beating down on us, the bush humming with heat, with the crickets singing their hearts out.

Pierre had put all the measurements and quantities on paper for me, and although I received some very strange looks when I walked into the yards—a woman with a toddler in tow, ordering bricks and timber—everything was duly written down and would be delivered the following day. It sure was a change to buying dresses!

50. HIGHS AND LOWS

Meanwhile, life in Wacol Migrant Hostel continued with a unique mix of the routine or mundane, and some unforgettable surprises and adventures as new frontiers were opened for our young family. What also became obvious was the wonderful and very generous welcome being extended by the wider Queensland community to migrant families like ours. It was also during this time that Corry's love for Australia, its people and its natural beauty, moved to another level!

September was a very social month, with different outings for the children, and their mother as well. First it was Peter's turn for a bus trip with his class to Tamborine Mountain. The girls' turn came a week later, but with the same destination. The children were terribly excited about this. 'We're going to have a picnic, Mum, and games and everything,' Peter told me. 'And we go on a bushwalk as well. Sounds fun, eh, Mum?'

'There are high mountains, and waterfalls and creeks, our teacher told us,' Mona added.

'That sounds extremely exciting. I think I'll come with you. Do you think the teacher will let me come?' I teased.

'Nooo! It's only for children,' three little voices sang in chorus, Brigitte joining in as well. 'Mothers aren't allowed on the bus!'

'Oh, then you better tell me all about it when you get back.'

On the day in question Peter was awake at dawn, too excited to sleep, and was dressed and ready to go at seven. When I finally waved him off, I heaved a sigh of relief. I felt as if I had walked to Tamborine myself, but I was so happy for him. The children had adjusted so well to their new lives in Wacol, and, almost from the start, had allayed any concerns about how they would settle.

The following week it was the girls' turn, and we went through the same procedure until they too went to school, full of expectation, then, arriving home later, falling over themselves to tell me all about their adventures.

That same week the Youth Chamber of Commerce invited eighty children from the migrant hostel to a picnic at Mandalay on the following Saturday, and I was invited to assist with supervision.

Saturday morning arrived with the usual excitement from our three eldest. Consequently, we were at the school nice and early. Soon other children joined us, accompanied by their parents. It was a glorious day, sunny and warm, not a single cloud in the sky.

Shortly before ten, a fleet of big sedans drew up at the school. This was our transport? Beautiful luxury cars, in perfect condition and polished to a shine, and here was I expecting to travel by bus. This was fantastic. We would be travelling in style today. We found a seat in a luxurious black car; our chauffeur a genuinely nice gentleman, who addressed me during the whole journey as 'Madame', no doubt thinking this was very continental.

On arrival at the picnic grounds, I noticed we were expected. In a large tent, tables were laid out with a most appetising morning tea. Ladies stood waiting, ready to serve us and, although hanging back at first, the children needed little encouragement to help themselves to the cakes, lamingtons, scones and biscuits these ladies had prepared. They must have been cooking for days.

It was a marvellous morning, warm, but not yet hot. While the children sat on the grass, we talked with our hosts. I found them very friendly and full of interest in our stories. Some had travelled to Europe, which made it so much easier to talk about the places we had seen. While it was probably daunting for them to interact with so many newcomers to their country, they were so very generous in their efforts in giving our children such a lovely day out.

After morning tea, the men devised several games, in which all the children took part, with much hilarity and laughter. Competition was fierce, and the winners duly rewarded with small monetary prizes. When all the races were run, we had a marvellous spread for lunch, and I wondered how they could have transported all this to the grounds. This had been a massive exercise. No one hung back this time and all tucked in with much enthusiasm.

On the trip home the children chirped like little birds. Not so my driver, however. I do believe he was very shy. Maybe it was his first experience with people from overseas, and I know we probably seemed like such a strange lot to get used to. However, I hoped he realised how much we appreciated this outing and, on arrival at Wacol, I thanked him most sincerely for this pleasant day. Luckily, the children remembered to say 'thank you' as well, which pleased me. For once I didn't have to remind them. After all, these people did all this voluntarily. It was one of the things I found very endearing in our new countrymen (and women). They did not have to do this.

On the very next day, my day out with the Catholic ladies was a great success as well. We boarded the bus at eight o'clock and drove to Tamborine Mountain, where we arrived in time for Mass at a Brothers' monastery. I am afraid I was rather distracted by the lovely views and didn't catch much of the sermon. But I suppose admiring nature is a kind of prayer as well. I have always believed this. What nicer way to pray than to say, 'You did such a good job, Lord. Thanks for everything.'

The air was fresh and crisp so high up, and I inhaled deeply. The Netherlands is such a small, flat country, in such contrast to this landscape. I fell in love with the mountains that day, and, when we walked to the waterfall later, I suddenly wished to be alone, no one to talk to, no others around me, so I could drink in this beautiful spot. I promised myself I would come back later, to enjoy it all at my leisure. At that precise moment, I knew I loved this country, and with a certainty I had never experienced before. In some strange way, it was as if I had come home, as if I had waited all my young life to experience this.

We later had lunch at the hotel, which was a rare treat, used as we were to the fare at the centre. The food was cooked to perfection, and the service exceptional. There was a nice atmosphere; ladies out for the day, and we certainly made the most of it.

On the return journey we were high. Not from that single glass of wine at lunch but with the joy of a carefree day. We sang all the way to Wacol—all the school songs most of us remembered—and we received some odd looks from other motorists on the highway. We were, like our children before us, celebrating life. Life was still hard, the food still bad, but we could face it again.

Another support which helped carry all of us through our first year was the help of our families in the Netherlands.

Our 'home front' was terrific. Not one week passed when there wasn't a letter from Mum or my sisters; often a parcel with a surprise for the children. Pierre's brother Ted kept the comics for them (he was addicted to them), and Mama wrote and kept contact as well with letters and parcels.

Nevertheless, it seems that our Dutch 'support crew' could simply not comprehend the enormous step we had taken and the adjustments our family had already been making and would continue to make. They hadn't travelled very far from the Netherlands, so couldn't grasp our new way of life, despite Corry's best efforts in her letters to help them understand at least a little better what we were experiencing in our adopted country.

In the letters from her mother and brother, the news about Corry's dad, who we children knew as Opatje Oudenbosch, continued to be very worrying, the more so because, being on the other side of the world, there was just nothing we could do, except pray.

The news about Dad, however, was worrying. His health seemed to deteriorate slowly, and he was aging quickly from what I read in Mum's letters. I often wished I could go home for a couple of days, just to convince myself Dad was still all right.

This could not be, however, and I found this very hard. I knew Mum was the best nurse he could have and that she would look after all his needs, but it was a constant and tiring job. It would be very demanding for her, and I worried about them. Collecting the mail filled me with apprehension with the thought of more bad news. All I could do was pray, and we did this fervently every night.

A few days later, Peter was looking rather peaky. He didn't have much of an appetite, which was most unusual. It worried me and I kept a close eye on him. Next morning when he got up, I noticed his skin had a faint yellow tinge, which gave me quite a fright. 'Peter, come here a minute, son,' I said. 'Let me have a look at you.' I took him into the light at the windows and looked at his eyes. The whites seemed yellow as well.

'I think I better take you to Sister this morning, Pete. You can't go to school today, love.' I was terribly upset. I had recognised the signs. I had jaundice as a child and was home from school for eleven weeks until I was finally declared fit again. This time with Peter, I hoped it would not be so severe. At the surgery, the doctor confirmed my fears, but luckily it was still in the early stages.

He saw how upset I was when I told him, 'I'm so careful with everything. I keep the children as clean as possible. How could this happen now?'

'It's not your fault, Mrs de Haas, believe me. You're living in far from ideal circumstances and infections do happen, despite how careful you are.'

Within a few weeks, however, the yellow faded, my little son's energy returned, and I started to relax again.

Amidst all such challenges and difficulties of adjusting to our new lives in Australia, albeit within the relatively protected (but not always healthy) environment of the migrant hostel, there continued to be many special moments which were deeply cherished.

From the start, we had joined the English classes, where Mr Milton, the principal of the migrant school, not only taught the language, but told us about the Australian way of life, which made it most interesting. There was often much laughter when we compared the different cultures which we all came from, and the one we were entering. There would be many mistakes, he reminded us, sometimes with hilarious consequences, but if we could keep our sense of humour we would soon learn to interact with our new countrymen.

On certain occasions Mrs Milton came with him, a charming lady who quietly sat beside him and followed the proceedings with keen interest. Shortly after the August school holidays, she attended once again. Afterwards, Pierre and I stayed behind and talked with them for a while. She asked us to wait, disappeared into the teacher's room, then came back carrying a big bunch of flowers, which she handed to me saying, 'I brought you some flowers from our garden, Mrs de Haas. I hope you like them. I picked them just before we left.' I thanked her, blushing with pleasure at this most kind gesture.

This was so unexpected and was something I missed, for I always had fresh flowers at home. In spring the house had been full of daffodils and hyacinths and their perfume, more than anything else, proclaimed spring had finally arrived. I was absolutely thrilled, thanked her and said, 'These will certainly bring colour to our rooms, Mrs Milton. They are lovely.'

We said goodnight and walked home arm in arm; I with this lovely warm feeling inside. It is amazing, I thought later, how some small gesture can take the hard edges off life and replace them with something of beauty. The flowers brightened our hut for a week.

At about the same time, I noticed how our children had progressed. During teacher's week we parents were invited to visit the school and sit in the children's classes. I found it extremely interesting to see the children at their lessons. I was amazed at their mastery of English. Peter's face was a study in concentration. Mona was doing sums, while Brigitte was writing on a slip of paper, trying out the different letters of the alphabet. There were no more worries about the children fitting in. They were fine.

Then later, twenty young voices sang 'Waltzing Matilda', Australia's most well-known ballad, children from Hungary, Denmark, Germany, Yugoslavia, the Netherlands, England and Greece, Italy and Malta; clear voices, bright voices, happy voices … happy children. I felt the soft, reassuring pressure of the teacher's hand on my arm. He understood the tears that blinded my eyes.

Arrival at Wacol Migrant Hostel

So Hot!!

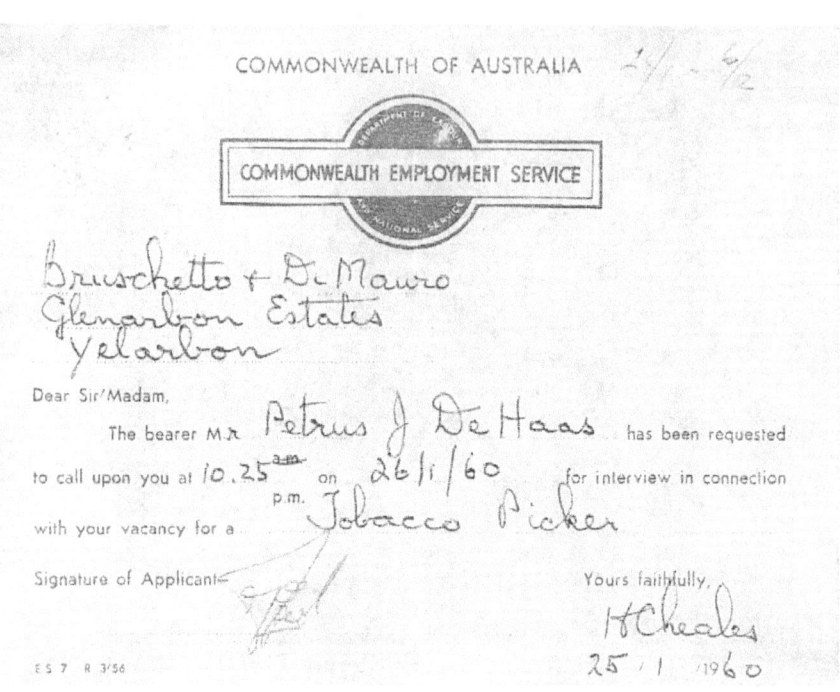

Pierre's first job in Australia – a tobacco picker

Our Wacol hut ... and makeshift sunshade

A new experience!

'Give me a home among the gum trees'

The photo that appeared in the *Courier Mail* in May 1960, with the caption: 'She likes our State'

Mona in her Dutch costume at Brisbane City Hall

Brigitte with some of her young friends at the kindergarten at Wacol Migrant Hostel

PART 7: MOVING ON

51. AN EMOTIONAL ROLLER COASTER

So, within a period of less than nine months since our arrival in Australia, most of the big adjustments were behind us: Pierre had found a steady job, or so he thought; Corry had already touched upon a genuine connection with the land (and probably its *spirit*) during her excursion to Tamborine; we children had learnt the language, knew how to sing some of its ballads, and were back in our proper grades at school, doing very well; as a family we had acquired three little pieces of Australia, in Redcliffe, Chermside and Darra; and Pierre had commenced building our home. Little could we know, however, that the next few months would bring some big surprises, some welcome, others not, taking us all on an emotional roller coaster which would also thoroughly test the resilience of my parents.

Of course, none of this was planned …

The first 'surprise' came at the end of October.

By then, I was sure I was expecting our sixth baby and didn't know how to cope with this news. Not because of the baby, but the primitive circumstances in which we lived made everything so much more difficult. Pierre also knew the signs; I didn't have to tell him. As soon as I lifted my head from the pillow in the morning, I was sick.

We both found it extremely hard to accept this; this on top of all that had happened in our lives recently. It was a very subdued couple who went about their everyday routine those first weeks. There was one bonus, though: we lived far enough from the kitchen and from the cooking smells; it helped a bit with the morning sickness.

I wanted to find out about procedures in a situation like this, so I went to see the Sister at the clinic. She was immensely helpful and told me I would have to go to the hospital in Brisbane for my monthly check-ups. She also explained mothers had to go into hospital to have a baby, which I found very strange. I had had all my children at home, assisted by my own doctor and midwife. I didn't like this arrangement at all. It all seemed so clinical.

On coming home, I put Veronique down for her nap, made myself a cup of coffee and had a good cry. Why, oh why, did this have to happen now, as if life wasn't difficult enough already? After a while I dried my tears and felt a little better. I well knew that the realities of life had to be faced and overcome, but it took me a long time to accept this new burden gracefully. I didn't feel very graceful at the time. I dreaded the months ahead.

The second surprise arrived the very next day and gave Corry a much-needed lift.

> I received a letter from *Wereld Post* and a cheque for ninety guilders in appreciation of my articles. This cheered me up considerably and lifted my spirits. It was lovely to know that my articles found such an eager readership, and I hoped it helped some people come to terms with all the changes an emigration brings.

Number three arrived on the day of Pierre's birthday, 11 November 1960. When he arrived at work that morning, he found out that he would be losing his job.

> 'I'm sorry, Pierre but I will have to let you go. The job is nearly complete, and I can't keep everyone on now.'
> This was a terrible setback and Pierre said as much. 'This is quite a blow, and on my birthday as well.'
> 'Oh, well, many happy returns, anyway,' he'd said, and, shrugging

his shoulders, had walked away, probably not knowing what else to add. It was a shame, for they had worked well together and often talked about their years in the army.

What now? What else could happen? Still, for the children's sake we acted as if nothing had happened. They were always so enthusiastic and joined in so happily. They had made lovely cards and we still sang 'Happy Birthday' and, with this, put work worries on hold for a few hours.

Surprise number four arrived the next morning.

As soon as he arrived on the job, his boss drew him aside and said, 'I've reconsidered, Peter. I have decided to keep you on until Christmas.'

Pierre thanked him most sincerely, and when he came home that night, he absolutely glowed. 'Guess what?' he said.

'What?'

'The boss told me this morning I can work till Christmas.'

My arms around him, I hugged him tight. 'Oh, what a relief. We can have a good Christmas after all. What a shame though for the others. What are they going to do? No one wants to employ people with the holidays coming.'

'I don't know, Corry. A shame eh?'

It would be our second Christmas in the tropics, and it certainly would be different this time.

Then, in early December, a bombshell ...

We received a message on the intercom to come to the post office. Apparently, they had a telegram for us. A dreadful apprehension filled my mind and the thought, 'It's Dad, it's Dad,' kept repeating itself. I ran to the post office and, out of breath, I gasped, 'I'm Mrs de Haas. You have a telegram for me?' The girl behind the counter handed it to me. I tore at it with fingers that seemed to have lost all feeling and read, 'Mama died 3 December. Letter follows.' It was signed: 'Ted.'

I grew cold all over, then burst into tears, while the poor girl looked on and said, 'Oh, I'm so sorry. I didn't know it was bad news, Mrs de

Haas.'

I couldn't speak, just nodded that I understood. My first thought was: How to tell my husband? Pierre and his mother had always been so remarkably close ... Mama was in good health when we left the Netherlands and, although she was diabetic, it had not stopped her from living a full and busy life; and now this. Blinded by tears I slowly walked home, trying to figure out how I could reach my husband. On arrival, I read the telegram again and again while trying to come to terms with its contents. Her last letter had been cheerful; there was no indication she wasn't feeling well.

Since we arrived in this country, I had held secret hopes that, once we were settled, Mama would be able to visit us here and stay for an extended holiday. I sat at the table, numb with shock, not able to do anything. Two hours later Pierre arrived home. There were no words between us. We embraced and held each other, trying to find the courage to face this, while my tears flowed anew.

Later, much later, we talked and wondered how this could have happened, so quickly, without warning. In her last letter she had told us she was playing indoor bowls again, her favourite pastime on weekends. Apparently, there had been no indication of any lasting effects from her slight heart attack a few months before.

At last, I asked, 'Would you like a cup of coffee?'

'Okay, yes, but nothing to eat. If you don't mind, I think I'll go to the land in Darra and do a few jobs there. I think that's what Mum would have wanted.' His voice broke. 'Yes, that's what I'll do.'

I knew he had to deal with this in his own way; by building on our future. 'You do that, Pierre, and we'll talk more later.'

He finished his coffee and left soon after, and I also started on the daily chores. I dreaded having to tell the children; they were so young to understand this great mystery. Mama wrote nearly every week, and with her part of our 'home front' fell away as well. We would miss her dearly; nothing was ever too much for her.

After dinner that night, we all sat around the table, and we told the children gently that Oma had gone to heaven and was living with the angels now. We also said a prayer together. It was Peter who asked, 'Won't Oma come and see us anymore, Dad?'

'I'm afraid not, Peter,' Pierre replied, 'but she can see us, and she'll look after us, just as Oma did when we were in the Netherlands. And you can talk to her any time you want, maybe at night before you fall asleep. She would like that.'

'Oh, yes, okay.'

To this day, I have very fond memories of Oma. She was very kind when I stayed with her during our last weeks in the Netherlands. I attended the local school, the gate of which was just at the back of the lane running alongside the de Haas house and shop in Helmond. Every lunch time, she would be waiting for me at that gate to give me my lunch, and I am sure to check up on me and assure herself that I was okay at my very temporary, or transit, school.

A few quiet days followed and, although we didn't talk about it, our thoughts were in the Netherlands, where the family had to organise a funeral and go through the trauma that accompanies such a sad occasion. At least we were spared all this. We could remember Mama as we had seen her last, smiling through her tears as she kissed us goodbye.

Shortly afterwards, we received three parcels from the Netherlands. One from Pierre's brother Jan, and his wife, one from Mum and Leny, and the third from Mama, which brought new tears to my eyes—we could not even thank her anymore. Her place in our hearts would never be filled. Once again, our families had shown their support for us. We had not been forgotten. I put them all away until Christmas; we would have a real Dutch Christmas after all.

Later that week, we received a letter from Ted, in which he told us about Mama's Requiem Mass and funeral. It was all incredibly sad, especially now, the time of year when families gather to celebrate. With the same mail was yet a bigger parcel from her with toys and a lovely pair of new shoes for each of the children. I could picture her joyfully shopping for all this ...

Life certainly throws up big challenges at times, but we couldn't put our sorrow on the children's shoulders. Somehow it made Pierre and I try even harder to make this a wonderful Christmas for them, our first in Australia.

As if timed precisely to deliver a much-needed lift in spirits, a few days

Part Seven: Moving On

later our family was completely overwhelmed with the wonderful experience of our first work Christmas Party, something we could not even have imagined. As far as awesome surprises go, this one was hard to beat.

The Christmas party from Pierre's work was a picnic at Mandalay on 6 December. When Pierre's boss found out we didn't have a car, he assured Pierre, 'That's no problem, you can book a cab on me.' When Pierre told me this, I could not believe it at first; we had never experienced something like this before.

It was a beautiful summer day, the Brisbane river a silver shawl winding itself around the old stately suburbs of Brisbane. The afternoon was a magnificent occasion. The tables were laden with food with a traditional Christmas cake, beautifully iced and decorated, as its centre piece. What a treat this was. The children each received a present. There were games organised in which they all took part, and it was lovely. (And me worrying myself sick about them before we left the Netherlands—they had never been spoilt like this!) When I saw their happy smiling faces, I sent up a quick prayer of thanks.

But more was to come! Mona and I were invited to be part of a group of European migrant children invited to sing their traditional Christmas carols on television, so another week of great excitement followed, with practices every night before the big event.

On Monday night, 20 December, we were picked up in several Commonwealth cars and were driven to the studio where the program would be filmed. The children were fantastic. Each little group sang in turn, their voices as clear as Christmas bells, and I ended up quite teary-eyed at the finish. It was a wonderful evening. I was so sorry we did not have a television so Pierre and the other children could have seen it as well. What a wonderful lead-up to Christmas.

Our Christmas at home was as nice as we could make it under the circumstances. We unpacked the crib and statues which had made the journey undamaged, apart from one of the shepherds, who had lost his head, as shepherds are known to do at times. That was soon fixed, however.

After Mass we all gathered around the table for a lovely festive breakfast, and with the contents of the parcels it was a special one indeed. Later, with everything cleared away, as tradition dictated in our family, it was present time. Each in turn received a parcel to unwrap, so we could all enjoy it, and the excitement would last a little longer. The children were thrilled, and Santa must have had sore ears at the end of it from all the shouted: 'Thank yous.'

On Boxing Day, the management of the migrant hostel organised a huge party, and Santa, who may have forgotten his way home (!) was there again with another huge load of presents ... another surprise which was beyond any expectations. Very exciting, a day filled with much laughter and fun!

A babble of excited children's voices filled the air around us while we waited for Santa to arrive. Just as the waiting almost grew too much for our little people, a ute arrived on the scene, with Santa sitting in the back, ringing a big brass bell. To a thunderous sound of hundreds of voices Santa stepped down, a big sunny smile on his face, and shouted, 'Ho!' and he too had not come empty handed. On the back of the utility were hundreds of parcels, all wrapped in colourful Christmas paper.

Once again, I marvelled at the generosity of the organisers, this time the centre's management. All of this was free, and we had not contributed in any way. Our little people had never experienced such 'high-rolling' lives before.

After the ute was emptied, the children's names were called on the microphone, so each in turn could collect a present. This took quite a while, but finally Santa's job was finished. He departed with much cheering and clapping from adults and children alike, and once the tables were cleared, afternoon tea was served. The chefs had excelled themselves. There wasn't a hard, hairy bean in sight, replaced instead by a feast of delicious party food: cakes and fresh sandwiches, lamingtons, crackers and cheese, and many little dishes with Christmas lollies.

So, these special, festive days wound up, but there was just one more surprise, a bitter note in what was otherwise such a happy time (at least for

Part Seven: Moving On

we children) ... Pierre had lost his job after all ...

The job he had been working on was finished, and his boss had told him to come back in three weeks' time. Maybe he would have something for him then. Pierre had received forty-seven pounds holiday pay plus his wages, which was a nice little sum to see us through the holidays. We decided not to worry; the future could take care of itself for a change.

There was more to come, however. In January, Mona was invited to participate in the citizenship ceremony to be held at Brisbane City Hall on Australia Day. She was one of five girls, each from a different European country, to present flowers to the official guests. Each girl would be wearing the traditional costume of their native country.

Well, I was struck dumb for a moment. What a wonderful opportunity for our little girl. How lovely to be asked to take part, but that was not all. Mona would be presenting flowers to Lady May, wife of the Queensland Governor, Sir Henry Abel Smith. I was immediately assured that a local seamstress had been organised to make Mona a traditional Dutch costume.

I could not wait to tell Mona. What excitement there was at the de Haas dinner table that night. Mona absolutely glowed. I saw she was a bit apprehensive, but I knew she would do a great job.

Consequently, January was a month of great activity. We practised curtsies until I was sure Mona could do it in her sleep, fitted costumes, found out about times and dates, designed the lace cap, which was the hardest part, and wondered whether we would finish it all before the twenty-sixth. We certainly did; and the seamstress made a wonderful job of the costumes. Our girl would be a true Dutch girl indeed.

When I later enquired about the time the children had to be ready, I was then told the children and their mothers had also been invited to have afternoon tea with the official party. Another huge surprise!

Finally, the long-expected day arrived, and Mona and I left, waved off by Pierre and the children, and walked to the office, where Commonwealth cars were waiting to take us to City Hall. All the children looked gorgeous, their little faces glowing with excitement. I sensed they were a bit nervous as well, but I tried to put them at ease with, 'You'll do fine I'm sure. You have practised so many times, it will all go well.' I could talk! I had a hard time of it. My heart was pounding, and my stomach was tight with nerves. Five hundred and forty-two people would be watching. Oh dear!

On arriving at City Hall, photographers were waiting to take photos of each girl in turn, after which we were escorted into the big hall and seated on the side near the stage. When the official guests arrived, we all stood, and the ceremony started with the national anthem, 'God save the Queen'.

After everyone was seated, the children presented the flowers to the official guests. They managed beautifully and I was so proud of them. If only Mum and Dad could have seen our little girl now. There were several speeches, followed by the Oath of Allegiance to the Queen, which made the hair on my neck stand on end. I then knew that one day we would stand, as a family, in this great hall and would leave it as Australians. I knew this with unwavering certainty.

With so many people present, the handing out of the citizen certificates took forever, but finally it was done and a great roar of applause went up, followed by a word of thanks by a German migrant, who spoke for all new Australians. By that time, I was overcome with emotion.

Afterwards, our little party was escorted to a special reception room, where afternoon tea was waiting for us. We stood quietly waiting in the background until the official party arrived. Our hosts took turns to introduce us to Sir Henry and Lady May, to the Lord Mayor and the Lady Mayoress and several aldermen and their ladies. Everyone was very friendly and easy to talk to, and we had a wonderful time.

The afternoon was one I—and I'm sure the children—would never forget; certainly not when afterwards the Lord Mayor took them to a different room where he presented them with a beautiful photo book of Brisbane. They also received a nice badge of City Hall. The Lord Mayor had signed and dated the books, so the children would always have a nice souvenir of this wonderful afternoon.

I was touched and again marvelled at the warm-hearted kindness of our future countrymen. I thanked him most sincerely. We said our goodbyes and, stepping outside, saw two black Commonwealth cars

Part Seven: Moving On

waiting for us to take us back to Wacol, where on arrival all the children were told that they could keep their national costumes to remind them of the wonderful job they did.

Well, this was the icing on the cake. This was such an unexpected and generous gesture I was speechless. When, finally, I had swallowed yet another big lump in my throat and trusted I could find my voice, I thanked him most sincerely. I knew we could never repay all this. But we could try and be good Australian citizens. I hoped we had made a start that very afternoon.

We walked home, my little Dutch girl dancing at my side, and when we walked into the hut, Pierre had one look at our faces and said, 'You're all smiles. It must have been a wonderful afternoon.'

'It was fantastic.'

We talked for two hours, hardly stopping to take a breath.

Then, a few weeks later, the emotional roller coaster plunged into the depths; a devastating blow ... another telegram from the Netherlands, this time announcing the death of Corry's father.

I received a call one morning to come to the post office as there was a telegram for me. I dropped everything and almost ran, one thought on my mind. 'It's Dad; something's happened to Dad.' I was not surprised, therefore, when I tore it open and read, 'Dad passed away this morning. Letter will follow, Nell.'

I started to shake while tears ran down my face. I could not speak and turned around to go home, when I found Peter standing behind me, his eyes big with worry. 'What's wrong, Mummy, why are you crying?'

I knelt and held that little boy in my arms as if to gather strength from his small frame and whispered, 'It's Opa, Peter, Opa has gone to live with the angels in heaven now.

'Is it Opaatje Oudenbosch?'

'Yes, Opaatje Oudenbosch,' I sobbed. 'Come, we'd better go home.' Hand in hand we walked home while I tried to find some solace in his little fist. When we arrived at the house, one of our friends, Nell, was waiting at the door. She had heard the message as well. One look at my face was enough. She put her arm around me, made me sit down, and poured me a glass of water from the container in the fridge, then sat down beside me without words, just holding my hand.

After a while, she asked quietly, 'Bad news, uh?' Without a word I handed her the telegram.

She read it, then put it on the table beside her and said to Peter, 'Will you stay with Mummy so I can phone Dad?' Peter nodded yes. Then to me, 'Have you got his work number?'

Just as she left to call Pierre, I felt the first movements of the baby I was carrying, a sign of new life where one had just ended. Pierre had just decided the other day, if the baby were a boy, we would name it after Dad. Now he would never know about it. The thought brought a new flood of tears, while Peter stood by my side, trying to help.

'Pierre will be home in five minutes,' Nell said as she walked into the room. 'I talked to the headmaster, Corry. Apparently, he had heard the message as well and sent Peter over to be with you. He feared it was bad news, you see. Did he know your dad was sick?'

'I don't know. Maybe one of the children might have mentioned it.' Nell stayed with me until Pierre arrived, then quietly slipped away. He took me in his arms, and I sobbed and sobbed.

When the other children came home from school, Pierre told them what had happened. We walked to the dining hall together, the children for once strangely subdued and quiet. Brigitte held my hand as if she would never let go, looking up every now and then to see if I was okay. I tried to swallow my tears to not make it harder on the children. They didn't know about life and had every right to be saved from grief at such an early age.

I tried to eat something, but the food stuck in my throat. In the end I just had a cup of tea. Pierre didn't fare much better and grabbed hold of my hand to reassure me, also lost for words.

A thousand pictures flashed through my mind: Dad at a family party, entertaining the relatives with his jokes and songs; Dad in the workshop, singing, while he plied his trade; my walks with Dad, always an adventure as he pointed out the different trees and flowers; Dad, shaving in the kitchen, reciting lines from the plays in which he acted, snippets of dialogue he still remembered; Dad, who when his clients were down on their luck, forgot about payment for a job. I grieved for his gentle soul. He always saw the best in people and made

Part Seven: Moving On

excuses for their shortcomings. Although small in stature, he was a great man.

Day followed day and I was not aware of them. I did the usual chores and, when the children were home, I tried to show some interest in their tales from school and kindy, but my mind was in the Netherlands with Mum and the family. One morning, I was washing the floor, tears streaming down my face, when Nell walked into the room. One look was enough. She took the mop from me. 'Leave this for now. Come on, we'll have a coffee.' She took my arm and steered me to the hut, where she pulled up a chair and ordered, 'Sit down and rest. I'll have the coffee ready in a tick.'

Soon the lovely aroma of freshly brewed coffee pervaded the air, and after she poured, she sat beside me and said, 'Come, drink it while it's hot. Later you can cry all you want.' I did. After a second cup, I calmed down and she let me talk while she sat beside me, holding my hand, while I talked and talked …

Somehow, I could face life again.

It was on the fifth of May, when, finally, I could write a letter to Mum. Dad had been gone five weeks by then.

52. New Births ...

As Corry was approaching full term, life was steadily becoming harder with every passing day. Now she was required to go to the Mater Hospital in Brisbane every second week for a check-up, and each of these was a major excursion on foot and by train and bus. Despite her increasing discomfort, Corry still carried the major responsibility for our young family as Pierre was mostly absent at work (including overtime whenever it was available) and house building in any spare time.

> One morning I was having a cry when Nell walked in unexpectedly. I looked up and asked her, 'Do you have any good jokes up your sleeve?' As it happened, she had a few, so I ended up crying and laughing at the same time. It helped me over the worst again.
> Later we walked (or rather ... I waddled) to the office together, to find out about procedures when the baby announced its arrival. Arrangements were also made for the barrier to be up for the ambulance to enter the centre.
> Then the manager said, 'There is also something else I wanted to talk to you about, now that you are here, Mrs de Haas.' He continued, 'I want you and your husband to think seriously about getting into proper accommodation once the baby is born. We can arrange—within three weeks—for a Housing Commission home for you in Inala. This is no place for a baby; the risk of infections is too great. Why don't you talk this over with your husband and let me know what you decide and, please, as soon as possible? I know you would like to wait until your home in Darra is finished but believe me, I have your best interests at heart.'
> 'Yes, of course, I understand. Thank you. I'll talk it over with Pierre and let you know what we decide.'
> 'It will be the best for your young children as well to live in a normal society. Believe me it will be the right decision for all concerned. This will also take the pressure off your husband, knowing

Part Seven: Moving On

you're in a decent home, and much more comfortable than you are here.'

At 3 am that same night I had to raise the alarm. I woke up Pierre by nudging him in the ribs, saying, 'Pierre, wake up, I think the baby is coming. You'd better get dressed and call the ambulance.' He was up and dressed in minutes, went to the supervisor's hut and on the way back woke up Nell as well. Nell had promised to stay with the children if I had to go into hospital during the night.

Three hours later, at 6 am, June 28, 1961 our beautiful baby, Diana, was born; a big baby indeed at ten pounds and two ounces. To me she looked like a three-month old baby. Although she was our sixth, that special moment when you hold your baby in your arms for the first time is still magic. I laughed and I cried, studied her little face, those perfect fingers and toes. The wonder of it is forever new. I was almost delirious with happiness to have a perfect little girl again. We were blessed, and the difficult months were left behind as so many puffs of smoke. Gone and forgotten, already in the past.

Pierre came to visit that afternoon, after he had fulfilled the official procedures following the birth of a child, anxious to meet his beautiful new daughter. He came in, carrying a big bunch of pink carnations and, never one to show his affection in public, gave me a chaste peck on the cheek, saying, 'How are you? How did it go?'

'Hard work, as usual,' I said, all the pain and agony forgotten, 'but if you see the baby ...'

'When I phoned up this morning, the Sister said she weighed ten pounds, two ounces. She must be as big a baby as Mona.'

'She is, Pierre. She looks three months old. She's beautiful.'

'When I told the children this morning, they wanted to come with me. They can't wait to see her. Before he went to school Peter wrote you a note.' He handed me a scrap of paper, I opened it and read,

Dear Mummy,

I'm so sorry you are sick, Mummy, just now when we have a new baby. I hope you are better soon. What does she look like? Does she have a nice little face? Not so ugly as Mona, eh, Mum, for she's a pest, Lots of kisses, from Peter.

New Births ...

The week I spent at the Mater Mothers' Hospital was special. I treasured my times with the baby, for once I was home there would be five other children who wanted my attention. Pierre visited every night, bringing the children in turn, so they could meet their new sister. We always walked to the nursery together, and the wonder in their eyes was a joy to see. On the nights he came on his own, we went downstairs to the cafeteria for a coffee, which was a real treat.

As usual I recovered quickly and could go home on the fifth day, back in the usual routine of looking after the family. This time, however, there were complications, and I was rushed back to hospital for another five days of rest. When the matron spotted me, she asked, 'But, Mrs de Haas, what are you doing back here with us?'

'You looked after me so well, Sister, I just wanted a bit more of that spoiling,' I answered. It was not until the doctors gave their okay, however, that I could go home, but this time I made sure I had a rest while the babies had their nap.

Diana was a placid baby, and the children were absolutely thrilled to have her home. Veronique was totally fascinated by her and slipped into our bedroom each time she had a chance. Thumb in her mouth, she stood beside the cot, watching her little sister sleep. As soon as she saw me get ready to bath the baby, she dropped what she was doing. Holding on to the bath at my side, she put her hand in the water to sprinkle some drops on the baby's head. When I was feeding Diana later, she stood leaning against me totally absorbed in the proceedings.

While Corry was in hospital, she and Pierre discussed at length what to do about the housing situation and decided to accept the offer of a new Housing Commission house in Inala. Taking this important step would finally conclude our family's migration journey, which had commenced more than two years previously with those first tenuous discussions between Corry and Pierre in our Nijmegen apartment.

We would now be leaving the relatively safe and supportive cocoon of the migrant hostel. So, our family was now on the very threshold of entering into the Australian community, and what that would involve was yet unknown. In many ways, it was just like a birth ...

Part Seven: Moving On

To celebrate our little girl's arrival, we invited a few friends for drinks one night. Pierre had just filled our glasses, when he stood up and said, 'I propose a toast for this,' and held out a set of keys to me, 'the keys to our new home in Inala, Corry.' He handed them over, and I promptly burst into tears, laughing and crying at the same time. He had not told me he had received the keys already, so it was quite a surprise. I could not believe we would soon be living in a normal house, and in a brand new one at that. I hardly slept that night.

Now we had to do some shopping. Because I couldn't get away, Pierre had to go into town instead. He had quite a few items on his list, a lounge suite, inner spring mattresses, extra blankets etc. to re-stock our house.

We later heard we would be moving in two weeks. When Pierre went to the office to ask about procedures, the manager told us not to worry about a removalist. They would look after it, and the groundsmen would give us a hand. This was a great help and one less worry. The move therefore went very smoothly.

On the day of our departure, we both went to the office to say goodbye to the managers and staff. We wanted to express our heartfelt thanks for everything they had done for us during the nineteen months we had spent at the migrant hostel. They had always been very understanding, compassionate and generous, always happy to 'go the extra mile'. We also made a point of saying goodbye to Sunny Boy. He was such a nice person and always had a kind word for the children. I would really miss his, 'Beautiful sunny Australia, eh Missus?'

53. AUSSIES IN THE MAKING

Once again, I marvel at the resilience and ingenuity of my parents, and by then it seemed to have been ingrained in us children as well. Once more, we had to adjust to completely new and different circumstances, learning to live in a developing suburb on the outskirts of Brisbane, with few facilities and little infrastructure … a huge change, not only from both the supportive, but always temporary, migrant community in Wacol, but also from the relatively luxurious CBD living we had grown accustomed to in the Netherlands. The first days and weeks were concerned with making ourselves comfortable …

> Our Housing Commission home was newly built and had three bedrooms, a bathroom with shower and bath, a big family kitchen with a free-standing laundry a few steps down at the back. The only setback was there was not a single cupboard in the house, other than a small one under the sink.
>
> At last, I had my stainless-steel sink, but there was no indoor toilet. The Brisbane City Council was working on a sewerage system for the city, but this had not reached our area yet, and we would have to make do with the dreaded 'thunderbox', not something I looked forward to. I hated the thought of it.
>
> I suspected we would be living out of suitcases for quite a while longer, until Pierre suggested he could make some clothes racks from conduit which he could buy at work. It was done quickly and would have to do for the time being. It was a question, then, what to unpack. We had no shelving or dressers, so most of our possessions had to stay in their boxes, and these we stored in a small room at the back, which would be Peter's bedroom. For the moment we all camped on the floor, except the two babies who had their own cot.
>
> One of the highest priorities was to work out the schedules (rounds) of the milkman, butcher, baker and greengrocer. So, I

engaged the children as lookouts. I told them to call me when they saw any activity in the street, and they did a marvellous job. Each time they saw someone coming, they called out, 'Mum, the baker's coming,' or 'Mum, I think I see the milkman,' with the result that by the end of that first day we had the various schedules worked out. We also found a Dutch butcher, who called in for orders twice a week, and Pierre took over the grocery shopping for me on his way home from work.

How we enjoyed our home-cooked meals again: cuts of meat prepared the way the butchers did in the Netherlands, and the delicious small goods in a variety we had not seen in nearly two years. It was a pleasure to cook, and the children ate like ravenous young cubs. Pierre also enjoyed the meals, and I hoped it would put some flesh on his bones. He looked almost gaunt from the long hours he spent on the job and his 'free' time on the house.

Mona, Brigitte and I were enrolled at Serviceton State School, which had only recently been completed to service this newly developing suburb. Gone were the understanding and compassionate school supports we had as migrant children in Wacol, and we were now expected to cope in a normal, mainstream Australian school. I was quite confused and uncertain in those first few days, thinking that somehow, all my classmates seemed smarter and much more able to understand the lessons. But soon afterwards, I found my bearings and school life took on a more familiar and reliable rhythm. I settled in and regained my confidence. My sister, Brigitte, however, found those first days at school rather frightening, especially with corporal punishment still in vogue.

Brigitte came home most days with a pinched, pale little face and looked extremely tired. I soon realised something was very wrong. When I had her on my own for a minute, I asked her, 'What is it, love? Aren't you happy at school? Are the children teasing you?'

She started to cry. 'I'm afraid, Mummy. The teacher is so angry all the time. And she hits the children.'

'But you're a good girl, aren't you? She wouldn't hit you?' meanwhile thinking, *She'd better not try!*

'No, I'm good, but I am still afraid.'

I took her in my arms and reassured her. 'Well, if you listen to what the teacher says and you're not naughty, then you don't have to be scared. I'll tell you what, each time the teacher gets mad, you think of something nice and you'll forget all about being scared. Do you think you can do that?' She nodded.

'Yes? And I'll tell you what, each day you're not scared we'll do something special together, or I'll have a little surprise for you, okay?'

I gave her a nice new hanky, and a few days went by where I made a big fuss of her, and each day after school she came to me and whispered, 'I wasn't scared today, Mum,' and I praised her and gave her an extra treat.

Another early concern was to arrange for the regular monitoring of Diana's health and progress. Corry discovered that the nearest baby clinic was two miles (about three kilometres) away. So, a second-hand pram was quickly found for Diana. A car didn't enter their thinking, and, in any case, Corry had never learnt how to drive ... and never would.

We liked what we saw (it was almost brand new), and so our little girl had her chariot. It would serve us well for as long as we needed it. It also had a little seat fitted to the front, so Veronique could have a ride as well.

The first time we used it, Veronique sat there triumphantly, thumb in her mouth, eyes big like saucers, and took in everything around her, while the baby slept. It was my first 'outing' in weeks, and I had a good look at my surroundings. It all seemed so bare; there were few established gardens, and most houses were in the finishing stages. They stood in neat rows, the concrete walls painted in pastel colours, which looked quite pretty. It seemed the builders had cleared an area of bushland, as the tree line finished right at the backyards, so providing a natural screen. It was incredibly quiet. There seemed to be nobody around, something I doubted I could ever get used to. There was no traffic other than the occasional builder's truck and, away in the distance, the dull thud of hammering.

It took me about half an hour to walk the distance and I was pleased the worst of the heat had gone as there was no shade at all.

Part Seven: Moving On

On arrival I introduced myself to the Sister in charge, who was quite friendly and chatted non-stop while she filled in the necessary details on Diana's chart.

Then, out of the blue, Veronique piped up, 'Where's Mummy's tummy now?'

What could I say to that? The nurse was in stitches, and so was I, but I managed, 'Mummy left it in hospital, with the doctor.' That little imp had timed her question to perfection.

Diana did quite well; the scales showed eleven pounds one ounce. I was immensely proud. Never had I managed to breastfeed my babies for more than a few days. This was a first.

When we moved into Inala, we didn't move into an established suburban community. Rather, the community gradually became established as houses were completed around us and other families moved in, as is still the case in new real estate developments. Nevertheless, our experience was a happy one, and I remember that there were often impromptu neighbourhood parties which were most enjoyable, not only for the adults but also for the throngs of children.

Behind the houses across the street from us was virgin bush, which we freely explored with our new-found friends in the neighbourhood. I distinctly remember walking by myself along one of the tracks on my way home late one glorious afternoon, the soft glow of the setting sun setting the tree tops alive in a blaze of orange and red colours. I was deeply moved, so much so that I was inspired to build a make-shift altar there and then knelt at it to pray.

Since we had left Wacol Migrant Centre, the children were blooming, especially Brigitte. The only one still very slim was Pierre, but no matter how much I tried to get some meat on his bones, I failed, due to the long hours he put in. Because he had to work so much overtime, he couldn't spend much time building, and so progress was very slow.

Soon, I met my new neighbours, the ice comfortably broken while pegging out the washing. A shy hello was soon followed by an invitation to morning tea, which I accepted graciously. One of my neighbour's little boys was two months older than Diana, and when she found out I didn't have transport, she offered to take us to the clinic. From then on, my long trek in the hot sun thankfully became a thing of the past, as we aligned our clinic days.

Our neighbours all had young families like ours, and it was inspiring to meet with other young women, and we certainly got on well together. It was like the United Nations at times, a girl from New Zealand, and a German lass, two Australians, Hetty from England and me. We usually had a lot of fun, and these coffee mornings nurtured firm friendships, also helping each other by minding the children now and then.

I had little trouble integrating into the Australian way of life and often had my new friends in stitches when I used a word in the wrong context. However, I was learning fast and my English improved quickly. What really confused me, however, were expressions like saying 'hooray' when they left or 'see you' when they had no plans to do so. They never just said 'goodbye' like normal people do! On occasion, when I thanked them for something, the 'no worries' had me worried. 'She'll be right' had me trying to figure out who SHE was. It was even worse when their husbands were home. You had to be quick off the mark to catch on, and I'm sure they had a lot of fun confusing me.

Some of our new neighbours were quite keen to learn about our ways, others were quite shy and probably uncertain as to how to take these strange people with their funny accent. However, after a few jokes everyone started to relax and laughed when I reminded them, 'When we have visitors in the Netherlands, we always start with coffee. So, don't run away now when you've finished your coffees. There will be drinks afterwards.'

The once quiet street now rang with children's voices, and I had eleven playing in the backyard on some days. Children make friends so easily, and they brought the parents together as well. Ours certainly enjoyed the company of their young friends. Hearing them talk we couldn't hear any difference between the Australian-born littlies or ours.

Then there was the 'scone disaster'!

Part Seven: Moving On

I thought it was time to write a letter to Mr and Mrs Milton, the principal at Wacol school, and invite them to visit when it suited. They replied immediately and accepted for the following Saturday. I baked a fruit flan and a Dutch honey cake, and then decided to be very daring by baking some scones as well, to have an Australian treat for them. The flan and cake turned out beautifully, but I didn't then know what happened to the scones. They didn't look even remotely like the scones I had seen at the different parties I'd attended!

Despite my being worried about this, we had a wonderful evening. They were so pleased to see the children again, and we had plenty to talk about. They congratulated Pierre on his big project, very happy to hear how well it was progressing.

Then, the moment of truth arrived. I arranged some slices of flan and cake on a nice oval dish, jammed and creamed the 'scones' and offered them to our guests, saying, 'I also made some scones for you, so you have something Australian as well.' The nasty little things were the size of big marbles. However, they squared their shoulders and took one, which I thought was very brave. I tasted one as well. The less said of this the better, but after they left Pierre said to me, carefully, 'The scones were a bit hard, weren't they?'

I didn't answer, just wished the ground had swallowed me and hoped our guests would survive them. Did I know you had to use self-raising flour?

Meanwhile, Pierre worked, and worked and worked … Any hopes that Corry may have held for more time together with Pierre in Australia had not been realised, but, fortunately, she quickly had a supportive network of neighbours around her.

Pierre never did rest after all the brickwork was finally finished in early October. Shortly afterwards, he finished making beds and, finally, we were all off the floor.

No sooner was that project finished when he told me, 'I've found someone to do the roof. He's a builder and specialises in building them. He said he'll come over on Saturday. Apparently, he charges by the day and he has a few jobs lined up, so we were lucky to get him.'

'Oh, that's great. I didn't particularly want you crawling all over those beams.'

'Well, I'll have to give him a hand, of course, and once the wood is up, I can then order the fibro sheets. After it's up, I can then work in all weather and out of the hot sun.'

'I can't believe we've come this far, Pierre. It's wonderful to see it grow, and I can't wait to see the house finished.'

'It will be a while yet. There's a lot to be done inside.'

'Yes, of course, I realise that.'

'Now come all the tricky bits. I'll have to put the conduit in and order the windows and doors, get a plumber etc. Luckily, I can do the electrical installation myself.'

'Honestly, Pierre, I don't know how you keep going at times. Don't you ever get sick of it all?'

'No, I still enjoy it. Each day I look forward to what I can do.'

'Still, I think you should have a break once the roof is up.'

'What's the difference, Corry? I'll be working here, then.'

'That's true.' Despite the fact we had decided not to put too much work in this house seeing we were renting, we still needed some work done to make it liveable, with cupboards a priority. Still, I didn't want to put more pressure on Pierre.

And so, after only a few months, we had settled into our first Australian community in Clipper Street, Inala, knowing all the time that this would also just be a temporary home.

As an indicator of how well we children had adjusted, Corry records that at the end of the 1961 school year:

> All the children came home with magnificent report cards from Serviceton State School. Brigitte was second in her class, Mona eleventh and Peter seventh, this in classes with an average of forty-five pupils. We were extremely pleased with these results, and I realised yet again all my worries about how the children would cope had been in vain. Still, nobody can look into the future, can they?

54. SETTLED

The year 1961 melted into 1962 with another very hot summer. Not that Pierre ever rested from the heat, or his extraordinary mix of working overtime and house building. He used every available spare day of the Christmas/New Year period to work on the house. Nevertheless, it would not be finished until early December … nearly another year away.

In the meantime, our life as a family in Inala resumed its now established pattern, thankfully without the emotional rollercoaster ride of the previous year. There was, however, a most significant and memorable milestone in Corry's personal migration journey. It was triggered by the settlement of the estate of Pierre's mum, leading to their first day out together in two years.

> What a lovely lunch it turned out to be. It was a rare treat indeed, and the food was delicious. The atmosphere a reminder of our trip through Europe, the soft background music of popular songs we remembered, and the food an epicure's dream.
>
> Pierre ordered a bottle of Spumanti, and we took our time, talking, planning, and, of course, reminiscing. Having a big family didn't leave much time for leisurely meals. Nor time to touch on subjects that were important to us.
>
> 'How do you feel about our migration now, Corry?' Pierre asked.
>
> 'Things certainly have looked up since we're in a proper home. But you know, Pierre, even after just a few months here, I did not want to leave, and still don't. Of course, I miss Mum and the family, but by writing every fortnight we have kept in close contact, and so do they.
>
> 'We have only seen such a small part of this country, but it has something undefinable. It feels good. I can understand now how you felt in the Netherlands, after spending three years in the tropics. But for me it is not the weather alone. The mountains for one. When we made that trip to Mt Tamborine, I could have stayed there, be there

on my own for a while and let it all sink in; maybe because the Netherlands is so flat and small. I think the grandeur of nature here, the wide vistas ...

'This country grows on you. Maybe it is because I have always thought of myself as a nature child. Do you feel this? It is that same kind of feeling I had when I went home and stopped at the basilica for a moment. Sitting alone in a pew, I just let the atmosphere of that grand building seep into me. I wasn't praying or anything, it just felt ... I don't know ... complete somehow. I feel that here and very strongly at times ...'

'I know what you mean. I told you, when I was in Indonesia, I often thought I could easily stay here. Wide horizons, I think, Corry. Wide horizons ...'

Years later, Corry wrote this poem, which captures something of these 'wide horizons' and what they meant for her, even now, only months after arriving in Australia.

Part Seven: Moving On

The roads that run between

Take me to the country byways, to the roads that run between,
which seem without beginning without end.
Where the pasture spreads before me, dressed in palest shades of green,
and I can feel the heartbeat of the land.

Take me to the rolling hills, to valleys dipping deep,
blue mountains dozing in the midday sun.
Where the ghost gums dot the landscape like a pre-historic feat
on routes the hasty traveller will shun.

Take me to a wider vista, stretching far as I can see,
where the wind combs waving grasses in a style that
compliments the scenes around me in a special rural way
and Nature bids me welcome with a smile.

Let me watch an outback sunset, firing far-reaching hills,
painting scarlet landscapes on the sky,
while I sit and dream away the fading hours of the day and
I can feel your Spirit pass me by.

Take me from the bustling city where the neons dress the night
in false glamour—where the lost and lonely tread.
Show me next the splendid setting of a shimmering starlit night
with the Southern Cross stringing sequins overhead.

There is where I sense your Being, hear you voicing Dreamtime truths
and find myself reborn in your arms.
With your Spirit close beside me, we will dance to distant tunes
and celebrate the outback's rustic charms.

Corry de Haas
(This poem is featured on an ABC CD, titled 'Outback Visions')

Settled

By mid-year, the house in Darra finally was at the lock-up stage, and, on coming home one night, Pierre announced to Corry that while he was working, a chap came in and asked if the house would be for sale once finished.

'What? He wanted to buy the house?'
'Yes; said he'd had his eyes on it for a while. I couldn't believe it.'
'What did you say?'
'What could I say? I never gave selling a thought. Did you?'
'No, of course not. Goodness, that's something else to think about. Would you sell?'
'I really don't know. I don't want to live here longer than absolutely necessary, but we always intended to move in ourselves, didn't we?'
'Of course, after all the hard work you put into it. When it's finished, it's ours and fully paid for. That's something to consider isn't it? It will put us right on track.'

We talked again till late that night and sat down working everything out on paper. In the end we decided to stick to our plans and move into the house ourselves. After all, this had been the whole idea; we would never have to pay rent or a mortgage, just the rates and the usual bills. The school was around the corner, the station a five-minute walk away, which was ideal with a young family. This would make a comfortable home while the children were all so young. We could always sell later and buy another house once the children had grown up.

I was keen to move in. I had made frequent visits to the house, and this had made me realise what an enormous task Pierre had undertaken. It would certainly give him much satisfaction to finally see his family move in. I think he deserved this. It would make us a delightful home.

And so it would prove to be!

In early October, the family had great fun in preparing an audio tape which was sent to our families in the Netherlands and survives to this day. Some of it is hilarious, an attempt at a *Day in the Life of the de Haas Family in Australia*, regularly interrupted by we children giggling and laughing in the background. Significantly, because he left no written accounts of our entire migration journey, Pierre comments how wonderful it is to feel the sun on his face every single day, noting also that our first two winters in Australia had been comparable to the very best summers in the Netherlands. He also remarks how relaxed and at ease he has found the Australians he has met, and how much he has enjoyed the various informal house parties that had become a regular feature of their life in Inala.

Then it was time for our final move!

> In early December, with the children at school, Hetty and I took the bus to Darra and walked to the house. I finally had the key, and it felt so good to see it nearly finished. Only the doors needed to be painted and the back wall in the kitchen to be finished.
>
> We planned our move for 14 December 1962, just a little over three years since leaving the Netherlands, and the final day of school that year. Pierre was so excited.
>
> By then, we had already enrolled the girls at the Sisters of Mercy Convent School in Darra for the start of the new school year. After much deliberation, we enrolled Peter with the Marist Brothers at Rosalie. We had made enquiries about the school and had heard particularly good reports. Apparently, it had an excellent academic record, which we considered particularly important. Peter could travel by train to Milton, and it was only a small distance from the station to the school.
>
> On the day of our move, our neighbour arrived with his truck at 8 am, and had also brought a friend so Pierre had plenty of help. Another neighbour had invited me to come in for a cup of coffee before I left. As she put it, 'You won't have a chance to relax with a coffee for the next few weeks, I'm sure. So, make the most of it. I'll drive you and the children to Darra afterwards.' I accepted happily.
>
> Later that morning Pierre stood in the doorway and watched us arrive. No, he didn't carry me over the threshold, but his eyes said it all. Full of expectation, he looked at me, watched me as I walked inside. The house looked so fresh and welcoming. Everything was polished and clean. It felt like home immediately.
>
> Pierre had a beer ready for the men, while the children and I checked out the bedrooms. Peter was delighted with his. The desk his

dad had made for him stood in front of the window, ready for some serious study. He would be quite comfortable there.

This was indeed home. Finally.

Once our helpers had gone, we stood, arms around each other, and walked the rooms. He took me in his arms and whispered, 'Welcome home.' I could only nod, overcome with emotion. I was quite unable to speak. It was almost too good to be true. After two years of incredibly hard, physical work, he had achieved what he had set out to do. Build a house for his family.

Now, at last, the migration upheaval was completely behind us. We could settle into our new home and once again find stability. Our future in Australia was waiting ... and we were ready

Our first Australian house provided by the Housing Commission, in Inala

Finally, space to relax and room to move!

Pierre working on our own home

Brick by brick, day by day …

Roof is on!

Lock up!

...and after moving in, the first BBQ albeit on a makeshift grill

Then the permanent entertainment area plus pool was added!

And ... not that much later, the dream of their own home, complete and with plenty of land

Peter, Simone and Veronique in the open lounge/kitchen in the Darra home, with Pierre's Commando logo proudly displayed above the stove in the kitchen

Afterword

So, at last, the years of restless instability, dislocation and uncertainty, which commenced with Pierre's forced labour in Germany twenty years previously, were behind him ... and his young family! As their story has revealed, Pierre never fully came back to the Netherlands after his years of active service in the tropics. The land of his birth became too small, too cramped, and too cold and wet. He nurtured a dream of a place in the sun: a richer life with much wider horizons and opportunities than would ever be found in the Netherlands.

But this was not Corry's dream! Her horizons and earlier life experiences had been more 'normal', if that is the right word, without the high risk and high adventure of Pierre's extraordinary wartime odyssey. Yet, after an intense personal battle, she did take that leap of faith with Pierre, hoping that migrating to the other side of the world with five young children would eventually work out for the better, that they would indeed find their place in the sun. The dream then became theirs ...

When Corry finally agreed to put in the application forms to migrate to Australia, Pierre had promised: *I will make it work for us* ... And how he held himself to this commitment, as we have seen! This editor—and son—still shakes his head in awe at what Pierre was able to achieve, building our own home mostly on his own when he wasn't working overtime. How does one do justice to what was such an incredible project so bravely undertaken ... all the time learning how to do this in a new country? The commando had, seamlessly, become a self-taught builder, yet another risky step into the unknown, just like some of his wartime exploits! That he completed the house in just over two years is a testimony to his amazing endurance and resilience, and his determination to give his young family the best possible start in Australia.

We can only imagine the sense of achievement Pierre felt when we were finally able to move into our own home. Not that the project was finished then—there was still the garden to establish and other infrastructure, such as a small pool and barbeque, to build. Nevertheless, we now had our place in the sun … a home Pierre had built himself.

Corry's account of our migration journey reveals her to be an incredibly strong and resilient woman. Time and again, she was completely caught off guard by one of Pierre's latest schemes, or the unexpected circumstances and hardships with which they were confronted at various stages. Nevertheless, every time a difficult decision was carefully weighed and then agreed with Pierre, Corry fully committed to it regardless of the personal cost to her, or the sacrifices that would need to be made. Throughout these turbulent and formative years, Corry gave everything she could to care for her young family, always providing a stable and secure home environment from which we could all embrace our adopted country and its people, who made us very welcome in so many different, and generous, ways.

Sadly, one of her hopes in migrating, namely that there would be more time for her and Pierre to spend together, would not be realised until many years later when Pierre retired from work on his sixtieth birthday in 1983. My recollection is that for most, if not all, of the 1960s, Pierre continued to work exceptionally long hours, taking overtime whenever he could, and was rarely home for evening meals or on Saturdays. His energy was amazing, perhaps the reason he never did put on any weight!

Nevertheless, that old, second-hand bike, with no gears and a shoddy brake, which was his main, and energy sapping, transport while building the house, was retired not long after we moved in. I inherited it! Then we bought our first car, a Morris Major, and I will leave it up to you, the reader, to picture how a family of eight managed to squeeze into it!

On Australia Day 1966, the entire family was naturalised as Australian Citizens at Brisbane City Hall, Lord Mayor Clem Jones presiding. While this would have been an incredibly significant step for Corry and Pierre, for their children it was just a formality as we were all well and truly on the way to thinking of ourselves, and behaving, as 'Aussies'.

Corry's first trip back to the Netherlands in 1967 was a surprise gift from Pierre. He recognised both the ongoing homesickness she had been experiencing and the need for a break from the continuing demands of caring for her family. While she was very eager to see her mother and family, Corry was concerned about leaving her six children, given Pierre's long hours at work. Anyway, the necessary adjustments were made, and so Corry flew to the Netherlands for a long-anticipated reunion.

Our family remained in our Darra home until 1974, by which time I was already a lieutenant in the Australian Army after completing four years of training at the Royal Military College, Duntroon, in Canberra. Corry and Pierre had built a new home at Chapel Hill, another suburb of Brisbane—this time using a builder—and received a Housing Industry Award for their design! They continued to live there until Pierre retired at the end of 1983. With their children by then all having left home, they relocated to another new home, this time at Helensvale on the Gold Coast.

From that base, they travelled extensively, both overseas and within Australia. There were several trips back to the Netherlands, until the time came when they felt that their country of origin had changed too much and decided not to return for another visit.

Most importantly, in their later years they both discovered the joy of writing, without which this book would not have been possible. In addition, Corry always loved poetry. Indeed, some of her earliest available writings include poems written in Dutch. She became a prolific writer of short stories and poetry, and self-published several books.

What soon becomes clear in her poetry is the deep love for Australia that took root in her within months of our arrival and continued to grow deeper with each passing year. She relished its sunny weather, wide open spaces, and great natural beauty and the opportunities that it did, indeed, give her children. At the same time, she never forgot her roots in a vastly different place and in an altogether different time. Nevertheless, she seemed able to gently hold both stages of her life in harmony.

This is but one accolade for her work:

At the young age of 60, Corry de Haas started out on a late writing career. It was Australia's greatest, Henry Lawson, who introduced her to Bush Verse. On reading his books, she discovered and more clearly understood the real Australia.

Since the late nineteen eighties, Corry has been a contributing member of the Australian Bush Poets Association, has had work published in 'The Bronze Swagman Book of Bush Verse,' numerous other anthologies and several publications world-wide.

Reading Corry's poetry and prose stands to make native Australians wonder at the amount of knowledge and depth of understanding she has about her new country, and like Lawson, she will take readers on a journey that will not only amaze but will create an eagerness to take the trip over and over again.

Frank Daniel, President Australian Bush Poets Association. Inc.

So, this very, very reluctant emigrant became a recognised Australian bush poet!

Corry's works that she self-published, include:

Goudstukjes, (Gold Pieces) 1990, a book of Dutch poetry
Whispers, 1991, a book of poetry in English
Blue Remembered Mountains, 1997, a book of poetry and short stories in English
Twilight Dreaming, 2004, her final book of poetry and short stories.

These are two of her better-known poems:

WHISPERS OF THE PAST

I wanted to write me a bush-verse,
—I'm almost addicted to them—
But I found I lacked the right background
For my pen to produce such a gem.
For suddenly as I sat writing,
My lines seemed to fade clean away,
And a memory stirred that was hidden between
Of a small country's crisp autumn day.

What I wrote was a song from my childhood,
Where the whirr of the windmills kept time;
With a far different tone to its music,
A much sadder note to its rhyme.

I searched for some fresh inspiration,
Read Lawson and Paterson too;
They showed me the past and its struggles,
The back-breaking plight of the few.
But as I was reading their verses
The themes of my youth filtered in,
I smelled the fine tang of the heather,
Felt a bitter-sweet yearning begin.

And the scenes became songs of my childhood,
With their lyrics etched deep in my soul.
When my footsteps would pace out the rhythms
on the cobblestones I used to stroll.

Your bards told of mountains and rivers,
Of brolgas that dance on the plains.
Of young springtime growth in the valleys
And life-giving monsoonal rains.
They wrote about fierce floods and fires,
Of bushrangers everyone feared,
The bullockies, shearers and swagmen
And the yarns that—with them— disappeared.

Deep down inside mists were swirling,
On the low-lying fields I once knew,
Where the willows stood guard at the ditches,
With cattle near hidden from view.

They write of the rush to the goldfields,
Where fortunes are lost as they're made,
And tell of the slow rate of progress
When the early foundations were laid.
Then, later, when shadows grow longer,
And mirages of riches have gone,
They speak with the pride of a nation
That was so reluctantly won.

Still the pictures I see are the memories
Of pine forests dressed in pure white,
And of dreamy, long summery evenings
When the skies were aflame with the light.

But now, as I read recent verses,
That are written by poets so fine,
I feel that their roots are beginning
To be interwoven with mine.
I can still hear the whispers of childhood,
And my heart can still treasure the past,
But the new songs I hear of this country
I can truthfully call mine at last.

Corry de Haas, January 1991
(This poem won the Reciter's Award at the Poet's Dinner of the 25th National Folk
Festival held in Adelaide at Easter, 1991)

THE STRANGEST ORACLE

At times I read it in your eyes
—your face a puzzled frown—
'What is this woman doing here
when the poets come to town?
Does she belong amongst us, when
her background's overseas?
Her accent places her abroad …
Can someone tell us, please?'

Yet bravely I face the 'Lion's Den'
where Australia's poets stroll;
and try to lend my foreign voice
to the music in my soul.
    For I have lived here many years
no longer will I roam,
for none could love this country
    more
this country I call home.

So, lead me to a park somewhere
and let me drink the view of
    poplars in their autumn gown
which hearten me anew.
And let me weep a silent tear
when I hear 'My Country' sung
in remnants of an Irish brogue
and lilt of native tongue.

And let me marvel at a sky
My eyes then write a thousand lines
    that
numerous books could fill.
But I won't need any words at all
    when writing with their quill.

Lend me your ear and let me sing
like bards are wont to do.
Though early footsteps lie abroad,
my words will ring so true.

Then my soul awash with rhyming
    verse
can take a little spell;
for restless is a poet's pen
where pure emotions dwell.

I play only such a little part
in the theatre of this land,
and stake the tiniest of claims
where weathered gum trees stand.
The songs that linger in my heart
will be my legacy
so they who follow come to know
the one that's truly me.

(But take heart, my valued friends,
perhaps soon—in 2099—I'll then
recite my poetry in pure Australian
strine.)

This is a performance poem Corry recited on many occasions at bush poetry gatherings.
Written after attending the 'Oracles of the Bush' Festival in Tenterfield April 1997

Pierre, although not nearly as prolific as Corry, and not as well known or awarded, also had 'a way with words'. The transcript of his war diaries includes many poems in Dutch and English (some written to Corry) and deep, insightful reflections about his experiences written during those rare quiet periods when not on operations and, more extensively, during the long journey back to the Netherlands. He self-published *Toen en Nu (Then and Now)*, a book of poetry in Dutch, in 1991.

In reflecting on his work, *Dreams and Tears for Souvenirs*, which took two and half years to write, he records this rather sad conclusion:

> If writing brings such rich rewards by expressions put to paper, then why do I feel so poorly? Every word I use is a memory unfolded, a distant world revealed, a long-forgotten place revisited. They are my own experiences, no one else's. Why am I disclosing my secrets to complete strangers? Once written down, they become public.
>
> Is it because I am writing an autobiography? How can a reader appreciate what I am saying when I cannot even find myself? Does the colour of eyes, shape of face, a profile etc., mean that much or is the soul the important factor?
>
> Is youth such a faraway dreamworld that it is beyond recall, even though your memory is excellent? I still have no answer to the question: 'Does writing make you richer or poorer?' If putting words to paper gives a relief from built-up emotions, like a release-valve, then, in consequence, each creation used in such a manner becomes a loss ...
>
> A farewell of imaginations, a goodbye to reflections ... is that what writing is all about? Losing part of yourself, word by word as they leave you, never to return to the safety of deep within?
>
> Writing about yourself brings on the real danger of finding a different personality at the end when all is revealed. In fiction such problems do not eventuate; but trying to write an honest account of your own life—this during a time when an endless war was disturbing the world at large—is so totally different.
>
> Try and put a person, only known to yourself, into true perspective ... make him come alive from a period more than forty years ago. Make him a hero one day, a coward the next ...! Let him kill and let him die a thousand deaths ...! Portray one who feared, cringed,

crawled in a desperate attempt to escape, who ran and fled, stood up to become a man when the world around him disintegrated, yet stayed down long after life moved on …

Over the period of one year, I have written more than 200,000 words about a life that choked me at times or held me in a tender embrace on many occasions. As yet, I have not been able to find the person who should be me! Whatever happened to him, I do not know.

His star sign, Scorpio, contains over 500 words … reading those lines brings an icy chill travelling up my spine. That's how close they are to the truth …! However, he is still a stranger. The more I write about him, the more he develops that cunning ability of fading between sentences, hiding behind words, camouflaging himself in no-man's land. Reading my book over and over again is no solution either. I know he is there all right … but like a mirage, he—in front of my eyes—evaporates.

My diaries—kept faithfully up to date for four long years as a commando— stare at me with accusing eyes. I betrayed them, divulged their intimate secrets of love and war they shared with me, to an outside world in which they play no part …!

I used those diaries to try and find myself, but somewhere in the cauldron that was Europe in wartime, or later in the jungle of the Far East, I lost track and let him escape …

As was (and still is) the choice of many veterans, Pierre quietly carried and mostly kept to himself the emotional scars of his wartime experiences. The nightmares abated from time to time, but they didn't stop for years. Nevertheless, he always cared deeply for his family, and his consistent and sacrificial actions as a husband, and as a father, always spoke for themselves.

Pierre died from a stroke on 15 April 2005. Corry continued to live in their home at Helensvale for some years. Never having lived alone, she found the isolation of her final years extremely hard, made even more difficult by the onset of Alzheimer's. In 2014 she moved into ARCARE Aged Care at Helensvale on the Gold Coast, where she died peacefully on 18 September 2017.

Corry's and Pierre's ashes are interred together at Allambe Memorial

Park, near Nerang on the Gold Coast, in full view of Tamborine Mountain, a place which always remained special in their hearts, from their very first visits shortly after arriving in Australia.

Their headstone enshrines the words of their very first meeting:

If you are Corry ... I am Pierre.

And so ends this incredible story, a story of adventure and chance encounters, of great risks taken and challenges faced, a story of committed love and sacrifice, and a story of faith, hope, sheer guts and hard work.

Who could have possibly imagined this incredible, yet true, story ... their story of finding a place in the sun!

Yet the story lives on, in the souls, hearts and minds that were directly formed and shaped, or otherwise influenced, by their witness and example. At the time of writing, Corry and Pierre are survived by all their children, twelve grandchildren, and fourteen great grandchildren, with another on the way.

I think I can state this on behalf of my siblings: we are all proud Australians, and most thankful to be living in this great country!

The house that Pierre built for us is still standing and recognisable. While it now looks so very small, if only those walls could speak ...

Corry and Pierre's 50th Wedding Anniversary, 2001, from L to R: Diana, Veronique, Simone, Pierre, Corry, Brigitte, Mona and Peter

Corry at her word processor

Pierre also hard at work; they had to negotiate sharing their one machine!

One of Corry and Pierre's last photos together, with their family, taken at Pierre's 80th birthday party in 2003

Corry enjoying the visit of one of the Australian natives!

May they rest in peace!

www.ingramcontent.com/pod-product-compliance
Lightning Source LLC
Chambersburg PA
CBHW070247010526
44107CB00056B/2365